A YEAR IN L

Two Things To Do Every Day

David Hampshire

ROYAL ALBERT HALL

Survival Books • Bath • England

Copyright © Survival Books 2014
Illustrations & Cover © Jim Watson

Survival Books Limited
Office 169, 3 Edgar Buildings
George Street, Bath BA1 2FJ, United Kingdom
☎ +44 (0)1225-462135, ✉ info@survivalbooks.net
💻 www.survivalbooks.net

British Library Cataloguing in Publication Data
A CIP record for this book is available
from the British Library.

ISBN: 978-1-909282-68-1

Printed and bound in China by D'Print Pte Ltd.

Acknowledgements

The authors would like to thank all those who helped with research and provided information for this book, unfortunately too many to list here. Special thanks are due to for Robbi Atilgan for editing; Alex Browning for proof-reading; David Woodworth for final proof checking; Di Bruce-Kidman for design, DTP and photo selection; Jim Watson for the superb illustrations and cover design; and the author's partner (Alexandra) for continuing with the pretence that writing is a proper job with a proper salary. Last, but not least, a special thank you to the many photographers who provided images – the unsung heroes – whose beautiful photographs add colour and help bring London to life.

IMPORTANT

While every care has been taken to ensure that the information in this book is accurate, the dates and timing of events can change at short notice, while some may even be cancelled! Bear in mind that the exact dates for some events had not been confirmed when this book went to press – and some days/dates change each year (shown by ⓘ after the address) – therefore it's advisable to confirm by telephone or check the website before travelling.

DISABLED ACCESS

Many buildings – particularly old buildings – don't offer wheelchair access or may allow access to the ground floor only. Wheelchairs are provided at some venues, although users may need assistance. Contact venues if you have specific requirements.

Readers' Guide

The notes below will help you get the most from *A Year in London*:

♦ **Contact Details:** These usually include the address, telephone number, website and the nearest tube or rail station, where applicable. You can also travel to most venues by bus and to some by river ferry, although some are best reached by car. Bear in mind, however, that parking can be difficult or impossible in many areas, particularly in central London, and even parking nearby can be a problem. You can enter the postcode to display a map of the location on Google (and other map sites).

♦ **Timing:** This book suggests two things to do a day, usually in the same area. We are not suggesting that readers necessarily do both in one day – indeed it may not be feasible to do so – but simply offering a choice. However, as one suggestion is often a café, pub or restaurant, it's often possible to enjoy both activities on the same day.

♦ **Bookings:** While the majority of places listed in this book can be visited spontaneously and are open on most days, some require you to make bookings or buy tickets in advance. For example, bookings are usually required for popular restaurants and gastropubs. When it's necessary to book or buy tickets before visiting, it's indicated by a telephone symbol (☎) after the contact details (a telephone symbol with a line through it indicates that booking isn't possible and you just have to turn up).

♦ **Cost:** We haven't listed entry fees as these are liable to change at short notice (and can be checked via websites). Places and events offering free entry – which includes many museums and galleries – are indicated by 'free' after the address. Note that a few churches and cathedrals charge non-worshippers an entry fee (indicated).

♦ **Restaurants, Pubs & Cafés:** We have provided a price guide for eateries – based on two courses and a drink – as follows:

£   **Inexpensive:** less than £20 per head
££   **Moderate:** between £20 and £40 per head
£££   **Expensive:** from £40 per head (the sky's the limit!)

The vast majority of eateries listed in this book fall into the first two categories. Where no price guide is given, e.g. some cafes and pubs, you can assume that the venue is relatively inexpensive.

Note that prices are subjective – one man's moderate is another's very expensive – and London prices are often much higher than in other parts of the UK (and worldwide!). However, many restaurants – even the most expensive and exclusive – offer good value set menus at lunchtime and early evening, e.g. pre-theatre meals. These can be a real bargain, given the general high quality of food on offer.

Contents

Introduction

George Inn, EC1

Welcome to *A Year in London*, an exhaustive guide to 365 days in the most exciting, inspiring, beguiling, engaging city in the world! London is a vast, sprawling collage of a city that's like no other, with so much to thrill, fascinate, divert and intrigue you. What began as a Roman trading port 2,000 years ago has swallowed up a thousand villages, hamlets and settlements, and now covers an area of more than 600 square miles with a population of over 8 million. London wasn't planned as a grand design but evolved piecemeal over many centuries to become what it is today: a chaotic and haphazard ever-changing metropolis with a wealth of attractions, both ancient and modern.

London is a world leader in many fields, including architecture, art, business, design, fashion, film, gastronomy, music, publishing, shopping, sport, theatre, television and much more. It's also (officially) the world's most cosmopolitan and racially diverse city, which adds immeasurably to its cultural and culinary wealth (in London you can literally eat your way around the world). Its social scene is a lot like the city itself – vibrant, diverse and in a constant state of flux – blending traditional and cutting-edge, world-class and run-of-the-mill, brilliant and bizarre, grimy and glorious. Above all, London is a cool city that doesn't take itself too seriously.

London is also the world's leading tourist destination – attracting over 30 million visitors a year – with more world-class attractions than any other city: fascinating museums and galleries; beautiful parks and gardens; majestic palaces and grand houses; superb restaurants and bars; innovative theatre, cinema and comedy; pioneering music

Notting Hill Carnival

Parliament Hill, Hampstead Heath

and dance; and much more. While **A Year in London** doesn't neglect the star attractions, it also takes you off the beaten track to many lesser-known but no less worthy places – the 'secret' hidden corners beloved by long-time Londoners.

peacock, Kew Gardens

Whether your idea of a good time is a stroll around an art gallery or a frenzied dance at a hip nightspot, an evening at the theatre or a night in a pub downing pints of real ale, you'll find it in London. Whether you're nine or 90, a drinker or a thinker, gay or straight, night owl or early bird – you'll never lack things to do in this charismatic capital. From refined to hair-raising, laid-back to frantic, arty to artless, we've included activities that will add a bit of spice to anyone's life.

The variety and number of London's leisure opportunities is boundless – conservative estimates put it at over 1,500 events every week – and **A Year in London** can only provide a snapshot of the possibilities. Nevertheless, we've tried to include something for everyone – singles and couples, families and kids, the young and young at heart, and everyone in between. There are two suggestions for every day of the year – contrasting or complementary

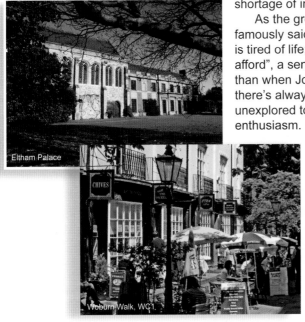

Eltham Palace

Woburn Walk, WC1

– adding up to around 750 activities, so there's no shortage of inspiration.

As the great man of letters Samuel Johnson famously said, "When a man is tired of London, he is tired of life; for there is in London all that life can afford", a sentiment that's even more relevant today than when Johnson voiced it in 1777. In London there's always something new, unexpected or unexplored to capture your imagination and fire your enthusiasm.

So when you're seeking something to prise you off the sofa on a Sunday afternoon or a diversion to keep the kids amused, entertaining an out-of-town friend or trying to impress a special date, you're bound to find something interesting to do in London. **All you need is a sense of adventure, an open mind – and this book!**

Long live London!

David Hampshire

August 2013

January

1 January

Happy New Year!

S tart the new year with the spectacular London New Year's Day Parade. From humble beginnings in 1987, the parade has evolved into one of the world's great street spectaculars with up to 10,000 performers from across the world. The cast of dancers, acrobats, cheerleaders, musicians and more assembles in the heart of the city for a colourful celebration combining exuberant contemporary performance with pomp and ceremony. The parade starts around 11.45am on Piccadilly (outside the Ritz Hotel), wending its way along Piccadilly Circus, Lower Regent Street, Waterloo Place, Pall Mall, Cockspur Street, Trafalgar Square and Whitehall, finishing in Parliament Street at around 3pm.

London New Year's Day Parade (londonparade.co.uk, free).

R ound off a splendid start to the year with a five-star meal at Lima, one of London's most innovative restaurants. Chic and cool, Lima is representative of the recent gastronomic renaissance in Peru, combining Britain's best ingredients with unique organic and wild produce from small Peruvian growers. The result is a treat for the eyes and taste buds. Start with the Pisco cocktail menu, where the *Cuento del Diablo* (Devil's Story) – spicy with a sweet strawberry kick and devil horns – is a knockout! Dishes are meant to be shared, particularly the starters, so don't hold back. A lovely restaurant with a chic ambiance, fantastic food, friendly service and cocktails to die for. Booking essential. *¡Buen provecho!*

Lima, 31 Rathbone Place, W1T 1JH (020-3003 2640, limalondon.com, Tottenham Court Rd tube, £££, ☎).

If you can't get a table at Lima, try 10 Greek Street (W1D 4DH), Burger & Lobster (29 Clarges Street, W1J 7EF), MEATliquor (74 Welbeck Street, W1G 0BA), Pitt Cue Co. (1 Newburgh Street, W1F 7RB) or Polpo (41 Beak Street, W1F 9SB). You may have to queue, but none of these acclaimed restaurants (and many others) accept bookings in the evenings.

2 January

Keeping Up with the (Peter) Jones's

Indulge yourself at the new year sales at Peter Jones in Sloane Square, noted for its stylish fashion and homewares. PJs was founded in 1877 in two small shops and was acquired by John Lewis in 1905. The current department store (Grade II* listed) was built between 1932 and 1936 and was the first modern use of the glass curtain wall in Britain.

Peter Jones, Sloane Sq, SW1W 8EL (020-7730 3434, johnlewis.com/ our-shops/peter-jones, Sloane Sq tube).

Round off the perfect day with a play at the Royal Court, London's coolest theatre. The Royal Court Theatre occupies a splendid Victorian-era building and is the de facto home of modern English theatre; it staged John Osborne's *Look Back in Anger* in 1956, seen as the starting point of modern British drama, and the *Rocky Horror Show* also premiered at the theatre in 1973.

Royal Court Theatre, Sloane Sq, SW1W 8AS (020-7565 5000, royalcourttheatre.com, Sloane Sq tube, ☎).

Peter Jones

3 January

Bones & Boots on Bankside

Pay homage to the 'Winchester Geese' in Cross Bones Graveyard, a post-medieval burial ground in Southwark. It's believed to have been an unconsecrated graveyard for 'single women' – a euphemism for prostitutes – known locally as Winchester Geese as they were licensed by the Bishop of Winchester. There's no access to the actual burial ground, but the site has become a shrine for those buried here.

Cross Bones Graveyard, Redcross Way, SE1 1YJ (crossbones.org. uk, Borough tube).

Cross Bones Graveyard

Enjoy a glass of wine at The Boot & Flogger, which looks and sounds like a pub but is actually a wine bar. Although almost 50 years old, the atmosphere is redolent of a much earlier period, its wood panelling and leather armchairs suggesting the bonhomie of a gentlemen's club. The list of fine wines contains some serious Bordeaux and Burgundy vintages.

The Boot & Flogger, 10-20 Redcross Way, SE1 1TA (020-7407 1184, davy.co.uk/bootandflogger, Borough tube, £).

4 January

At the Sharp End

Enter the magical world of glassblowing at the London Glassblowing Studio & Gallery. Established by Peter Layton in 1976, the LGS was among the first hot-glass studios in Europe and remains one of its leading glassmaking workshops, noted for its flair in the use of colour, form and texture. The gallery is an Aladdin's cave of unique works of glass art.

London Glassblowing Studio & Gallery, 62-66 Bermondsey St, SE1 3UD (020-7403 2800, londonglassblowing.co.uk, Borough tube, free).

See London in miniature from Europe's highest building, The Shard, completed in 2012. You can experience the view from The Shard's viewing platform (68th floor, 800ft), but it's best to avoid the astronomical fee and have lunch or dinner at one of the Shard's three restaurants: Aqua Shard, Hutong and Oblix. Not a cheap option, but at least the view's 'free'!

The Shard, 32 London Bridge St, SE1 (020-7478 0540, shard.com/restaurants, London Bridge tube, £££, ☎).

The Shard

5 January

Thumbscrews & Corkscrews

Do some time in the Middle Ages at the Clink Prison Museum, which tells the story of one of England's oldest and most notorious prisons. The Clink (which gave rise to the expression 'being in clink') was the Bishop of Winchester's infamous jail from 1144 to 1780, when it was burned down during anti-Catholic riots.

Clink Prison Museum, 1 Clink St, SE1 9DG (020-7403 0900, clink.co.uk, London Bridge tube).

Raise a glass (or three) and have a tasty meal at Vinopolis, a temple to Bacchus housed in the stunning Victorian railway arches of London Bridge. Vinopolis offers a self-guided wine tour (at your own pace) of the world's most famous wine regions (with tastings along the way) employing the latest technology and interactive features. Round off your visit with a delicious meal in Vinopolis' excellent restaurant, Cantina.

Vinopolis, 1 Bank End, SE1 9BU (020-7940 8300, vinopolis.co.uk, London Bridge tube, ££, ☎).

6 January

On the Twelfth Day of Christmas…

Celebrate Twelfth Night or Epiphany in Bankside, the twelfth day of Christmas and traditionally the end of the festive season (the day before the general return to work on Plough Monday). The festival combines ancient seasonal customs – The Green Man, The Mummers, King Bean and Queen Pea, The Kissing Wishing Tree and Wassailing – along with contemporary festivities. It's free to all and takes place whatever the weather.

Twelfth Night (thelionspart.co.uk/twelfthnight, free, ⓘ).

———————

Drop in at The Anchor & Hope, one of London's best-known gastropubs. It's a no-frills venue, with minimal décor, bare wooden tables and bright art on the walls, while the menu is chalked on a board. The food is robust British fare, served in 'hearty portions using the finest fresh ingredients'. If you need to wait there are inventive bargain-priced cocktails.

The Anchor & Hope, 36 The Cut, SE1 8LP (020-7928 9898, Southwark tube, ££, 🚇).

7 January

Read all About it!

See the *Magna Carta* and Shakespeare's *First Folio* (and much more) at the British Library's Sir John Ritblat Gallery. Named in honour of its major donor, it contains a permanent display of over 200 of the world's rarest and most precious manuscripts and books, including sacred texts, historically important documents, landmarks of printing, masterpieces of illumination, and much more.

British Library, Sir John Ritblat Gallery, 96 Euston Rd, NW1 2DB (0843-208 1144, bl.uk/whatson/permgall/treasures, King's Cross St Pancras tube, free).

Have a wee dram or a pint of Guinness at Filthy MacNasty's Whiskey Café in the City. This popular venue specialises in whiskey (or whisky) and Guinness, but isn't a clichéd theme bar. As you might expect, there's a wide selection of whisky (Scotch) and whiskey (Irish and American) – but MacNasty's is also noted for its live music, music quizzes and literary readings.

Filthy MacNasty's Whiskey Café. 68 Amwell St, EC1R 1UU (020-8617 3505, filthymacnastys.co.uk, Angel tube, £).

8 January

Power-Packed Portobello

Enjoy a meal or pre-movie snack at the Electric Diner, adjacent to the Electric Cinema, open from 8am to late (midnight Mon-Wed, 1am Thu-Sat, 11pm Sun). It's an on-trend, gleaming/grungy, traditional American-style diner, with a long row of bar stools flanked by booths (banquettes), a no-reservation policy and an American soundtrack from the diner's reel-to-reel tape machine.

The friendly, efficient staff serve a French-American menu – in American-size portions (one serving is more than enough for two) – including the fried house-made bologna sandwich, roasted bone marrow with beef cheek marmalade, cheeseburger, and honey-fried chicken with chilli and sesame seeds, followed by chocolate pie topped by a mountain of cream – all very tasty but not for the faint-hearted (or dieters!). The bar is a handy spot to enjoy well-mixed cocktails, a thoughtful wine list and a choice of some 20 beers.

Electric Diner, 191 Portobello Rd, W11 2ED (020-7908 9696, electricdiner.com, Ladbroke Grove tube, £).

See a movie at the beautiful Electric Cinema (next door to the Electric Diner), London's first purpose-built cinema which opened in 1910. Since then it has been renamed (in the '30s), re-launched (in the '60s) and even had a notorious mass murderer (John Christie) work there in the '40s. In the '90s it was purchased by architect Gebler Tooth, who upgraded the building with new WCs, air-conditioning, a restaurant and an upstairs private members club. Now Grade II* listed, once you step inside you're transported back to the '30s, with comfortable leather armchairs, footstools and side tables offering unparalleled comfort. There are even a number of 2-seater sofas (at the rear) and double beds (!) in the front row, providing a unique cinematic experience; individual cashmere blankets complete the picture. Cinema heaven! The films aren't bad either.

Electric Cinema, 191 Portobello Rd, W11 2ED (020-7908 9696, electriccinema.co.uk, Ladbroke Grove tube, 🎦),

9 January

Carnivores' Celebration

Get up early to visit Smithfield Market (Mon-Fri from 3am), carnivorous hub of the capital's food industry and one of the world's largest meat markets. Smithfield is London's oldest market – dating back over 800 years (when it was also a place of execution) – housed in an imposing Victorian building. Don't leave without buying a few tasty morsels for dinner.

Smithfield Market, 201-232 Charterhouse St, EC1M 6JN (020-7248 3151, smithfieldmarket.com, Barbican tube).

Smithfield Market

There's nowhere better to celebrate man's love of meat than to have a mighty carnivorous meal at the St John Bar and Restaurant Smithfield. Housed in a former Georgian townhouse/smokehouse around the corner from the market, St John's is one of Britain's (and the world's) best restaurants and a London institution. Not cheap, but somewhere for a special treat.

St John Bar & Restaurant Smithfield, 26 St John St, EC1M 4AY (020-7251 0848, stjohngroup.uk.com/smithfield, Barbican tube, £££, ☎).

St. JOHN

10 January

Nuns, Martyrs & Michelin Stars

Take a tour of Tyburn Convent, founded in 1901 and dedicated to the memory of the martyrs executed at nearby Tyburn Tree gallows (and elsewhere) for their Catholic faith. Around 105 Roman Catholics were hanged at Tyburn during the Reformation (1535-1681). It's a cloistered community of around 25 Benedictine contemplatives who never leave their enclosed walls.

Tyburn Convent, Hyde Park Place, W2 2LJ (020-7723 7262, tyburnconvent.org.uk, Marble Arch tube, free),

---

Enjoy lunch or dinner – and a glass of champagne – at the Texture Restaurant & Champagne Bar, which is both conventional and inventive at the same time, and won a Michelin star in 2010. Texture's cuisine is modern European with Icelandic influences, including Icelandic Cod, Icelandic Lamb from Skagafjordur, and Icelandic herbs and skyr (yogurt).

Texture Restaurant & Champagne Bar, 34 Portman St, W1H 7BY (020-7224 0028, texture-restaurant.co.uk, Marble Arch tube, £££, ☎).

TYBURN CONVENT

GLORIA DEO
A Film Documentary

An unique inside portrait of the world of Tyburn Nuns
written, narrated and co-produced by the Tyburn Nuns

 DVD

11 January

Whatever Floats Your Boat

Cast off at the London Boat Show, one of Europe's largest exhibitions of boats and water craft. It features some 500 exhibitors showcasing everything from 1.4m sailing dinghies to 37m tri-deck motor yachts, while displays include indoor canoeing, sailing, tall ships, historic vessels and a marina (in the Royal Victoria Dock) containing some of the largest boats in production.

London Boat Show, ExCel Exhibition Centre, 1 Western Gateway, Royal Victoria Dock, E16 1XL (londonboatshow.com, Custom House DLR, ⓘ).

Have a delicious Chinese meal at Yi-Ban, one of Docklands' best restaurants. The vast, sleek dining room – with a bar and terrace – overlooks the London Regatta Centre and London City Airport. Yi-Ban has a traditional vast Chinese menu, including classic dishes and dim sum, with particular emphasis on fish and seafood.

Yi-Ban, London Regatta Centre, Dockside Rd, Custom House, E16 2QT (020-7473 6699, yi-ban.com, Custom House DLR, ££, ☏).

London Boat Show

12 January

Put Your Best Foot Forward

See how the pros do it at the Sadler's Wells Theatre, the UK's leading dance house showcasing the most dynamic and innovative dance. Sadler's Wells is dedicated to producing, commissioning and presenting the best of international and UK dance, and crossing the boundaries between different art forms. Get your heart racing – without working up a sweat!

Sadler's Wells Theatre, Roseberry Ave, EC1R 4TN (020-7863 8198, sadlerswells.com, Angel tube, ☏).

Dance the night away at Fabric, a 'super club' with a 2,500 capacity housed in a 25,000ft² ex-cold meat store (opposite Smithfield Market) in Clerkenwell. The club has five sound systems and Europe's first bass-loaded 'bodysonic' dance floor, where sections are attached to 400 bass transducers that emit bass frequencies allowing you to feel the music in your body. With unisex toilets!

Fabric, 77A Charterhouse St, EC1M 6HJ (020-7336 8898, fabriclondon.com, Farringdon tube, £).

13 January

Spectacular St Pancras

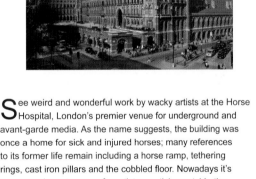

Admire the architecture and sculptures at St Pancras International Station, London's most majestic railway terminus. The famous roof contains some 2.5 acres of glass, equal to almost two football pitches or 38 tennis courts! The station underwent a major redevelopment in the last decade, when the stunning Midland Grand Hotel (1873-1935) was reincarnated as the St Pancras Renaissance Hotel. It's home to two of London's most beloved statues: *The Meeting Place*, a 9m tall bronze by Paul Day, and the *Betjeman* statue by Martin Jennings which pays tribute to the poet Sir John Betjeman (1906-1984) who was responsible for saving the station from demolition in the '60s; there's also a station pub, The Betjeman Arms, named in his honour.

St Pancras International Station, Euston Rd, N1C 4QP (020-7843 7688, stpancras.com, King's Cross St Pancras tube).

The Meeting Place, Paul Day

See weird and wonderful work by wacky artists at the Horse Hospital, London's premier venue for underground and avant-garde media. As the name suggests, the building was once a home for sick and injured horses; many references to its former life remain including a horse ramp, tethering rings, cast iron pillars and the cobbled floor. Nowadays it's a progressive arts venue for artists practising outside the mainstream, whether it's painting, film, fashion, literature, music or performance art.

Horse Hospital, Colonnade, Bloomsbury, WC1N 1JD (020-7833 3644, thehorsehospital.com, Russell Sq tube).

Enjoy a glass of champagne or lunch at Searcys St Pancras Grand Brasserie & Champagne Bar (searcyschampagnebars. co.uk, ££), the longest in Europe at 96m, a haven from the hustle and bustle of the station concourse.

14 January

Mime & Dine

Celebrate the art of storytelling while keeping schtum at the London International Mime Festival, which spans two weeks of the freshest and most inventive physical theatre, dance, circus, puppetry and live art at top arts venues across London. If you thought mime was all about white-faced clowns plagued by invisible glass and strong winds, the Mime Festival will make you think again. Encompasses a breathtaking range of work.

London International Mime Festival (mimelondon.com, ☏, ⓘ).

Enjoy an elegant dinner at Bob Bob Ricard, which serves eclectic English-Russian cuisine to its cosseted clientele in one of London's most glamorous all-booth dining rooms (a deluxe diner). While invariably good, the food gets mixed reviews, but the sumptuous, decadent décor (in turquoise, pink and gold!) is a riot and the banquettes have a champagne button – how cool is that?

Bob Bob Ricard, 1 Upper James St, W1F 9DF (020-3145 1000, bobbobricard.com, Piccadilly Circus tube, £££, ☏).

15 January

Behind the Scenes at the Beeb

BBC Broadcasting House

Take a tour of BBC Broadcasting House, the Beeb's Art Deco HQ since 1932. The tours (daily, 1½ hrs) are informative, interesting and fun, with tour guides bringing to life the work of the BBC's new, state-of-the-art, multimedia broadcasting centre. Experience a camera's eye view via a big screen of some of the live studios, such as the Six O'clock News and Radio 1.

BBC Broadcasting House, Portland Place, W1A 1AA (bbc.co.uk/ showsandtours/tours/bh_london.shtml, Oxford Circus tube, ☏).

Embark on a sensory dining journey at Archipelago, amid the glow of golden Buddhas, dwarf palm trees and giant peacock feathers (Indiana Jones would be at home here). If you fancy yourself as an intrepid diner you should enjoy Archipelago, where hallmark dishes include (ethically-sourced) crocodile, wildebeest, kangaroo, ostrich and zebra, among other exotic creatures (there are also 'normal' and vegetarian dishes).

Archipelago, 110 Whitfield St, W1T 5ED (020-7383 3346, archipelago-restaurant.co.uk, Warren St tube, ££, ☏).

16 January

Horniman of Plenty

Spend the day in darkest Forest Hill at the eclectic Horniman Museum & Aquarium, founded by Victorian tea trader Frederick John Horniman (1835-1906) to house his collection of cultural artefacts, ethnography, natural history and musical instruments – a total of over 350,000 objects! The museum opened in 1901 and occupies a lovely, purpose-built Arts & Crafts/Art Nouveau style building. For many the highlight is the striking, recently renovated, aquarium.

Horniman Museum & Aquarium, 100 London Rd, SE23 3PQ (020-8699 1872, horniman.ac.uk, Forest Hill rail, free except aquarium).

Have lunch or tea at the Horniman Museum's Gallery café overlooking the 16 acres of award-winning, beautifully maintained gardens, which include a conservatory, bandstand, animal enclosure, nature trail and ornamental garden. The café offers a range of tasty hot and cold snacks and refreshments, and you can picnic in the gardens or in a dedicated area on the bandstand terrace.

17 January

Eye of the Beholder

See cutting-edge art at the London Art Fair, one of the city's most vibrant and longest-running art shows, and a showcase for the country's young, up-and-coming artists. The fair caters for all, whether you're 'just looking' or a serious collector, with exhibits from over 100 of London's (and Britain's) best galleries representing over 1,000 artists. Interesting for both amateur collectors and professionals.

London Art Fair, Business Design Centre, 52 Upper St, N1 0QH (020-7359 3535, londonartfair.co.uk, Angel tube, ☏, ⓘ).

Enjoy a play at Upstairs at the Gatehouse, a combination of historic pub and award-winning fringe theatre, producing a varied programme of comedy, drama and musicals. The theatre has a knack of finding future smashes, such as musicals based upon Take That (*Never Forget*) and *Big Brother the Musical*. The Gatehouse also stages the Camden Fringe in July-August.

Upstairs at the Gatehouse, 1 North Rd, N6 4BD (020-8340 3488, upstairsatthegatehouse.com, Highgate tube, £, ☏).

18 January

Golly GOSH!

Be amazed by St Christopher's Chapel at Great Ormond Street Hospital (GOSH), a stunningly decorative building (1875) and the most sumptuous hospital chapel in the country, dedicated to St Christopher, the Patron Saint of children. When the old GOSH was replaced in the '90s the small chapel was 'simply' moved by sliding it along a purpose-built runway.

St Christopher's Chapel, Great Ormond Street Hospital, Great Ormond St, WC1N 3JH (020-7405 9200, gosh.nhs.uk/about-us/our-history/gallery, Russell Sq tube, free).

St Christopher's Chapel

Feed your senses and your stomach at Sketch, a restaurant with a difference, where it's difficult to know where the art ends and the food begins. One of the city's wackiest OTT restaurants, Sketch houses three restaurants with varying prices: The Lecture Room & Library (Michelin-starred, £££), The Gallery (££) and The Glade (£), which are fun, unique and downright weird. Be sure to visit the amazing loos!

Sketch, 9 Conduit St, W1S 2XG (020-7659 4500, sketch.uk.com, Oxford Circus tube, ☎).

19 January

A Formula for Fun

Go karting in Bermondsey with TeamSport, where the track's hair-raising bends and elevated flyovers will push your driving skills to the limit. And what's more it's eco-friendly, as the track is equipped with Electric Eco Karts which are lighter, have faster acceleration, better handling and of course, being electric, zero emissions. Maybe the F1 boys will follow suit? Awesome fun day out.

TeamSport, Tower Bridge Business Park, 100 Clements Rd, SE16 4DG (0844-998 0000, team-sport.co.uk/london-tower-bridge, Bermondsey tube, ☎).

Chill out with a pint of ale at the historic Mayflower pub in Rotherhithe, close to where the Pilgrim Fathers set sail in 1620. The charming 18th-century pub has an upstairs dining room, although the main draw is the view of the Thames from its rear deck. Visit after 6pm on a 'Blackout Sunday', when it's lit only by candlelight.

The Mayflower, 117 Rotherhithe St, SE16 4NF (020-7237 4088, themayflowerrotherhithe.com, Rotherhithe rail, £).

20 January

Divine Dulwich

See the Old Masters at the Dulwich Picture Gallery, one of London's 'secret' galleries. Designed by Sir John Soane and opened in 1817, the Dulwich Picture Gallery was England's first purpose-built public art gallery and has been called 'the world's most beautiful art gallery' – an elegant piece of abstract classicism, made from brick with Portland stone detailing.

The collection itself was mainly bequeathed by Frenchman Noël Desenfans (1745-1807) and his Swiss partner Sir Francis Bourgeois (1753-1811), who together formed one of the most successful art dealerships of Georgian London. The dealers were commissioned by Stanislaus Augustus, King of Poland to create a Royal Collection-cum-National Gallery, but Poland was partitioned by its more powerful neighbours, leading (in 1795) to the King being forced to abdicate – and the dealers were left with a royal collection on their hands!

> Have lunch or afternoon tea at the Dulwich Picture Gallery Café, acclaimed by Square Meal as 'one of the top ten places in London for afternoon tea'.

The collection was eventually left to Dulwich College to be put on permanent public display in a specially-built gallery, which is enclosed by peaceful gardens, mainly lawns, with a number of old and unusual trees. The collection is a small-but-beautifully-formed gem, largely comprising well-chosen European old masters, mainly from the 17th and 18th centuries, including works by Canaletto, Constable, Gainsborough, Hogarth, Murillo, Rembrandt, Reynolds, Rubens and Van Dyck.

Dulwich Picture Gallery, Gallery Rd, Dulwich, SE21 7AD (020-8693 5254, dulwichpicturegallery.org.uk, West/North Dulwich rail, free).

If you visit the gallery on a Tuesday, take the opportunity to see the beautiful Christ's Chapel of God's Gift (open 1.30-3.30pm), consecrated in 1616 by George Abbot, Archbishop of Canterbury. It can be accessed from the Dulwich Picture Gallery's cloister. You can also attend a service on Sunday mornings.

Christ's Chapel of God's Gift at Dulwich (thedulwichestate.com/beneficiaries/christs-chapel-of-gods-gift-at-dulwich).

January

21 January

The Norsemen Cometh

Enjoy lunch or tea at the Nordic Bakery, a delightful, cool Finnish café and peaceful haven close to the West End. Offerings include the house favourite cinnamon buns (and many other varieties), plus delicious dark rye sandwiches filled with prawns, gravadlax, pickled herring and hard-boiled egg, and other tasty northern European treats. Coffee is good and strong. *Hyvää ruokahalua!* (bon appétit).

Nordic Bakery, 14A Golden Sq, W1F 9JG (020-3230 1077, nordicbakery.com, Piccadilly Circus tube, £).

Cinnamon Bun

Indulge yourself with an evening at the Nordic Bar, an understated Scandinavian basement bar near the Telecom Tower in Fitzrovia. It isn't particularly smart or trendy, but it's friendly, welcoming and fun, with a wide choice of drinks, as may be expected from our famously alcohol-loving Scandi friends. Nordic's speciality is cocktails based on Scandinavian mixes and ingredients, including fruit and berries. *Skol!*

Nordic Bar, 25 Newman St, W1T 1PN (020-7631 3174, nordicbar.com, Tottenham Court Rd tube, £).

22 January

A Whole New Ball Game

Experience the excitement of a Six Nations rugby match at Twickenham Stadium, the home of England rugby seating an impressive 82,000 spectators, and the largest dedicated rugby union venue in the world. You'll need to check match days and book tickets in advance (see website). Twickers is also a popular venue for megastar rock concerts.

Twickenham Stadium, 200 Whitton Rd, Twickenham TW2 7BA (0871-222 2120, rfu.com/twickenhamstadium, Twickenham rail, ☎ ①).

Have a pint at The White Cross, a historic, 18th-century Young's pub on the river near Richmond Bridge; it has some unusual features, such as a fireplace tucked under a window. The large terrace is glorious on sunny days but just as atmospheric in winter, especially at high tide when the river can reach almost to the door (bring your wellies!).

The White Cross, Riverside, off Water Ln, TW9 1TH (020-8940 6844, thewhitecrossrichmond.com, Richmond tube, £).

23 January

Splendours of Southwark

Soak up the atmosphere at Southwark Cathedral, a beautiful and historic cathedral and London's first Gothic church. Often overlooked in a much-visited part of London (the buzzy south bank of the Thames), it's been a place of worship for over 1,000 years and is the mother church of the Anglican diocese of Southwark. The cathedral is a popular venue for concerts and organ recitals (see website).

Southwark Cathedral, London Bridge, London SE1 9DA (020-7367 6700, cathedral.southwark.anglican.org, London Bridge tube, free).

Feast like Pavarotti at Zucca, a shiny, modern Italian restaurant employing first-class ingredients with the maximum of flavour – cooked with passion and perfection. Wonderful starters include sea bass carpaccio, salt cod and roasted tomato bruschetta and ox tongue, while the superb silky pasta is to die for – as good as you'll find anywhere in London. *Buon appetito!*

Zucca, 184 Bermondsey St, SE1 3TQ (020-7378 6809, zuccalondon. com, London Bridge tube, ££, ☏).

24 January

Ladies' Day

Have a splurge at Fenwicks, one of London's first department stores that's been a beacon of effortless style since 1891. Today it's fashion heaven in the city's most fashionable street, with five floors of fabulous designer frocks and timeless stylish accessories. There's also a gleaming beauty department and spa services to cater to your every whim. Fenwicks is chic, unflustered and beautifully groomed – just like its clientele.

Fenwicks, 63 New Bond St, W1A 3BS (020-7629 9161, fenwick.co.uk/ bond-street, Oxford Circus tube).

Indulge your passion for accessories at Liberty & Co, housed in a mock-Tudor masterpiece constructed (1924) from old warships. Synonymous with luxury and outstanding design since 1875, Liberty is one of London's most famous retailers, specialising in fashion, accessories, cosmetics, gifts, homewares and furniture. If you're peckish, treat yourself to a sumptuous afternoon tea in the airy restaurant on the second floor.

Liberty & Co, Great Marlborough St, W1B 5AH (020-7734 1234, liberty.co.uk, Oxford Circus tube).

25 January

For Auld Lang Syne

Explore the Fleming Collection, the finest collection of Scottish art in private hands and the only dedicated museum granting public access to Scottish art year round. Assembled by bankers Robert Fleming & Co, the collection contains over 750 oils and watercolours dating as far back as 1770, including works by Raeburn, Ramsay and Wilkie.

Fleming Collection, 13 Berkeley St, W1J 8DU (020-7042 5730, flemingcollection.co.uk, Green Park tube, free).

Attend a Burns' Night Supper to celebrate the life and poetry of the poet Robert (Rabbie) Burns, Scotland's most famous son. What better way to mark the occasion than with a traditional Scottish feast at Boisdale Belgravia, featuring cock-a-leekie soup, haggis with neeps and tatties, followed by cranachan, sprinkled liberally with poetry and pipers – and a few wee drams. Kilts are optional.

Boisdale Belgravia, 15 Eccleston St, SW1W 9LX (020-7730 6922, boisdale.co.uk/belgravia, Victoria tube, £££, ☎).

The Turn of the Tide, John Duncan

26 January

Tales of the Unexpected

Escape the hustle and bustle of Covent Garden and have your fortune told at the Mysteries Shop, an Aladdin's Cave of all things spiritual and other-worldly. Mysteries is a world-famous new age resource and the perfect one-stop shop for body, mind and soul enthusiasts. There's a choice of psychic readers, including tarot cards, aura readings, palm readings and Reiki, plus various classes.

Mysteries Shop, 9-11 Monmouth St, WC2H 9EQ (020-7240 3688, mysteries.co.uk, Covent Garden tube, ☐).

Enjoy a traditional French brasserie lunch or dinner at Les Deux Salons in London's Theatreland. The Michelin-starred team of Will Smith and Anthony Demetre ensure that it isn't just style which packs them in, but the excellent, affordable food (the *prix-fixe* menu is a bargain) and efficient service, without any of the pretensions associated with some French restaurants. *Bon appétit!*

Les Deux Salons, 40-42 William IV St, WC2N 4DD (020-7420 2050, lesdeuxsalons.co.uk, Charing Cross tube, ££, ☎).

27 January

Movie Magic on the BIG Screen

BFI IMAX cinema

Experience a film at the amazing BFI IMAX cinema, located in a *futuristic* seven-storey, glass-enclosed cylinder. With its vast 26m x 20m screen – the largest in the UK – and 12,000w digital, surround-sound system and stunning IMAX technology, BFI IMAX is the most technically impressive cinema in the country. Great fun for kids and adults alike.

BFI IMAX, 1 Charlie Chaplin Walk, South Bank, SE1 8XR (0330-333 7878, bfi.org.uk/imax, Southwark tube, ☏).

Have a drink or meal at the BFI Benugo Bar & Kitchen, widely regarded as one of the area's most atmospheric venues. The restaurant serves modern British food but the main attraction for drinkers is the large, buzzy bar area, called Loungeside, where the comfortable mismatched chairs and sofas invite you to kick off your shoes and relax.

BFI Benugo Bar & Kitchen, BFI Southbank Centre, Belvedere Rd, SE1 8XT (020-7401 9000, benugobarandkitchen.com, Waterloo tube, ££).

28 January

Beautiful Bloomsbury

Stroll along Sicilian Avenue in Holborn, so-named because of its authentic old-world southern Italian feel, one of London's most charming and peaceful streets, with colonnades at each end. Sicilian Avenue was completed in 1910 and was designed as a pedestrianised shopping street with pavement cafés and restaurants, which include a number of gems including the Orchard vegetarian café, Patisserie Valerie, the Spaghetti House restaurant and the Holborn Whippet pub.

Sicilian Ave, Holborn, WC1A (Holborn tube).

Sicilian Ave

Visit nearby St George's Bloomsbury, a church of startling originality and a monument to the genius of Sir Nicholas Hawksmoor (1661-1736). Consecrated in 1731, St George's was reopened to the public in 2006 following a five-year restoration. It's the architect's most idiosyncratic work, combining Baroque splendour with classical references, topped by the most eccentric spire in London. There's an exhibition, 'Hawksmoor and Bloomsbury', housed in the undercroft.

St George's Bloomsbury, 6-7 Little Russell St, WC1A 2HR (020-7242 1979, stgeorgesbloomsbury.org.uk, Holborn tube, free).

January

29 January

Village with a View

Promenade in Primrose Hill village, one of London's most beautiful and charming villages with a wealth of lovely cafés, quaint Victorian shops, attractive galleries and stylish boutiques. Not surprisingly, the village is among the most expensive and exclusive in north London – noted for its roll-call of famous residents – with an air of middle-class bohemian chic. Try Odette's for a drink or lunch (130 Regents Park Rd, 020-7586 8569, ££, ☎).

Primrose Hill village, NW3 (primrosehill.com, Chalk Farm tube).

Take in London's skyline from Primrose Hill at dusk, one of the city's most scenic spots celebrated for its grassy slopes and stunning views. At 256ft, Primrose Hill isn't particularly high, but is sufficiently so to provide wonderful views of central London; on a clear day you can see landmarks such as St Paul's Cathedral, the Gherkin, the Shard and the London Eye.

Primrose Hill, Primrose Hill Rd, NW3 (0300-061 2300, royalparks. org.uk/parks/the-regents-park, Chalk Farm tube).

30 January

In the Footsteps of Charles I

Visit Banqueting House where King Charles I (b 1600) was executed on this day in 1649, marked by an effigy above the entrance. One of London's most beautiful buildings – and the only remaining segment of the Palace of Whitehall (1530-1698) – it was designed by Inigo Jones in Palladian style and completed in 1622. The stunning ceiling was painted by Peter Paul Rubens in 1635.

Banqueting House, Whitehall, SW1A 2ER (020-3166 6154, hrp.org. uk/banquetinghouse, Westminster tube).

Admire the equestrian statue of Charles I in Trafalgar Square, cast by the French sculptor Herbert Le Sueur in 1638 before the English Civil War. Following the war it was sold by Parliament to John Rivet (a metalsmith) to be broken up; however, he hid the statue until the Restoration, when it was placed on a pedestal at its current location at the official centre of London.

Equestrian statue of Charles I, Trafalgar Sq, WC2 (Charing Cross tube).

Charles I, Anthony van Dyck

31 January

Chinese New Year – a Moveable Feast

Dance with the dragons in Chinatown for the Chinese New Year celebrations (2014 = horse, 2015 = goat). The city's original Chinatown was located in Limehouse in London's East End, moving to the Gerrard Street area after World War II. Today's Chinatown – with its stone lions, pagoda and impressive gates – isn't just about restaurants but is the heart of a thriving Chinese community with its own tea shops, bakeries, supermarkets, souvenir shops and other Chinese-run businesses. A lively place any time, Chinatown really comes alive at Chinese New Year with one of the largest celebrations outside Asia, including a parade through the West End, a lion dance, food and craft stalls, live performances and a fireworks display. *Kung Hei Fat Choi!*

Chinatown, Gerrard St, W1 (chinatownlondon.org, Leicester Sq tube, free, ⓘ).

Tuck into a Chinese feast in one of London's wealth of superb Chinese restaurants. If you fancy dim sum – the best way to sample Hong Kong style Cantonese cooking – you can do no better than **Yauatcha** (15-17 Broadwick St, yauatcha.com/soho, £££, ☎), a contemporary dim sum teahouse – with a rare Michelin star – which specialises in modern authentic dim sum, wok-friendly dishes and other 'small eats'. If you prefer your dim sum served the traditional way, wheeled from table to table on trolleys where you 'grab' dishes as they pass, then you should visit buzzy **New World** (1 Gerrard Pl, newworldlondon.com, ££, ☎) or **Chuen Cheng Ku** (17 Wardour St, £, ☎).

For more of a street-food experience – although housed indoors – go to the **Baozi Inn** (26 Newport Ct, baoziinnlondon.com, £, ☎), where the flavoursome food is perfectly priced. If crispy duck is your favourite, then **Four Seasons** (12 Gerrard St, fs-restaurants.co.uk, £, ☎) serves some of the best in Europe.

February

February

1 February

One for the Lads

Treat yourself to a shave and haircut at Gentlemen's Tonic in Mayfair, a unique establishment that's a traditional barbershop but also offers a variety of lifestyle and grooming services. The private haircutting 'stations' and treatment rooms offer a combination of traditional wood, leather and marble, combined with high-tech music consoles and LCD screens. A man could get used to this…

Gentlemen's Tonic, 31a Bruton Place, W1J 6NN (020-7297 4343, gentlemenstonic.com, Bond St tube, 🚇).

Now you're all spruced up, enjoy an erotic evening with some mates at the Windmill International. The original Windmill Theatre was a variety and revue theatre, best known for its nude tableaux vivants which began in 1932 and lasted until its reversion to a cinema in 1964. Nowadays it's one of London's premier table dancing nightclubs (i.e. a classy strip joint).

Windmill International, 17-19 Great Windmill St, W1D 7JZ (020-3468 6721, windmillinternationa-px.rtrk.co.uk, Piccadilly Circus tube, ££, 🚇).

2 February

Get it Off Your Chest

Listen to a 'rant' at Speakers' Corner, where inspiring (and boring) orators, religious zealots and antagonists have their say on Sundays. Since 1872 it's been permissible to speak on any subject – provided it's lawful! Contrary to popular belief, there's no immunity from the law and no subjects are proscribed, but the police are unlikely to intervene unless they receive a complaint or hear profanity.

Speakers' Corner, Hyde Park, Marble Arch, W2 (speakerscorner.net, Marble Arch tube).

———————

Hop on board a 'green' bus for a London bus tour. The environmentally-friendly, hydrogen-powered RV1 buses connect various attractions such as the Tower of London, Tate Modern, the Southbank arts complex, London Eye and Covent Garden. For a more traditional tour, try one of the open-top tour buses, such as Big Bus (bigbustours.com/eng/london) which offers a hop-on hop-off service that takes in most of the city's famous landmarks.

RV1 Bus Route (londonbusroutes.net/times/rv1.htm).

3 February

Take the Plunge

Splash out on an early morning swim at Marshal Street Baths (Grade II listed), a stunning, marble-lined '30s swimming pool that's been restored to its former glory. There are also exercise/dance studios, fitness suites and a health suite with a sauna and steam rooms, offering a range of treatments and therapies. Short-term passes are available.

Marshal Street Baths, Marshall Street Leisure Centre, 15 Marshall St, W1F 7EL (020-7871 7222, westminster.gov.uk/services/ leisureandculture/active/marshallstreet, Oxford Circus tube).

Treat yourself to a coffee at Bar Italia, a family-run business opened in 1949 by Lou and Caterina Polledri and passed on through three generations. A Soho institution, the bar serves excellent – if pricey – Italian coffee and delicious pastries and cakes, with a smile. It's also an excellent place to people watch in summer from an outside table.

Bar Italia, 22 Frith St, W1D 4RP (020-7437 4520, baritaliasoho.co.uk, Tottenham Court Rd tube, £).

4 February

Galloping Galanthophiles

A special day for galanthophiles (snowdrop enthusiasts – after the Latin name, *galanthus nivalis*, for the most common variety) to admire the magnificent display of snowdrops at the Chelsea Physic Garden. The garden contains some 75 varieties of snowdrops, many of which are also for sale. There's also an excellent café.

Chelsea Physic Garden, 66 Royal Hospital Rd, SW3 4HS (020-7352 5646, chelseaphysicgarden.co.uk, Sloane Sq tube, ⒤).

Meet the Chelsea pensioners at the Royal Hospital Chelsea, a retirement and nursing home for British soldiers, commonly referred to as 'Chelsea pensioners', who are unfit for duty or retired. Founded in 1682 by Charles II and built by Sir Christopher Wren, the hospital remains virtually unchanged apart from minor alterations by Robert Adam between 1765 and 1782, and the stables which were added by Sir John Soane in 1814.

Royal Hospital Chelsea, Royal Hospital Rd, SW3 4SR (020-7881 5200, chelsea-pensioners.co.uk, Sloane Sq tube, free).

February

5 February

A Day of Knights

Explore the Museum of the Order of St John, which tells the fascinating story of the Order of the Hospital of St John of Jerusalem, founded after the first Crusade captured Jerusalem in 1099. The story spans over 900 years: beginning with the Crusades and continuing through revolutions, war and peace, it shows how warrior monks set out from Clerkenwell to fight for the faith and tend the sick. An official tour of the crypt and museum takes around 80 minutes, so allow around two hours if you're planning to explore by yourself.

Museum of the Order of St John, St John's Gate, St John's Ln, EC1M 4DA (020-7324 4005, museumstjohn.org.uk and sja.org.uk, Farringdon tube, free).

Soak up the atmosphere at Temple Church, a mysterious, spiritual space with wonderful acoustics, where you can hear some of the City's finest church music. It's also one of London's most striking and historic churches, with 800 years of unbroken history. From the Crusaders in the 12th century, through the turmoil of the Reformation, the Civil War, the Great Fire and World War Two bombs – it has survived virtually intact.

The church was built by the Knights Templar or Red Knights (after the red crosses they wore), the order of crusading monks founded to protect pilgrims travelling to and from Jerusalem in the 12th century. It's in two parts: the rare circular 'Round' from 1185 and the Chancel (the 'Oblong'), dating from 1240. The Round Church, made of Caen stone, is one of only four Norman round churches remaining in England, consecrated by Heraclius, Crusader Patriarch of Jerusalem. Its choir is said to be perfection, with stunning stained glass windows, an impressive organ and a handsome wooden altar by Sir Christopher Wren. The Round Church contains nine knightly effigies, which were believed to be tombs until restoration revealed no bodies.

Temple Church, Temple, EC4Y 7BB (020-7353 3470, templechurch. com, Temple tube, paid entry).

6 February

Treasures & Treats

Take in an exhibition at Two Temple Place, a Gothic Revival extravaganza and treasure house. Originally called 'Astor House', TTP is a masterpiece of irreverent excess and fun, built in 1895 for William Waldorf Astor (1848-1919), later first Viscount Astor. It's both an architectural gem and a treasure house of exquisite works by the leading artists and craftsmen of the day. See the website for upcoming exhibitions.

Two Temple Place, WC2R 3BD (020-7836 3715, twotempleplace.org, Temple tube, free, ☎, ⅰ).

Enjoy an alfresco lunch at Whitecross Street Market, one of London's coolest markets with the best street food in town. It's home to a general market on weekdays, but it's the superb food market on Thu-Fri that draws the crowds. Like most market streets, it has an eclectic, independent feel that's missing from many of the capital's high streets. Hosts the famous Whitecross Street Party in July.

Whitecross Street Market, Whitecross St, EC1 (Barbican tube, £).

7 February

Heaven Scent!

Experience some aroma therapy at Penhaligon's, a bastion of classic British style, which has built its reputation on traditional fragrances. Established in the 1870s, Penhaligon's perfumes and pomades quickly became a favourite with the aristocracy and it still boasts two royal warrants. You can book a free private perfume profiling appointment with a fragrance advisor who can help you select your perfect match.

Penhaligon's, 41 Wellington St, WC2E 7BN (020-7836 2150, penhaligons.com, Covent Garden tube).

Have lunch at the Giaconda Dining Room which occupies the ground floor of a 17th-century building (1688) in Denmark Street. The Giaconda might not look much, with its small plain room, basic bare tables and chairs, and carpeted floor, but it's the perfect spot for a delicious lunch (Mon-Fri from noon), with a classical French menu. Wine is a bargain!

Giaconda Dining Room, 9 Denmark St, WC2H 8LS (020-7240 3334, giacondadining.com, Tottenham Court Rd tube, ££, ☎).

8 February

Game, Set & Match

Find out how the Wimbledon Tennis Museum became the largest of its kind in the world, with some 15,000 objects dating back to 1555! The museum traces Wimbledon's rich history on paper, in photos and on film, and through a wealth of objects and memorabilia. Following a re-vamp in 2006 it's now a high-tech spectacular with hands-on exhibits, interactive displays, touch screens, films and audio guides in nine languages.

Wimbledon Tennis Museum, Church Rd, Wimbledon, SW19 (020-8944 1066, wimbledon.com/visiting/museum, Wimbledon Park tube).

Go to the dogs with some mates at Wimbledon Park Stadium on a Friday or Saturday night. Enjoy the greyhound racing from the comfort of the glass-fronted grandstand, with panoramic views of the track and no less than four bars and a restaurant. A great fun night out and – if you're lucky – you may even show a profit!

London Wimbledon Stadium, Plough Ln, SW17 0BL (0870-840 8905, lovethedogs.co.uk/wimbledon, Wimbledon Park tube, ££).

9 February

The Other Westminster Churches

Ascend the bell tower of Westminster Cathedral, London's distinctive Byzantine-style, Catholic cathedral built in 1903. The Campanile Bell Tower, 273ft high, is dedicated to St Edward the Confessor and has just one bell, 'Edward', the gift of the Duchess of Norfolk in 1910. The tower's viewing gallery offers impressive 360° views across the city.

Westminster Cathedral, Francis St and Victoria St, SW1P 1QW (020-7798 9055, westminstercathedral.org.uk, Victoria tube, free to cathedral).

St Margaret's Church

While you're in a worshipful mood, drop into St Margaret's church, a hidden gem in the shadow of Westminster Abbey. The original church was built in the latter part of the 11th century so that local people could worship without disturbing the Benedictine monks at the Abbey. It's dedicated to the now little-known St Margaret of Antioch, one of the most popular saints among the laity in medieval England.

St Margaret's, St Margaret St, SW1P 3JX (020-7654 4840. westminster-abbey.org/st-margarets, Westminster tube, free).

10 February

Full House with a Glorious Past

Eyes down in Tooting at the Gala Bingo Hall, the former Granada Cinema (Grade I listed) built in the '30s and considered by many to be the most spectacular cinema in Britain. This exotic treasure of 20th-century architecture is the ultimate example of the 'super cinema style' of the '30s, with a lavishly-decorated interior. A glorious building with a glorious past.

Gala Bingo Hall, 50 Mitcham Rd, SW17 9NA (020-8672 5717, galabingo.com/clubs/tooting, Tooting Broadway tube).

Gala Bingo Hall

Watch an ice hockey match at Planet Ice in Brixton, the home of Streatham Redskins (streatham-redskins. co.uk), who were exiled from their previous home at Streatham Ice Rink when it closed in 2011. The Redskins are among the oldest British ice hockey teams (founded in 1932) and, although no longer in the Premier tier, you're guaranteed an enjoyable night out.

Planet Ice, 49 Brixton Station Rd, SW9 8PQ (020-7737 5034, planet-ice.co.uk/arena/brixton, Brixton tube, ☎, 🅸).

11 February

Concerts & Cream Teas

Take in a free lunchtime concert at the splendid 18th-century St Martin-in-the-Fields, one of London's most beloved non-cathedral churches, noted for its fine architecture (by James Gibbs, 1726), work with the poor and musical traditions. St Martin hosts a series of free lunchtime concerts showcasing new and emerging talent, plus atmospheric candlelit concerts (see website for information).

St Martin-in-the-Fields, Trafalgar Sq, WC2N 4JJ (020-7766 1100, stmartin-in-the-fields.org, Charing Cross tube, free).

Enjoy lunch or afternoon tea in St Martin's Café in the Crypt – *Les Routiers* Café of the Year 2012. The crypt's beautiful 18th-century architecture (with brick-vaulted ceilings) is a feast for your eyes, while the tantalising menu ensures that your stomach isn't left out. Open seven days a week for breakfast through to dinner (closes 6pm on Sundays), with live jazz on Wednesday evenings.

Café in the Crypt (stmartin-in-the-fields.org/cafe-in-the-crypt, £).

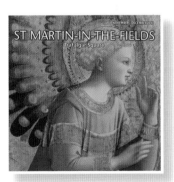

February

February

12 February

Come Dancing (After Brunch)

Tuck into a tantalising brunch at Yotam Ottolenghi's acclaimed restaurant in Islington (opposite the Almeida theatre). It's the take-away deli chain's only 'proper' restaurant, seating around 50 (mostly at communal tables with a few small tables for two) in a cool, sophisticated environment. Bookings are accepted only for dinner, so if you fancy weekend brunch you need to arrive early.

Ottolenghi, 287 Upper St, N1 2TZ (020-7288 1454, ottolenghi.co.uk/ locations/islington, Highbury & Islington tube, ££).

Shake a leg at the City Academy which offers a mind-boggling choice of dance classes and courses at venues across London, from ballet to ballroom, salsa to street dance, tango to tap dance, and much more. If you just want to dance to keep fit, there are also a range of fitness dance classes. Whatever your desires, the City Academy will fill your dance card.

City Academy, 51-53 Mount Pleasant, WC1X 0AE (020-7042 8833, city-academy.com/dance-classes, Farringdon tube, ☏).

13 February

Evolution of a Genius

Visit the Darwin Centre at the Natural History Museum on the anniversary of Charles Darwin's (1809-82) birthday. Experience world-class science in action in the museum's state-of-the-art £78m science and collections facility, which opened in 2009. See leading scientists at work, incredible specimens, and exciting wall displays and projections, as you journey through the futuristic Cocoon building.

Darwin Centre, Natural History Museum, Cromwell Rd, SW7 5BD (020-7942 5000, nhm.ac.uk/visit-us/darwin-centre-visitors, South Kensington tube, free).

Explore the Royal Geographical Society, where Darwin became a Fellow in 1838 and a member of the governing council in 1840. Founded in 1830 to promote the advancement of geographical science, today its work includes publishing, supporting field research and expeditions, lectures, conferences and managing its collections. The RGS organises over 150 free events annually across London, many open to the public.

Royal Geographical Society, Lowther Lodge, 1 Kensington Gore, SW7 2AR (020-7591 3000, rgs.org/whatson, South Kensington tube, free).

Natural History Museum

14 February

Be My Valentine

Indulge yourself at Ushvani, one of London's most luxurious day spas, acclaimed as the UK's Best Day Spa by both *Tatler* and *Condé Nast Traveler*. Housed in an Edwardian period building, the wood-panelled Ushvani specialises in traditional southeast Asian treatments such as Balinese massage. Before treatments you're invited to use the spa facilities, which include a hydrotherapeutic spa pool, themed showers and steam rooms. One clever touch is that you never actually see another client, so you feel like the pool and eucalyptus showers (the blasts of hot and cold showers are meant to replicate the rain in the rain forest) are exclusively yours.

Asmara Suite

Each room has a different theme, for example the Asmara (Malay for 'love') Suite is used by couples, friends and relatives, the Blue Room is the men's treatment room, while the Sentosa Studio is for yoga, Pilates and meditation classes. In keeping with Malaysian tradition, the spa treats men and women separately, so when necessary a screen is used to divide couples during treatments. The Balinese massage and the Ushvani signature facial massage are highly recommended. Only marginally cheaper than plastic surgery, but much more enjoyable!

Ushvani, 1 Cadogan Gardens, Knightsbridge, SW3 2RJ (020-7730 2888, ushvani.com, Sloane Sq tube).

Treat your partner to dinner at the Michelin-starred Galvin at Windows restaurant and bar, which has a glamorous interior evoking the golden age of the '30s. Situated on the 28th floor of the London Hilton in trendy Mayfair, its pièce de résistance is its panoramic views over the capital, including the gardens of Buckingham Palace. If you want to impress, Galvin at Windows boasts not only tempting cocktails in its decadent bar, but superb cuisine based around modern French haute cuisine with a twist, and an extensive wine list.

Galvin at Windows, Park Lane Hilton, 22 Park Ln, W1K 1BE (020-7208 4021, galvinatwindows.com, Hyde Park Cnr tube, £££, ☎).

February

15 February

Golf for the Hoi Polloi

Tee off with a round of indoor golf at Urban Golf, where anyone, from beginner to professional, can walk in off the street to play, practice or learn. Using the latest simulators, you can 'play' 60 of the world's best championship courses. And you aren't required to abide by any archaic dress codes or speak in whispers in the club house – there isn't one.

Urban Golf, 33 Great Pulteney St, W1F 9NW (020-7248 8600, urbangolf.co.uk, Piccadilly Circus tube, ☎).

Listen to some cool jazz at Ronnie Scott's, London's most famous jazz club founded in 1959 and inspired by the vibrant New York jazz scene of the '50s. Ronnie's was a key player in Soho's jazz explosion in the '60s and '70s, and despite the passing of Scott (1927-96) it still retains some of the original electrifying atmosphere.

Ronnie Scott's, 47 Frith St, W1D 4HT (020-7439 0747, ronniescotts. co.uk, Tottenham Court Rd tube, £).

16 February

Art for Art's Sake

Ghost, Kadir Attia

Prepare to be shocked and captivated in equal measure at the Saatchi Gallery, housed in the Duke of York's Headquarters (Grade II* listed) completed in 1801, one of London's most beautiful art spaces. It provokes extremes of critical reaction, but love it or hate it, it never fails to get a reaction and attracts over 1.4m visitors a year.

Saatchi Gallery, Duke of York's HQ, King's Rd, SW3 4RY (020-7730 8135, saatchi-gallery.co.uk, Sloane Sq tube, free).

Seek out artistic icons at Holy Trinity, Sloane Square, a ravishing Victorian, Anglican parish church built in 1880-90, dubbed 'the cathedral of the Arts & Crafts movement'. Built on a grand scale, it's London's widest church, even eclipsing St Paul's Cathedral. However, it's the interior that makes Holy Trinity stand out, the work of leading sculptors and designers of the day.

Holy Trinity Church, Sloane St, SW1X 9BZ (020-7730 7270, holytrinitysloanesquare.co.uk, Sloane Sq tube, free).

17 February

A Day With Dickens

Celebrate the anniversary of Charles Dickens' birth – on 7th February 1812 in Landport (Portsmouth) – with a visit to the Charles Dickens Museum in Holborn. The museum is spread over four floors of a typical Georgian terraced house, where the rooms have a traditional Victorian appearance. London's most famous author lived here for over two years from March 1837 (a year after his marriage) until December 1839: it's the only surviving house he occupied in London. He and his wife Catherine shared the house with the eldest three of their ten children, and their two eldest daughters were born here.

It was a productive time for the author, during which he completed *The Pickwick Papers*, wrote *Oliver Twist* and *Nicholas Nickleby*, and worked on *Barnaby Rudge*, therefore it's appropriate that it houses the world's most important Dickens' collection totalling over 100,000 items, including manuscripts, rare editions, paintings, personal items and a research library. The photographic collection contains over 5,000 photographs, 2,000 magic lantern slides, 1,000 35mm slides and a large number of colour transparencies. There are also over 500 portraits of Dickens, many interesting views of 19th-century London, illustrations from his novels, and cartoons and caricatures.

Charles Dickens Museum, 48 Doughty St, WC1N 2LX (020-7405 2127, dickensmuseum.com, Russell Sq tube).

———————

Toast the ghost of Dickens at the atmospheric George & Vulture in the City. Tucked away in an alley, it's the ultimate Pickwickian pub, mentioned at least 20 times in *The Pickwick Papers*. Pickwick and his friends Tupman, Winkle and Snodgrass make it their London base, enjoying a pint of 'particular port' in 'very good, old-fashioned and comfortable quarters'. Saved by the author's great-grandson when threatened with demolition, the George & Vulture is adorned with Dickens-related portraits and photographs.

The George & Vulture, 3 Castle Court, EC3V 9DL (020-7626 9710, Bank tube, £).

February

18 February

King of the Castle

Get in a spot of practice before tackling Everest at the Castle Climbing Centre in Stoke Newington. The Castle, housed in a former Victorian pumping station, is run by climbers for climbers, and is the premier indoor climbing centre in southeast England. Whether you're a complete novice or a rusty pro, the Castle is a good place to (re-)learn the ropes.

Castle Climbing Centre, Green Lanes, Stoke Newington, N4 2HA (020-8211 7000, castle-climbing.co.uk, Manor House tube, 🏛).

Take a stroll around Clissold Park, one of north London's finest green spaces offering a wide range of facilities, including a children's playground, paddling pool, sports fields, bowling green, table tennis, basketball and tennis courts, bandstand, a café and animal attractions, including an aviary, animal enclosures and terrapins in the lakes. Even the benches are beautiful in Clissold Park!

Clissold Park, Greenway Close, N4 2EY (020-8356 8428, hackney. gov.uk/clissold-park.htm/clissoldpark.com, Manor House tube, free).

19 February

An Orgy of Orchids

Be enchanted by the ravishing orchids at the Royal Botanic Gardens, Kew, on display in February or early March in the Princess of Wales Conservatory. Kew has the oldest living orchid collection in existence, dating back over 200 years, with around 5,000 species. Its annual Tropical Extravaganza features stunning displays of thousands of orchids – a wonderful way to brighten up winter with a burst of colour.

Royal Botanic Gardens, Kew, TW9 3AB (020-8332 5655, kew.org, Kew Gardens tube, ℹ).

See some first class art at the Orleans House Gallery overlooking the Thames in Twickenham, one of Greater London's best small galleries. Opened in 1972, it's home to Richmond's art collection, one of the most outstanding fine art collections in London outside the city's national collections. The Orleans has a reputation for innovative exhibitions, ranging from historical to contemporary art.

Orleans House Gallery, Riverside, TW1 3DJ (020-8831 6000, richmond.gov.uk/orleans_house_gallery, St Margaret's rail, free).

20 February

Potter Among the Tombstones

Find Beatrix Potter's beloved characters at Brompton Cemetery, one of London's 'magnificent seven' Victorian cemeteries. One of Britain's oldest (1840) and most distinguished garden cemeteries, it contains some 35,000 monuments marking the sites of over 200,000 burials. Among its most famous 'residents' is Beatrix Potter, who lived nearby and took the names of many of her animal characters from tombstones in the cemetery.

Brompton Cemetery, Fulham Rd, SW10 9UG (020-7352 1201, royalparks.org.uk/parks/brompton_cemetery and brompton-cemetery.org, West Brompton tube, free).

———————

Relax at the West London Buddhist Centre, where everyone is welcome to attend a drop-in meditation class without booking. There are lunchtime meditation sessions on weekdays (1-2pm) suitable for everyone from beginners (instruction is provided) to Buddha. On Saturday mornings there's a thorough introduction class to basic Buddhist meditation, with tips on posture, relaxation and body awareness.

West London Buddhist Centre, 94 Westbourne Park Villas, W2 5EB (020-7727 9382, westlondonbuddhistcentre.com, Royal Oak tube).

Brompton Cemetary

21 February

Lessons in Life

Recharge your batteries with a course or lecture at the School of Life, a cultural enterprise offering ideas on how to live wisely and well. You aren't brainwashed by dogma, but directed towards a variety of ideas – from philosophy to literature, psychology to the visual arts – designed to tickle, exercise and expand your mind.

School of Life, 70 Marchmont St, WC1N 1AB (020-7833 1010, theschooloflife.com, Russell Sq tube, ☏).

———————

Raise a glass at The Princess Louise on High Holborn, one of London's most stunning Victorian pubs. Its remarkable original 'gin-palace' interior is one of the best preserved and most attractive in London. Named in honour of Queen Victoria's fourth daughter, the pub was built in 1872 and refitted in 1891 during the golden age of Victorian pub design.

The Princess Louise, *208-209 High Holborn, WC1V 7BW* **(020-7405 8816, Holborn tube, £).**

February

22 February

EastEnders

Spend the Saturday at Broadway and Netil Markets in East London. Broadway Market runs from London Fields park to the Regent's Canal and forms part of a pedestrian and cycle-friendly route from the Hackney Empire through the park, over the canal and on to Haggerston Park and Hackney City Farm at the junction with Hackney Road. Barrow boys have been welcoming shoppers to Broadway Market since the 1890s, and although it suffered a decline over the years, it has gone from strength to strength since the Saturday food market was launched in 2004.

Today there are over 100 stalls selling delicious cheeses, breads, coffee, rare-breed meat, spices, cakes etc., along with stalls selling tasty ethnic snacks and drinks, while cosy cafés, trendy restaurants, bustling pubs, raucous indie music shops and myriad other independent shops line the street, The market is also popular for its vintage and designer togs, bric-à-brac, books, flowers and crafts.

The neighbouring **Netil Market** – an altogether more sedate and smaller affair – is just around the corner on Westgate Street, where you'll find vintage homewares, jewellery designers, illustrators, original artwork, vintage clothing, accessories and more, as well as more food stalls and a heated dining area.

Broadway Market, E8 (broadwaymarket.co.uk, London Fields rail) and Netil Market, 11-25 Westgate St, E8 3R (netilmarket.tumblr.com).

Visit Viktor Wynd's Little Shop of Horrors on a Saturday (noon to 7pm) or by *appointment. Opened by the* Last Tuesday Society (thelasttuesdaysociety.org), the Little Shop is a shop, art gallery and museum, designed in the style of a 17th-century *Wunderkabinett*: a collection of objects assembled on a whim for their aesthetic or historical appeal. It sells a wide variety of curiosities, including 19th-century shrunken heads, taxidermy, narwhal tusks, carnivorous plants and articulated skeletons.

Viktor Wynd's Little Shop of Horrors, 11 Mare St, E8 4RP (020-7998 3617, viktorwyndofhackney.co.uk, Cambridge Heath rail).

23 February

The Actors' Church & Beer Buffs' Pub

Step inside the other St Paul's – Covent Garden's parish church designed by Inigo Jones in 1631. Dubbed the actors' church, it contains a wealth of memorials dedicated to famous personalities of stage and screen. St Paul's is noted for its concerts and has its own resident chamber orchestra, the Orchestra of St Paul's, and a celebrated summer repertory season.

St Paul's, 31 Bedford St, Covent Garden, WC2E 9ED (020-7836 5221, actorschurch.org, Covent Garden tube, free).

Join beer aficionados for a pint of real ale at The Harp in Covent Garden, the CAMRA UK 'National Pub of the Year' 2010. Built in the 1830s, it has an attractive stained glass front and what's reputed to be the West End's best choice of real ale, with an ever-changing selection that includes regulars such as Dark Star, Harveys, Sambrook's and Twickenham Ales.

The Harp, 47 Chandos Place, WC2N 4HS (020-7836 0291, harpcoventgarden.com, Charing Cross tube, £).

24 February

Queen of Winter Flowers

Breathe in the fleeting fragrance of camellias at Chiswick House's spectacular conservatory, a national treasure and the oldest collection in the Western world. Known as the queen of winter flowers, the camellias at Chiswick bring a burst of glorious colour to the season. Visitors can also celebrate these beautiful blooms in the newly-restored 19th-century Italian Garden.

Chiswick House & Garden, Burlington Ln, W4 2RP (020-8742 3905, chgt.org.uk, Turnham Green tube, ⓘ).

Chiswick House

Sample South American flavours with dinner at Quantus (Latin for 'as great as') in Chiswick, a comfortable, romantic restaurant with an eclectic menu presenting a South American influence, created by 'Cocinero Argentino' Juan Zuliani. Using seasonal, locally sourced ingredients, Quantus offers a la carte and set menus which change frequently, plus a comprehensive wine list. There's also a bar with delicious cocktails.

Quantus, 38 Devonshire Rd, W4 2HD (020-8994 0488, quantus-london.com, Turnham Green tube, ££, 🍽).

February

25 February

Temples to Justice & Tea

Observe proceedings at the Royal Courts of Justice, a marvel of Victorian Gothic architecture, particularly the cathedral-like Great Hall. Opened in 1882, the finished building contained 35m Portland stone bricks, over 3.5mi of corridors and some 1,000 clocks. Visitors are invited to watch civil trials (criminal trials take place at the Old Bailey), although guided tours must be booked (see website).

Royal Courts of Justice, The Strand, WC2A 2LL (020-7947 7684, justice.gov.uk/courts/rcj-rolls-building/rcj/tours, Temple tube, ☎).

Pop across the road for a cup of Rosie Lea at Twinings, one of London's oldest companies trading continuously from the same site. It was founded in 1706 by Thomas Twining (1675-1741), who daringly introduced tea to a coffee house when it was an exotic drink enjoyed only by the wealthy. The shop contains a museum and offers tea tastings, as well as lunch and refreshments.

Twinings, 216 Strand, WC2R 1AP (020-7583 1359, shop.twinings. co.uk/shop/strand, Temple tube, £).

26 February

Chills & Thrills in Islington

Tuck into a big breakfast at The Big Chill House – a large Victorian pub in the heart of London's King's Cross – in the expansive arts café on the ground floor. The Big Chill House has pretty much everything you could want – freshly-roasted morning coffee, free wi-fi in the café area, an upstairs study room and a sunny terrace.

The Big Chill House, 257-259 Pentonville Rd, N1 9NL (020-7427 2540, bigchill.net/house, King's Cross St Pancras tube, £).

Take in a film at Screen on the Green, an Art Deco beauty opened as a cinema in 1913. With its huge neon sign and red velvet curtains, the Screen has maintained its retro style, with drinks served at your seat and plush sofas with foot stools. It delivers consistently classy movies, focusing on the more interesting mainstream releases, indies and world cinema.

Screen on the Green, 83 Upper St, N1 0NP (0871-906 9060, everymancinema.com/cinemas/screen-on-the-green, Angel tube, ☎).

27 February

The Wonders of Whitechapel

Catch a tour of the Whitechapel Bell Foundry, the oldest manufacturing company in Britain dating back to at least 1570. Bells cast here include Big Ben (the great bell in the Palace of Westminster) in 1858, and the first casting (in 1752) of the famous (US) Liberty Bell. Tours must be booked, but the interesting free museum is also worth a visit.

Whitechapel Bell Foundry, 32-34 Whitechapel Rd, E1 1DY (020-7247 2599, whitechapelbellfoundry.co.uk, Aldgate East tube, free).

The Liberty Bell

Wonder at Wilton's Music Hall – dubbed 'the oldest Grand Music Hall in the world' – which adds a new dimension to the term 'faded elegance'. This gloriously crumbling relic of a past age is one of the first generation of pub music halls that sprang up in London in the 1850s. Intimate concerts still take place in the auditorium.

Wilton's Music Hall, 1 Graces Alley, London E1 8JB (020-7702 9555, wiltons.org.uk, Aldgate East tube, ☎).

28 February

Peace in the City

Find some inner calm at St Bride's Church, dubbed the journalists' church, where the beauty of the architecture blends with the weight of history to provide a peaceful counterpoint to the clamour of the City. Designed by Wren and completed in 1703, its 226ft wedding cake spire – Wren's tallest – dominates the surrounding area. There are also lunchtime concerts and other frequent musical events.

St Bride's Church, Fleet St, EC4Y 8AU (020-7427 0133, stbrides. com, St Paul's tube, free).

Discover the Barbican Centre, a prominent example of British Brutalist concrete architecture and Europe's largest arts venue, staging a comprehensive range of art, music, theatre, dance, film and creative learning events. The 'ugly' building conceals hidden treasures and is full of peaceful places to enjoy, including high walkways, a music library, an indoor tropical conservatory, a lakeside terrace and gardens.

Barbican Centre, Silk St, London Wall, EC2Y 8DS (020-7638 4141, barbican.org.uk, Barbican tube, free).

29 February

Leap Year Luxuries

February

When you only get a birthday once every four years (2016, 2020, etc.) you need to do something special, so why not celebrate with a flight over the city in a helicopter? The London Helicopter company offers 20-minute flights over the city from the Barclays London Heliport in Battersea. The route follows the Thames from Putney in the west to Greenwich in the east, with the pilot pointing out landmarks along the way.

The London Helicopter, POD Building, Bridges Court, SW11 3RE (020-7887 2626, thelondonhelicopter.com, Clapham Junction rail, ☎).

Celebrate your dearth of birthdays at Dinner by Heston, Heston Blumenthal's acclaimed West End restaurant. It isn't mandatory to have dinner – you can also have lunch – but dinner is the prize ticket (and one of London's hottest). Widely acclaimed as one of the city's and the world's best restaurants – astonishingly good and huge fun – but astronomically expensive for normal folk. The good news is that you'll have plenty of time to save up – and you might even be able to secure a table if you book four years in advance!

Dinner by Heston, Mandarin Oriental Hyde Park, 66 Knightsbridge, SW1X 7LA, (020-7201 3833, dinnerbyheston.com, Knightsbridge tube, £££, ☎).

February

PICCADILLY CIRCUS

March

1 March

Captivating Cannizaro

Admire the crocuses at Cannizaro Park, one of London's most beautiful 'secret' parks situated on the edge of Wimbledon Common (although it sounds as if it should be in Italy). Cannizaro was a private garden for some 300 years before opening as a public park in 1949. It combines great natural beauty with a unique collection of rare and exquisite trees and shrubs, including sassafras, camellia, rhododendron and other ericaceous plants. It has a huge variety of green areas, from expansive lawns to small intimate spaces, such as the herb and tennis court gardens, lovely leisurely walks through woodlands, and formal areas including a sunken garden next to the park's hotel and an Italian Garden near its pond.

> The park has a long history of staging arts and musical events, including the Wimbledon Cannizaro Festival in summer.

Cannizaro Park, West Side Common, Wimbledon, SW19 4UE (020-8879 1464, cannizaropark.com, Wimbledon tube, free).

Book a table for two for lunch or afternoon tea at Cannizaro House, an elegant country house hotel on the edge of Cannizaro Park. It was built in the early 1700s, and the kitchen garden served the tables of its many famous residents and guests from the 18th century to the last private owners in the '40s. The restaurant, set in the hotel's historic dining room, is decorated with whimsical patterned wallpaper and regal high-backed chairs, and has a Gatsby-esque terrace overlooking the park, providing a sense of retro grandeur. The modern British menu is influenced by organic seasonal produce such as Cornish crab and cognac bisque with crayfish, avocado and coriander cress and slow-cooked belly and tenderloin of Wiltshire pork with paprika crackling.

Cannizaro House, West Side Common, Wimbledon, SW19 4UD (020-8879 1464, cannizarohouse.com, Wimbledon tube, ££, 🏨).

2 March

Chic on the Cheap

Go designer sample-sale shopping at Chelsea Old Town Hall, and revamp your wardrobe at rock-bottom prices. Sales may include brands such as Belstaff, Armani, D&G, Westwood, Chloe, Missoni, Lanvin, YSL, Jimmy Choo, Valentino, Ralph Lauren, Pringle, Paul Smith, Moschino, Hugo Boss and more. Not just womenswear, but accessories, jewellery, menswear and childrenswear, all selling at discounts of 60 to 90 percent below retail prices.

Chelsea Old Town Hall, Kings Rd, SW3 5EE (01273-858464, designersales.co.uk/tag/chelsea-old-town-hall, Sloane Sq tube, ⓘ).

Allons nous to the Institut français du Royaume-Uni (or French Institute) in Kensington, the official French government centre of language and culture in the UK. The Institut, founded in 1910, occupies a handsome Art Deco building in Kensington containing a cinema/theatre, library, bistro and reception rooms. A ray of French sunshine in west London.

Institut français du Royaume-Uni, 17 Queensberry Place, SW7 2DT (020-7871 3515, institut-francais.org.uk, South Kensington tube, free).

3 March

Picture Perfect

Join a free, one-hour guided tour (daily, 11.30am and 2.30pm plus Fridays at 7pm) at the National Gallery in Trafalgar Square. Designed specifically for first-time, adult visitors, tours are led by gallery lecturers and look at five or six paintings to help provide an overview of the collection. Have lunch at the National Dining Rooms (020-7747 2525, ££, ☎) or the more casual National Café (£).

National Gallery, Trafalgar Sq, WC2N 5DN (020-7747 2885, nationalgallery.org.uk, Charing Cross tube, free).

See a film in style at the Curzon Cinema Mayfair (Grade II listed), one of London's oldest and most prestigious art-house cinemas, with two screens and a stylish bar. Opened in 1934, the Curzon was one of the first cinemas to import and show foreign language films in the UK. Nowadays it also screens live performances from around the world.

Curzon Cinema Mayfair, 38 Curzon St, W1J 7TY (0330-500 1331, curzoncinemas.com/cinemas/mayfair, Green Park tube, ☎).

March

4 March

Flipping Good Fun

Cheer on competitors in the Great Spitalfields Pancake Race on Shrove Tuesday (the day preceding Ash Wednesday, the first day of Lent). Teams dressed in wacky costumes – from fashionable locals in specially-created outfits to construction workers in their hardhats – run up and down Dray Walk at the Old Truman Brewery, flipping pancakes to raise money for charity.

The Great Spitalfields Pancake Race, Old Truman Brewery, 91 Brick Ln, E1 6QL (020-7375 0441, alternativearts.co.uk, Shoreditch High St tube, free, ⓘ).

Buy some cool togs at Old Spitalfields Market, one of London's finest surviving Victorian market halls. The restored market is the perfect antidote to anonymous shopping malls, and offers a popular daily fashion, food, vintage and general market. Discover 'hidden gems' from fashion and arts to interiors and antiques, or delve into the profusion of independent shops, cafés and restaurants.

Old Spitalfields Market, 65 Brushfield St, E1 6AA (020-7377 1496, oldspitalfieldsmarket.com, Liverpool St tube).

5 March

A Night (& Day) at the Opera

Step backstage in the shadow of Fonteyn, Nureyev and Pavarotti on a tour of the Royal Opera House, one of the world's premier opera houses. The ROH 'Velvet, Gilt and Glamour Tour' focuses on the architecture and the history of the theatre, while the 'Backstage Tour' visits the backstage and front of house areas and includes the colourful history of the theatre.

Royal Opera House, Covent Garden, WC2E 9DD (020-7304 4000, roh.org.uk, Covent Garden tube, ☎).

Spend a memorable and unique evening at Bel Canto Restaurant, where (from Tuesday to Saturday) talented singers masquerade as 'waiting staff', one minute serving your starter or pouring your wine, the next belting out solos, duets or quartets from *Don Giovanni*, *Tosca*, *La Boheme* or *Carmen*, while balancing the plates and glasses. Great fun!

Bel Canto Restaurant, Corus Hotel Hyde Park, 1-7 Lancaster Gate, W2 3LG (020-7262 1678, lebelcanto.com/page.php?id=56&langue=1, Lancaster Gate tube, ££, ☎).

March

6 March

Glorious Greenwich

Feast your eyes on the magnificent Painted Hall in the Old Royal Naval College in Greenwich, part of the National Maritime Museum, the largest museum of its kind in the world. The Painted Hall (1708-1727), designed by Sir Christopher Wren and completed by Nicholas Hawksmoor and Sir John Vanbrugh, has been described as the 'finest dining hall in Europe'.

Painted Hall, National Maritime Museum, Park Row, SE10 9NF (020-8858 4422, rmg.co.uk/national-maritime-museum and ornc.org, Cutty Sark DLR, free).

Flutter along to the Fan Museum in Greenwich, the only museum in the world devoted entirely to fans and fan-making, housed in two early Georgian (1721) houses. The museum's collection numbers over 4,000 fans, fan leaves and related ephemera, with the oldest dating from the 11th century. Visit on a Tuesday or Sunday and you can have afternoon tea in the orangery.

Fan Museum, 12 Crooms Hill, SE10 8ER (020-8305 1441, thefanmuseum.org.uk, Cutty Sark DLR, ☏).

Painted Hall, Old Royal Naval College, Greenwich

7 March

Tuck in with the Jolly Friars

Enjoy a bite of culture at the Lunchbox Theatre at the St Bride Foundation & Library (1895), a unique cultural centre. Shows (1pm daily, ¾hr) include

everything from classics to new pieces by up and coming writers. Alternatively, you can attend an evening performance in the Bridewell Theatre (or have a drink in the Bridewell Bar).

Lunchbox Theatre, St Bride Foundation & Library, 14 Bride Ln, EC4Y 8EQ (020-7353 3331, stbride.org and sbf.org.uk, Blackfriars tube, £).

Join the brothers at The Black Friar pub which has London's most spectacular interior – a sumptuous blend of Arts & Crafts and Art Nouveau styles. The building dates from 1875 and stands on the site of a medieval Dominican Friary which is reflected in the decoration: friars feature everywhere in the pub's cascade of intricate friezes, mosaics, reliefs and sculptures.

The Black Friar, 174 Queen Victoria St, EC4V 4EG (020-7236 5474, nicholsonspubs.co.uk/theblackfriarblackfriarslondon, Blackfriars tube, £).

March

8 March

Chill Out in Camden

Rummage through the stalls in Stables Market, part of the vast Camden Market complex that once housed the horses that pulled the barges on nearby Regent's Canal. Nowadays it contains some 700 shops and stalls offering a bewildering array of goods, from the latest in adventurous alternative fashion to superb vintage clothing and the joy of collecting 'stuff".

Stables Market, Chalk Farm Rd, NW1 8AH (020-7485-5511, stablesmarket.com and camdenlock.net/stables/index.html, Chalk Farm tube).

———————

Roll up for a show at The Roundhouse, home to an exciting programme of live music, theatre, dance, circus, installations and new media. A former Victorian steam-engine repair shed, the Roundhouse became a legendary gig venue in the '60s hosting many of the world's top rock bands. It's now a charity – the Roundhouse Trust – which runs a comprehensive creative programme for 11-25s.

The Roundhouse, Chalk Farm Rd, NW1 8EH (0844-482 8008, roundhouse.org.uk, Chalk Farm tube, 🏛).

9 March

Get High in Hampstead

Fly a kite from Parliament Hill (Hampstead Heath), which although just 322ft high, provides excellent views of the capital's skyline. Parliament Hill – thought to take its name from its role as a defensive post for troops loyal to Parliament during the English Civil War – was purchased in 1888 for £300,000 and added to the Heath.

Parliament Hill, Hampstead Heath, NW3 (cityoflondon.gov.uk > green-spaces > hampstead-heath, Gospel Oak tube, free).

———————

Go star-gazing at Hampstead Observatory, one of only a few observatories in the world situated in the centre of a huge city, and the only one in London offering regular free viewings of the night sky. Situated at the highest point in the city, it's owned and operated by the Hampstead Scientific Society (1899).

Hampstead Observatory, Cnr of Heath St and Hampstead Grove, Lower Terrace, Whitestone Pond, NW3 7LT (hampsteadscience. ac.uk, Hampstead tube, free, ⓘ).

Hampstead Observatory

10 March

Bustling Brixton

Chill out in Brixton Market, London's most vibrant and colourful market in one of its most exciting areas. Once a wealthy part of London – home to the city's first purpose-built department store (Bon Marché in 1877) and its first electric street lighting (Electric Ave) – nowadays Brixton is renowned for its markets and as the focus of London's Caribbean community. Brixton Market is actually a number of markets, comprising a vibrant street market and covered market areas in the nearby arcades: Reliance Arcade, Market Row and Granville Arcade – the last now rebranded as 'Brixton Village' and packed with culinary treats.

The market is an important focal point for the black community and sells a wide range of foods and goods, but is best known for its African and Caribbean produce, including specialties such as flying fish, breadfruit and all manner of weird looking fresh meats, reflecting the diverse community of Brixton and the surrounding area. It has a heaving, bustling atmosphere that you won't find elsewhere in London, offering a wide choice of world produce at modest prices with minimum frills. The Atlantic Road part of the market offers more in the way of clothes, leather goods, household linen and children's toys, rather than food. Brixton Station Road also hosts a Sunday farmers' market (10am to 2pm).

Brixton Market, Electric Ave, Pope's Rd and Brixton Station Rd, SW9 (020-7926 2530, brixtonmarket.net, Brixton tube).

Enjoy London's best (and most reasonably priced) pizza at Franco Manca, housed in the covered section of Brixton Market. Franco's pays homage to the best Neapolitan pizzerias, serving delicious, slow-rise, sourdough-crust pizzas topped with simple sauce, the best Italian-style cheese, cured meats and seasonal vegetables – cooked for just 40 seconds at a high temperature in a brick kiln. *Bellissimo!*

Franco Manca, Unit 4, Market Row, SW9 8LD (020-7738 3021, francomanca.co.uk/pages/brixton.html, Brixton tube, £).

March

March

11 March

Towers of Power

Climb Big Ben's tower! If you're a UK resident you can book a free tour of Elizabeth Tower – which houses Big Ben – by contacting your local MP or a member of the House of Lords. Tours take you up the 334 spiral steps to the top of the tower (203ft) to see the clock mechanism and faces and hear Big Ben strike the hour.

Palace of Westminster, Westminster, SW1A 0AA (020-7219 3000, parliament.uk/visiting/visiting-and-tours/ukvisitors/bigben, Westminster tube, ☎).

See the Jewel Tower, one of only two surviving sections of the medieval royal Palace of Westminster (the other is Westminster Hall). Built in around 1365 to house the treasures of Edward III, the ground floor retains its superb original 14th-century ribbed vaulting adorned with 16 unusual bosses of animals, grotesque human faces and green men.

Jewel Tower, Abingdon St, SW1P 3JX (020-7222 2219, english-heritage.org.uk/daysout/properties/jewel-tower, Westminster tube).

12 March

Chocolate Nirvana

Forget the diet and unleash your culinary creativity at a chocolate-making workshop at My Chocolate. Under the guidance of a Master Chocolatier – using ingredients such as melted organic chocolate, dark chocolate ganache, milk chocolate praline and strawberry curls – you'll soon be making your own handmade organic chocolates, truffles, cupcakes, whoopee pies and even chocolate martinis. Mmmm…!

My Chocolate, Unit B1, Hatton Sq Business Centre, 16-16A Baldwins Gardens, EC1N 7RJ (020-7269 5760, mychocolate.co.uk, Chancery Ln tube, ☎).

Spend an entertaining evening at the Menier Chocolate Factory Theatre, a renovated Victorian (1870) chocolate factory that now houses an award-winning theatre. With original exposed wooden beams, unusual cast iron columns and brick feature interior, the Chocolate Factory is a stimulating environment in which to enjoy a high-quality and entertaining theatrical experience. Also a seductive restaurant (££) and bar.

Menier Chocolate Factory Theatre, 53 Southwark St, SE1 1RU (020-7378 1713, menierchocolatefactory.com, London Bridge tube, ☎).

13 March

It's a Woman's World

Attend the Women of the World (WOW) Festival at the Southbank Centre, part of Women's History Month in East London. WOW is an annual global festival where women (and men!) of all ages and backgrounds celebrate women's achievements and discuss the obstacles they face, with a diverse programme of keynote talks, performances, concerts, gigs, debates and music.

Women of the World Festival, Southbank Centre, Belvedere Rd, SE1 8XX (020-7960 4200, southbankcentre.co.uk, Waterloo tube, ☎, ⓘ).

Browse in the Women's Library @ LSE, Europe's largest collection of material relating to the lives of women and a key part of British heritage. The library concentrates especially on Britain in the 19th and 20th centuries and contains over 60,000 books and pamphlets, including scholarly works on women's history, biographies, popular works, government publications and works of literature.

The Women's Library @ LSE, LSE Library, 10 Portugal St, WC2A 2HD (020-7955 7229, lse.ac.uk/library, Temple tube, free).

14 March

Bait for Bookworms

Stock your library at Word on the Water, London's only floating second-hand bookshop, which offers a vibrant alternative world of poetry, music and novel browsing. The Dutch barge travels between Camden Lock, Angel, Hackney and Paddington, stopping for two weeks at each mooring to sell books donated by the public and charity bookshops. To find out the barge's present location follow its progress on Twitter.

Word on the Water (thewordonthewater.blogspot.co.uk, twitter@ wordonthewater, facebook.com/wordonthewater, ⓘ).

Hunt for a rare first edition at the Southbank Book Market, London's own *Bouquinistes* – a collection of stalls selling second-hand and antique books, maps and prints, open daily until 7pm whatever the weather. A great place to search for something special or that elusive first edition. Not as cheap as a car boot or charity shop, but a lovely spot to browse and maybe pick up a bargain.

Southbank Book Market, Beneath Waterloo Bridge/Queen's Walk (southbankcentre.co.uk/visitor-info/shop-eat-drink/shops/ southbank-centre-book-market, Waterloo tube, free).

15 March

Orient Excess

Marvel at Leighton House Museum in West Kensington, the former home of Pre-Raphaelite painter and sculptor Frederic, Lord Leighton (1830-1896), with one of the 19th-century's most remarkable and original interiors. The house's centrepiece is the stunning, two-storey Arab Hall, designed to display Leighton's priceless collection of over 1,000 Islamic tiles dating from the 13th-17th centuries. Magical!

Leighton House Museum, 12 Holland Park Rd, W14 8LZ (020-7602 3316, rbkc.gov.uk/subsites/museums/leightonhousemuseum.aspx, High St Kensington tube).

Discover Paradise by Way of Kensal Green, a charming, bohemian gastropub with a modern British menu, including treats such as Morecambe Bay shrimps, Lonk lamb and Dorset lobster – and a delicious Sunday roast. With its bizarre, banquet-sized dining room – containing an eclectic melange of antiques, mirrors and chandeliers – lovely courtyard garden and decked roof terrace, Paradise is a delight.

Paradise by Way of Kensal Green, 19 Kilburn Ln, W10 4AE (020-8969 0098, theparadise.co.uk, Ladbroke Grove tube, ££, ☏).

16 March

Going, Going – Gone to Chelsea

Buy something beautiful for your home at Lots Road Auctions on Sundays. At 1pm the 'Contemporary and Traditional Furnishings and Decorative Items' sale kicks off, followed at 4pm by 'Antique Furniture, Paintings, Carpets and Works of Art'. Lots Road Auctions provides a unique ever-changing collection of antique and contemporary items, filling two vast salesrooms to overflowing.

Lots Road Auctions, 71 Lots Rd, SW10 0RN (020-7376 6800, lotsroad.com, Fulham Broadway tube).

Refuel with lunch or dinner at Lots Road Pub & Dining Room (part of the Food & Fuel chain), a beautiful, tastefully-decorated gastropub with good food, drinks and service. It serves a wide range of beers and a mixture of tasty pub favourites (bangers and mash, fish and chips, etc.) and restaurant-style dishes that vary from season to season.

Lots Road Pub & Dining Room, 114 Lots Rd, SW10 0RJ (020-7352 6645, lotsroadpub.com, Fulham Broadway tube, ££, ☏).

March

17 March

What's the Craic?

Sport a shamrock on St Patrick's Day, dedicated to the Patron Saint of Ireland and traditionally celebrated with 'wearing of the green' by Irish expats around the world. With over 10 per cent of the capital's population claiming Irish ancestry, the London Mayor's St Patrick's Day Parade and Festival is one of the city's liveliest parties, featuring a colourful array of floats, marching bands and groups representing the Irish Counties. Starting in Piccadilly, the parade wends its way through central London to Trafalgar Square, which hosts a programme of acts on the main performance stage, showcasing the best of Irish music and dance, from traditional to contemporary. A great, free family day out and a delightful way to experience all things Irish, from food and dance to crafts, culture, music and more. *Sláinte!*

St Patrick's Day Parade (st-patricks-day.com/st_patricks_day_ parades_england_london.html, free).

For a more traditional Irish pub and perhaps a jig or two, make the trip north to the Auld Shillelagh (105 Stoke Newington Church St, N16), where good craic is guaranteed.

Carry on the celebrations with Guinness and oysters at The Cow in Notting Hill, a beautiful, cosy Irish pub with a traditional rural feel. Downstairs is a retro kitsch bar with a simple Anglo-Irish menu specialising in oysters, fish stew, crab and seafood platters (oysters, prawns, whelks and winkles) and Guinness, while upstairs is a dining room with flock wallpaper and (carefully) mismatched artwork, and a more formal menu, but also heavy on seafood. Roasts are also a speciality and are served with all the trimmings. The tasty seasonal food comes in huge portions, with friendly and efficient service and an impressive wine list. A bit expensive but a fine venue for a treat.

The Cow, 89 Westbourne Park Rd, W2 5QH (020-7221 0021, thecowlondon.co.uk, Royal Oak tube, ££, ☎).

March

March

18 March

Get a Handle on Handel

Celebrate the music of George Frideric Handel (1685-1759) at venues across London during the London Handel Festival, a six-week season (March/April) of concerts, talks and walks. Venues include the delightful St George's Church in Mayfair (stgeorgeshanoversquare.org), Handel's parish church, where the Handel Singing Competition and dozens of intimate performances take place.

London Handel Festival (london-handel-festival.com, ☎, ⓘ).

Visit the Handel House Museum in George Frideric Handel's (1685-1759) former home from 1723 until his death in 1759. London's only museum to a composer, it's where he composed some of his best music, including the *Messiah*, *Zadok the Priest* and *Music for the Royal Fireworks*. The house contains finely-restored Georgian interiors and an impressive permanent display of Handel-related items, and is dedicated to the celebration of Handel and his work, including weekly concerts and special musical events.

Handel House Museum, 25 Brook St, W1K 4HB (020-7495 1685, handelhouse.org, Bond St tube).

19 March

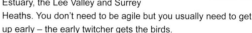

Springwatch

Spend a day twitching with Birding London, who specialise in arranging birdwatching trips for visitors and residents. The experienced guides will take you to some of the best habitats around London, including the Thames Estuary, the Lee Valley and Surrey Heaths. You don't need to be agile but you usually need to get up early – the early twitcher gets the birds.

Birding London (01923-237984, birdinglondon.co.uk/index2.html, ☎).

Stake your claim to a succulent steak at MASH, 'a sophisticated Modern American Steak House (MASH) with a twist of Danish informal eating and drinking'. The restaurant and bar occupies a vast room restored to its '30s Art Deco decadence with many original features. Specialising in delicious, premium aged beef from around the world, with starters including foie gras terrine and grilled lobster, you may guess that this isn't a budget venue.

MASH, 77 Brewer St, W1F 9ZN (020-7734 2608, mashsteak.dk/restaurants/london, Piccadilly Circus tube, £££, ☎).

20 March

Home Sweet Home

Get inspiration for your pad from the Ideal Home Show at Earls Court, the UK's largest and oldest home show founded in 1908 by the *Daily Mail* newspaper. Whether you're seeking a new kitchen or bathroom, furniture for the home or garden, gadgets, food, fashion, or just want to add a few finishing touches, you're bound to find inspiration here.

Ideal Home Show, Earls Court Exhibition Centre, Warwick Rd, SW5 9TA (0844-858 6763, idealhomeshow.co.uk, Earls Court tube, ⒤).

Put your feet up at the legendary Troubadour Café, a multi-faceted café/wine bar/art gallery and live music venue. The bohemian Troub hosted Jimi Hendrix, Joni Mitchell and Bob Dylan in the '60s and is still cluttered with paraphernalia from its hippie years. Nowadays it's one of London's most charming and relaxing hangouts, with an idyllic garden.

Troubadour Café, 265 Old Brompton Rd, SW5 9JA (020-7370 1434, troubadour.co.uk, Earls Court tube, £).

21 March

Chelsea Morning

Rejoice in the heavenly voices at Brompton Oratory (or Church of the Immaculate Heart of Mary, as it's officially known), an impressively ornate Catholic, Italianate church consecrated in 1884. As striking as the exterior is, it's the extraordinary interior – where Italian influence is at its greatest – that takes the breath away. The Oratory is also graced with no less than three renowned choirs.

Brompton Oratory, Brompton Rd, SW7 2RP (020-7808 0900, bromptonoratory.com, South Kensington tube, free).

———————

Treat yourself to lunch or afternoon tea at the Bluebird café in Chelsea, a popular refuge from bustling King's Road. The lovely courtyard is the perfect place for an alfresco lunch (try the crayfish salad or the classic Bluebird cheeseburger), afternoon tea (3-6pm) or perhaps a cocktail or glass of Pimms. The Bluebird also boasts a restaurant, bar, food store and wine cellar.

Bluebird Chelsea, 350 King's Rd, SW3 5UU (020-7559 1140, bluebird-restaurant.co.uk, South Kensington tube, ££, ☎).

Brompton Oratory

March

22 March

Tantalise Your Tastebuds

March

Fill your larder (and stomach) with artisan food at the Real Food Market in Southbank Centre Square behind the Royal Festival Hall – weekly on Fridays to Sundays. The market is dedicated to supporting the best artisan food, allowing you to buy directly from those who rear, grow and make your food. Here you'll find unique and delicious seasonal produce, including some of the freshest fish in London (brought daily from the nearby Kentish shores), high quality beef, artisan bread, delicious cheeses and charcuterie, beautiful fruit and veg, all manner of delicious cakes and desserts, coffee, the finest craft beers and wines, plus some of the city's most creative street food vendors.

There are also quarterly street food festivals at the Southbank Centre, Queens Walk on the Riverside (between the London Eye and Hungerford Bridge) presenting a line-up of the best quality and most passionate street food traders around, plus a live music stage (see website for information).

Real Food Market, Southbank Centre Sq, Belvedere Rd, SE1 8XX (020-7370 8624, realfoodfestival.co.uk/markets, Waterloo tube, ⓘ).

Feed your soul with a concert at the Southbank Centre, a complex of artistic venues on the south bank of the Thames built in 1951 as part of the Festival of Britain. It comprises three main buildings, the Royal Festival Hall, the Queen Elizabeth Hall and the Hayward Gallery, and is Europe's largest centre for the arts. Widely recognised as the most vibrant arts centre in the country, it attracts over 3m visitors annually who attend almost a thousand paid performances of music, dance and literature. Visitors can also take part in a wealth of free activities and events – in and around the performing arts venues – including over 300 free foyer events, and enjoy a wide range of restaurants, cafés and shops.

Southbank Centre, Belvedere Rd, SE1 8XX (020-7960 4200, southbankcentre.co.uk, Waterloo tube, ☎).

Joshua Bell

23 March

Hot Stuff!

Seek peace and quiet in Ravenscourt Park, a beautiful public park and garden established in 1888, although its origins lie in the medieval manor and estate of Palingswick (or Paddenswick), first recorded in the 12th century. The park's crowning glory is its magical, scented walled garden, a wonderful, Zen-like retreat secreted in the northeast corner of the park.

Ravenscourt Park, W6 (020-8748 3020, lbhf.gov.uk > parks and open spaces and s295963082.websitehome.co.uk/forp, Ravenscourt Park tube, free).

––––––––––

Order an authentic curry at the magnificent Kathmandu Inn in Shepherd's Bush, by popular consent one of London's best curry houses. Perfectly cooked and spiced authentic curries (not anglicised imitations) from Nepal and India – try Momo (dumplings in spicy sauce), lamb Nepal (with mango), ginger chicken or – if you have an asbestos mouth – the ferocious chicken ghorkali.

Kathmandu Inn, 6/7 7 Stars Cnr, W12 8ET (020-8749 9802, kathmanduinn.co.uk, Ravenscourt Park tube, £, 🍴).

24 March

The Home(s) of Arts & Crafts

Discover the William Morris Gallery in Walthamstow on the anniversary of the great man's birth in 1834 (he died in 1896). The building – which reopened in 2012 following a £5m redevelopment – was Morris's family home from 1848 to 1856, and is the only public gallery devoted to him. The internationally-important collection illustrates the life of Morris and his achievements and influence.

William Morris Gallery, Lloyd Park, Forest Rd, Walthamstow, E17 4PP (020-8496 4390, wmgallery.org.uk, Walthamstow Central tube, free).

––––––––––

Alternatively, visit The Red House (Grade I listed) in Bexleyheath, another of Morris's former homes. It was designed by Morris (with architect Philip Webb) and was his home for five years from 1860-1865. Designed as both a home and an artists' workshop, the house embodies Morris' aesthetic principles; a clever blend of the practical and the romantic with Gothic and medieval influences.

The Red House, Red House Ln, Bexleyheath, DA6 8JF (020-8304 9878, nationaltrust.org.uk/redhouse, Bexleyheath rail).

March

25 March

Spa Therapy

Spoil yourself rotten at the Sanctuary Spa in Covent Garden, established in 1977 to provide treatments for the female dancers from the nearby Royal Ballet School. A spa run by women for women, the Sanctuary is a place for indulgence, whether it's a glass of bubbly by the serene koi carp pools, a herbal compress facial or a blissful aromatherapy massage.

Sanctuary Spa, 12 Floral St, WC2E 9DH (0870-770 3350, sanctuary. com, Covent Garden tube, ☎).

Suitably refreshed and relaxed, indulge yourself further with a delicious lunch or afternoon tea at elegant Delaunay in Covent Garden, an all-day, café-restaurant inspired by the grand cafés of Europe. The glamorous and sophisticated dining room echoes a grand European brasserie with a vibrant cosmopolitan buzz. Whether you choose from the all-day middle-European menu or the decadent afternoon tea, Delaunay is a delight!

The Delaunay, 55 Aldwych, WC2B 4BB (020-7499 8558, thedelaunay. com, Holborn or Covent Garden tube, ££, ☎).

26 March

Send in the Clowns

Join the circus at Circus Space in Hoxton, one of Europe's leading providers of circus education housed in a magnificent former Victorian power station. Although running away to a circus isn't a viable option for most of us, you could learn a few handy skills such as flying trapeze, acrobatics and tight-wire walking, which should come in particularly handy if you're a City high-flier.

Circus Space, Coronet St, N1 6HD (020-7613 4141, thecircusspace. co.uk, Old St tube, ☎).

Round off the day with dinner at the Circus in Covent Garden, an innovative combination of cocktail bar and cabaret restaurant. The striking restaurant's pan-Asian food receives mixed reviews, but it's the circus acts that attract the punters – with a mishmash of fire-eaters, jugglers, acrobats and dancers who entertain you while you dine. It's certainly different and a cracking place for a celebration.

Circus, 27-29 Endell St, WC2H 9BA (020-7420 9300, circus-london. co.uk, Covent Garden tube, ££, ☎).

27 March

Only Here for the Beer

Tour Fuller's Brewery in Chiswick, where beer has been brewed since the Civil War, more than 350 years ago. Over the years Fuller's has established a reputation for brewing outstanding beers which have won numerous awards. In fact, three of their beers – London Pride, ESB and Chiswick Bitter – have been named Champion Beer of Britain, a feat unmatched by any other brewery. Cheers!

Fuller's Brewery, The Griffin Brewery, Chiswick Ln South, W4 2QB (020-8996 2175, fullers.co.uk, Turnham Green tube, ☎).

Continue the beer theme with a pint (or two) and dinner at The White Horse, a huge historic pub overlooking Parsons Green. A former 17th-century coaching inn, it's now a haven of Victorian elegance, with a vast horseshoe bar, sofas, huge tables, a lovely dining room and a beer garden. However, the main draw is the huge choice of ales. Beer heaven.

The White Horse, 1-3 Parson's Green, SW6 4UL (020-7736 2115, whitehorsesw6.com, Parsons Green tube, ££, ☎).

28 March

Cocktail Hour

Mix it up at 69 Colebrooke Row in Islington, one of London's most popular cocktail bars. Co-founder Tony Conigliaro has devised a series of informative and inspirational cocktail masterclasses, including how to make classics such as an old fashioned, daiquiri, dry martini, margarita, Manhattan and a champagne cocktail. You get to drink what you create, so pay attention – and take a taxi home.

69 Colebrooke Row, N1 8AA (07540-528593, 69colebrookerow.com, Angel tube, ☎).

Claridges Bar

See how the pros do it at Claridges Bar, one of London's finest cocktail bars at one of the city's finest hotels. Designed by David Collins, the sleek, opulent bar in Art Deco style has a silver-leafed ceiling, chandeliers and red leather banquettes. The atmosphere is both buzzy and sophisticated – you should dress appropriately – but isn't intimidating or snobbish.

Claridges Bar, 49 Brook St, W1K 4HR (020-7629 8860, claridges. co.uk/mayfair-bars/claridges-bar, Bond St tube, ££).

March

29 March

Riverside Revels

Cheer on the armada that takes part in the Head of the River Race, an annual Thames boat race that attracts over 400 crews of eights who follow the same 4¼-mile course as the Varsity Boat Race on Easter weekend – but backwards from Mortlake to Putney Bridge. Even if you aren't excited by the action, you can relax at one of the riverside pubs and watch the boats glide serenely past.

Head of the River Race (horr.co.uk, ⒤).

Take an afternoon stroll around delightful Bishop's Park near Putney Bridge. Home to Fulham Palace, the park has some lovely sculptures and memorials, including stone figures depicting *Adoration*, *Protection*, *Grief* and *Leda*, donated by the sculptor James Wedgwood. Bishop's Park's wealth of facilities include tennis courts, a bowling green, playgrounds, a beach, an ornamental lake and a café.

Bishop's Park, Bishop's Ave, SW6 3LA (020-8748 3020, lbhf.gov.uk > parks and friendsofbishopspark.com, Putney Bridge tube, free).

30 March

Mum's the Word

Buy your mum some hand-made chocolates at Rococo Chocolates in Knightsbridge, a pioneering artisan manufacturer, that creates a wealth of unusual flavour combinations and beautiful hand-painted eggs at Easter. The store is also home to the MaRococo garden café space, where you can sip an indulgent hot chocolate. There's even a Chocolate School, where you can learn to make your own heavenly creations.

Rococo Chocolates, 5 Motcomb St, SW1X 8JU (020-7245 099, rococochocolates.com, Knightsbridge tube).

Treat your mum to tea at The Ritz, where afternoon tea is an institution, impeccably served in the spectacular Palm Court accompanied by a piano or string quartet. Delicate sandwiches, freshly-baked scones with jam and clotted cream, and a choice of dainty pastries and scrumptious cakes accompany a wide range of teas. Expensive and pure indulgence but unforgettable – a once in a lifetime's treat.

The Ritz, 150 Piccadilly, W1J 9BR (020-7493 8181, theritzlondon. com/tea, Green Park tube, ££, ☏, ⒤).

31 March

Ripping Yarns

Walk in the footsteps of Jack the Ripper on a tour of the sites of his nefarious deeds in darkest Whitechapel. London's most notorious murderer was an unidentified serial killer who was active in and around the Whitechapel district between 1888 and 1891. A total of eleven unsolved murders of women were committed during this period – at least five or six of which were ascribed to Jack the Ripper (the name originated in a letter written by someone claiming to be the murderer). They typically involved female prostitutes from the slums whose throats were cut prior to abdominal mutilations.

The slayings have become the theme of a grisly London tourist attraction and nowadays numerous tours trace the serial killer's alleged footsteps and recount what's known of his (or her?) actions – to this day nobody knows for certain the identity of the murderer or even how many victims there were. So, if you dare, follow an expert guide and re-live those terrible times in Whitechapel when fear stalked the streets. Brrrr…!

Jack the Ripper Walks (020-8530-8443, jack-the-ripper-walks.com, Aldgate East tube, ☎).

Warm up in The Ten Bells in Whitechapel, once the haunt of some of victims of the Ripper or the Whitechapel Murders as the killings were also known. The pub luridly changed its name in the '80s to 'The Jack the Ripper' but has now reverted to its original name. Nowadays it's a uniquely decorated, lively and trendy East London pub, with a burgeoning reputation among fashionable East Enders. Although there are a few reminders of its past, it isn't (thankfully) a Ripper theme pub and no longer trades on its notoriety. Upstairs is a reasonably-priced (gastropub) restaurant serving excellent modern British, seasonal food.

The Ten Bells, 84 Commercial St, E1 6LY (07530-492986, tenbells. com, Aldgate East tube, ££, ☎).

April

1 April

A Cracking Good Time

Hunt the giant Easter eggs in the streets around Covent Garden, where you can pick up a guide book and get advice from one the 'Eggsperts' (sorry) on the best place to start your hunt. With 101 eggs to track down, it's an excellent way to discover hidden parts of the city while looking for the eggs, which have been decorated by leading artists, designers, architects and jewellers.

Big Egg Hunt (thebigegghunt.co.uk, Covent Garden tube, free).

Scoff some cakes to die for during afternoon tea at Patisserie Valerie, which opened its first shop in Frith Street (Soho) in 1926. Valerie specialises in high quality cakes and patisserie (delicious croissants and viennoiserie), plus continental breakfasts, lunches and the finest teas and coffees. Ice cream (gelato) and confectionary are popular too, and there's also a bespoke cake service.

Patisserie Valerie, 15 Bedford St, WC2E 9HE (020-7379 6428, patisserie-valerie.co.uk/covent-garden.aspx, Covent Garden tube, £).

2 April

Down on the Farm

Welcome the new-born lambs at Hackney City Farm. Established in 1984, the farm evolved from a derelict lorry park into a thriving community resource, and now houses a range of farm animals and a cottage garden. It offers children and adults the opportunity to interact with a variety of farmyard animals; see, smell and plant fruit and vegetables; and learn new skills.

Hackney City Farm, 1a Goldsmith's Row, E2 8QA (020-7729 6381, hackneycityfarm.co.uk, Cambridge Heath rail, free).

Catch a performance at The Sebright Arms – named after The Sebright Arms Music Hall (1865) – a great local pub with excellent ales and a long music tradition. In recent decades it's been a heavy metal venue, a disco and a cabaret pub, and is once again hosting a variety of live entertainment after locals managed to beat off the wrecking ball.

The Sebright Arms, 31-25 Coate St, E2 9AG (020-7729 0937, sebrightarms.co.uk, Cambridge Heath rail, £).

3 April

Just the Tonic

Learn to laugh more with Laughing Matters and the Laughter Network, both of which offer laughter coaching and therapy sessions to help you lighten your life and reduce stress. Come again – laughter coaching? Are you having a laugh? Apparently not. The aim is to learn how to laugh more easily – and not just at jokes or cartoons but at anything or nothing at all – it doesn't even matter whether it's real or fake laughter, any giggle will do.

Laughing in the face of anger, stress or anxiety – even if it's forced laughter – can actually lift your mood. And it's infectious, so you can expect to see those around you benefiting from a good chortle also. Laughter not only provides a full-scale workout for your muscles, it relaxes your body and unleashes a rush of stress-busting endorphins (natural painkillers) into the blood stream. The elation you feel when you laugh is a way of combating the physical effects of stress, so laughing more really can make you happier and healthier to boot.

Laughing Matters/Laughter Network (07789-954972, laughingmatters.co.uk and laughternetwork.co.uk, ☎).

Have a good belly laugh at The Comedy Store, opened by Don Ward in 1979 above a strip club in Soho. Inspired by a trip to see comedy clubs in the US, the aim was to re-create the same success in London – and, as they say, the rest is history. Nowadays, The Comedy Store is the daddy of all UK comedy clubs and has grown to become the most famous and respected brand in live comedy. It helped nurture the careers of numerous stars, including Alexei Sayle, Rik Mayall, Adrian Edmonson, Ben Elton, and French and Saunders, and still offers some of the best alternative stand-up, topical and improvised comedy in London.

The Comedy Store, 1a Oxendon St, SW1Y 4EE (0844-871 7699, thecomedystore.co.uk, Piccadilly Circus tube, ☎).

April

4 April

The Sounds of Soho

Buy the latest demos at BM Soho before your mates have even heard of them. London's longest running independent dance music record shop, BM Soho specialises in the latest club and dance music – house, minimal and techno, new and pre-release drum 'n' bass, dubstep, bassline and UK garage – it's all here. Just follow the apocalyptic bass sounds emanating from the sound system.

BM Soho, 25 D'Arblay St, W1F 8EJ (020-7437 0478, bm-soho.com, Oxford Circus tube).

———————

Listen to some cool jazz – and have a tasty pizza – at the Pizza Express Jazz Club in Dean Street, where the basement is one of Europe's best modern, mainstream jazz venues. Over the years many of the world's finest jazz musicians have taken to the stage, and although rarer nowadays there are still some excellent residencies.

Pizza Express Jazz Club Soho, 10 Dean St, W1D 3RW (020-7437 9595, tickets 0845-6027 017, pizzaexpresslive.com/jazzlist.aspx, Tottenham Court Rd tube, £, 🚇).

5 April

Barge into Battersea

Get on board one of London's most unique galleries, located on a fleet of permanently-moored Thames' barges. The Couper Collection exhibits artwork and installations by Max Couper, as well as hosting exhibitions and events by other artists. The barges are London's last remaining fleet of historic Thames barges on their ancient moorings.

The Couper Collection Barges, Battersea Beach, Thames Riverside Walk, Hester Rd, SW11 4AN (coupercollection.org.uk, info@ coupercollection.org.uk, bus routes 19, 49, 239, 319, 345, free).

———————

Wine and dine on the Battersea Barge, a Dutch barge built in 1932 and now moored on the Thames near the iconic Battersea Power Station. It isn't the easiest place to reach by public transport (see website), but it's well worth making the effort for a unique night out. The upstairs terrace offers a laidback atmosphere and views over the Thames.

Battersea Barge, Nine Elms Ln, SW8 5BP (020-7498 0004, batterseabarge.com, Vauxhall tube, ££, 🚇).

6 April

Up the Blues!

Watch the annual University Boat Race – now dubbed the BNY Mellon Boat Race – one of Britain's most popular sporting events. The contest between eights from Oxford and Cambridge universities takes place close to Easter each year on the River Thames in west London, between Putney and Mortlake (4.2mi). The first race was in 1829 and it has been held annually (apart from world wars) since 1856, making it one of the world's oldest sporting contests.

The Boat Race (theboatrace.org, ⓘ).

Visit Kew Bridge Steam Museum, a unique museum of water supply, housing a magnificent collection of steam engines and diesel-powered water pumping machines, including the world's largest collection of Cornish beam engines. It's a fascinating museum which records how London's water supply has evolved over the last 2,000 years, from Roman times to the present day.

Kew Bridge Steam Museum, Green Dragon Ln, Brentford, TW8 0EN (020-8568 4757, kbsm.org, Kew Bridge rail).

7 April

Seventh Heaven

Spend the day shopping, eating/drinking and chilling out in Seven Dials, one of London's most historic, atmospheric and quirky areas in Covent Garden. Seven Dials is a road junction where no fewer than seven streets converge, at the centre of which is a circular space containing a pillar bearing six (not seven) sundials – the pillar was commissioned before a late addition to the planned six roads.

Seven Dials, Covent Garden, WC2 (sevendials.co.uk, Covent Garden tube).

Tuck into classic moules and frites washed down with a glass (or two) of delicious Belgian beer at Belgo Centraal, who modestly claim to run 'the world's greatest Belgian restaurants'. Situated in the heart of Covent Garden, Belgo Centraal opened in 1995 occupying a vast 12,000ft² basement with two separate 'halls', one a 350-seat informal 'beer hall' and the other a more intimate restaurant.

Belgo Centraal, 50 Earlham St, WC2H 9LJ (020-7813 2233, belgo-restaurants.co.uk, Covent Garden tube, £-££).

April

8 April

Join the Literati

Peruse the books at the London Book Fair at the Earl's Court Exhibition Centre, London's premier publishing industry event, and second in importance internationally only to the Frankfurt Book Fair. It's a Mecca for international publishers, booksellers, rights agents and media trendspotters, and a global marketplace for rights negotiation and the sale and distribution of content across diverse media.

London Book Fair, Earl's Court Exhibition Centre, Warwick Rd, SW5 9TA (020-8271 2124, londonbookfair.co.uk, Earl's Court tube, ⓘ).

Tuck into *bigos* and *pierogi* (stew and dumplings) at the Patio Restaurant in Shepherd's Bush, a lively Polish family-run restaurant brimming with old world charm. Established in 1991, the Patio is very much a labour of love, offering a masterclass in how to prepare traditional Polish cuisine, accompanied by excellent Polish vodka. A truly super restaurant, dishing up some of London's best value food.

Patio Restaurant, 5 Goldhawk Rd, W12 8QQ (020-87435194, patiolondon.com, Shepherd's Bush tube, £, ☎).

9 April

Magical Mystery Tour

Take a 'photography mystery tour' of London with Hairy Goat, held on selected days throughout the year. Whether you're an old-timer or a newcomer, there's always something new to see – and photograph – in London, whether it's statues, elaborate doors and lamp posts, headstones or interesting architectural features, reflections, hidden gardens or old churches. You won't know where you're going until you get there, but there's sure to be something you haven't seen before.

Hairy Goat (hairygoat.net/london-photography-tour, ☎).

Sip cocktails in a secret location with the Candlenight Club, a clandestine pop-up cocktail bar which is – not surprisingly – entirely lit by candles, with an authentic '20s speakeasy flavour. Each event features a one-off cocktail menu with special themes, plus dancing to live (period) jazz music and vintage DJ-ing. It's the closest you'll come to a real Jazz Age experience, so pull on a flapper dress or your dandy duds and party!

Candlenight Club (thecandlelightclub.com, ££, ☎).

10 April

The Brilliant Brunels

This fascinating museum also has a riverside terrace and gardens, a café and a bookshop.

Brunel Museum, Railway Ave, Rotherhithe, SE16 4LF (020-7231 3840, brunel-museum.org.uk, Rotherhithe rail).

Drink a toast to the Brunels in the canal-side gastropub – The Engineer – in Primrose Hill, built by Isambard Kingdom Brunel between 1845 and 1850 for the brewers Claverts. The recently refurbished (Grade II listed) handsome building is built in Italianate style, with striking iron light fixtures in the form of dragons alongside the entrances. The Engineer is a relaxed, informal neighbourhood pub, specialising in fresh, seasonal food, excellent ales, a carefully-selected wine list and friendly service.

The Engineer, 65 Gloucester Ave, NW1 8JH (020-7483 1890, theengineerprimrosehill.co.uk, Camden Town tube, £, ☎).

Mark the anniversary of Isambard Kingdom Brunel's birth in 1806 with a visit to the Brunel Museum, which celebrates the life and work of three generations of the legendary Brunel engineering family: Sir Marc Isambard Brunel (1769-1849), his more famous son, Isambard Kingdom Brunel (1806-1859) – widely considered to be Britain's greatest ever engineer – and Isambard's second son, Henry Marc Brunel (1842-1903), also a civil engineer.

The museum is situated above the Thames Tunnel in the Brunel Engine House in Rotherhithe, designed by Sir Marc, part of the infrastructure of the Thames Tunnel. An exhibition tells the story of the construction and history of the tunnel, including display panels, models of the tunnel under construction, original artefacts and a video presentation.

Isambard Kingdom Brunel built dockyards and the fastest railway in the world, the 7ft broad gauge Great Western; constructed a series of steamships, including the first propeller-driven transatlantic steamship; and engineered numerous important bridges and tunnels. His designs revolutionised public transport and modern engineering.

> On certain days (see website) the museum opens a 'secret' underground chamber where Isambard Kingdom Brunel almost drowned.

April

11 April

Catch Up With Constable

Seek out some of John Constable's (1776-1837) finest paintings at the National Gallery in Trafalgar Square, on the anniversary of his birth in 1776 (East Bergholt, Suffolk). Constable was England's greatest romantic painter, known principally for his landscape paintings of Dedham Vale in Suffolk; the area surrounding his home is now dubbed 'Constable Country'. Nowadays his paintings are among the most popular and valuable in British art, although he was never financially successful and wasn't elected to the Royal Academy until the age of 52.

The National Gallery displays a number of works by Constable, including arguably his best known, *The Hay Wain*, which records a pastoral idyll in Suffolk near Flatford on the River Stour. Constable completed the painting in his studio in 1821 and it was exhibited at the Royal Academy the same year, but failed to find a buyer. In 2005 it was voted the second-best painting in any British gallery – JMW Turner's *Fighting Temeraire*, also in the National Gallery, took first place – and satisfyingly, the cottage and river path it captured remain much as they were when Constable painted them some two centuries ago.

National Gallery, Trafalgar Sq, WC2N 5DN (020-7747 2885, nationalgallery.org.uk, Charing Cross tube, free).

The Hay Wain

Visit John Constable's grave at St John-at-Hampstead, which has one of London's prettiest and most historic graveyards (with its own website – tombwithaview.org.uk). The church, dedicated to St John the Evangelist, is a sumptuous Georgian Church of England church with a stunning interior. However, most visitors come to see the tranquil graveyard, whose monuments and gravestones include many of historical significance, notably that of John Constable. Other famous 'residents' include novelist and historian Walter Besant, writer and comedian Peter Cook, actress Kay Kendall, Labour Party leader Hugh Gaitskell, and inventor of the marine chronometer and discoverer of longitude, John Harrison.

St John-at-Hampstead, Church Row, NW3 6UU (020-7794 5808, hampsteadparishchurch.org.uk, Hampstead tube).

12 April

Westminster Wonders

Delight in the unique and uplifting Westminster Methodist Central Hall, a magnificent, richly-decorated Methodist church built in 1905-11 to mark the centenary of the death of John Wesley (the founder of Methodism) in 1791. It was funded by the 'Wesleyan Methodist Twentieth Century Fund', which raised one million guineas from one million Methodists – the first large-scale example of crowdfunding.

Methodist Central Hall Westminster, Storey's Gate, SW1H 9NH (020-7654 3809, methodist-central-hall.org.uk, Westminster tube, free).

Westminster Methodist Central Hall

Take refuge in Westminster Abbey's hidden, tranquil gardens – a lovely place to escape the crowded confines of the abbey – and you don't have to pay a Pope's ransom to enjoy them as entrance is free! There are four gardens: the three originals (the Great Cloister Garden or Garth, the Little Cloister and College Garden) plus St Catherine's Garden, created more recently.

Westminster Abbey Gardens, 20 Dean's Yard, SW1P 3PA (020-7222 5152, westminster-abbey.org, Westminster tube, free).

13 April

Runners & Rangers

Cheer on the brave souls at the start of the London Marathon in Greenwich Park, one of the world's leading marathon races. Attracting more than 35,000 competitors – chosen by ballot from over 100,000 applicants – it's the world's largest fundraising event of its kind. The race, run annually since 1981, starts in Greenwich (from three separate starting points which converge after 3mi) and culminates in The Mall alongside St James's Palace.

London Marathon (virginlondonmarathon.com, [1]).

Admire Ranger's House (and The Wernher Collection), an elegant, red brick, early 18th-century Georgian villa adjacent to Greenwich Park. The official residence of Greenwich Park's ranger since 1816, the house's main attraction is the Wernher Collection, which includes jewellery, paintings, porcelain, silver and much more, assembled by Sir Julius Wernher (1850-1912). Viewing only by pre-booked guided tour.

Ranger's House & Wernher Collection, Chesterfield Walk, Blackheath, SE10 8QX (tours 020-8290 2548, english-heritage.org. uk, Cutty Sark DLR,).

April

14 April

Flying High

Enjoy spectacular views and a unique 'flight' across the Thames on the Emirates Air Line cable car between Emirates Greenwich Peninsula (South Terminal) and Emirates Royal Docks (North Terminal). Operated by Transport for London (TfL), the journey offers panoramic views over East London, including the Thames Barrier, Canary Wharf and the Olympic Park.

Emirates Greenwich Peninsula, Unit 1, Emirates Cable Car Terminal, Edmund Halley Way, SE10 0FR (TfL 0343-222 1234, emiratesairline. co.uk, North Greenwich tube).

Take a walk on the roof of the O2 Arena (Millenium Dome), now a spectacular entertainment complex which includes bars, restaurants, a cinema, live music venues, a nightclub and the British Music Experience. The roof walk is an exhilarating (up to 90 min) experience which takes you on an journey across the roof of the O2 via a tensile fabric walkway.

The O2 Arena, Greenwich Peninsula, Peninsula Sq, SE10 0DX (020-8463 2000, theo2.co.uk/upattheo2, North Greenwich tube, ☎).

15 April

Walking on Water

Walk the Thames Path from Tower Bridge to the Thames Barrier. There's a choice of routes; the north bank route (5.5mi) to Island Gardens – from where you cross to Greenwich via the foot tunnel – or the south bank route (10mi). The latter takes in atmospheric Shad Thames in Bermondsey, through historic Rotherhithe to the splendours of Maritime Greenwich, and on past the O2 Arena to the iconic Thames Barrier.

National Trail (nationaltrail.co.uk/thamespath/downloads. asp?PageId=79 and walklondon.org.uk/section.asp?section=52, Tower Hill tube).

Get up close to the Thames Barrier, one of the world's largest movable flood barriers, commissioned in 1982. The barrier spans 1,700ft across the Thames and protects 48mi² of central London from flooding caused by tidal surges. The barrier consists of ten steel gates – each weighing 3,300 tonnes – which when raised stand as high as a five-storey building.

Thames Barrier Information Centre, 1 Unity Way, SE18 5NJ (020-8305 4188, environment-agency.gov.uk/homeandleisure/ floods/38353.aspx, Woolwich Dockyard rail).

April

16 April

Join the Country Set

Practise your swing at Hainault Forest Golf Club, a public course that offers golfers of all abilities a choice of two picturesque and challenging courses set in over 300 acres. The club offers a range of reasonable casual pay-and-play rates, block tickets and season tickets for those who wish to play regularly.

Hainault Forest Golf Club, Romford Rd, Chigwell, IG7 4QW (020-8500 2131, hainaultgolfclub.co.uk, Fairlop tube, ☎).

Explore Hainault Forest Country Park which surrounds Hainault Forest Golf Club, a remnant of what was once the Forest of Essex (Epping Forest and Hatfield Forest are others). The forest once belonged to Barking Abbey and until the Dissolution of the Monasteries (1536-41) extended to some 3,000 acres. It remains one of the best surviving medieval forests of its kind and is a haven for flora and fauna.

Hainault Forest Country Park, Romford Rd, Chigwell, IG7 4QN (020-8500 7353. hainaultforest.co.uk, Hainault tube, free).

17 April

Huguenots There?

Be inspired by the Huguenots of Spitalfields Festival, a celebration of the contribution that the Huguenots – French Protestant refugees who fled persecution in Catholic France in the 16-18th centuries – made to Spitalfields, where they sought the freedom to practice their faith. Centred around Spitalfields, where some 25,000 Huguenots settled, the festival is designed to highlight the talents and culture of the Huguenots, who made a valuable contribution to East London.

Huguenots of Spitalfields Festival (huguenotsofspitalfields.org, free, ⓘ).

Be touched by a visit to the Museum of Immigration and Diversity, Europe's only cultural institution dedicated to the movement of people in search of a better life. It's appropriately situated in Spitalfields, a refuge for waves of dispossessed immigrants since the 16th century. It's housed in an unrestored 18th-century house, once home to Huguenot silk merchant Peter Abraham Ogier.

Museum of Immigration & Diversity, 19 Princelet St, E1 6QH (020-7247 5352, 19princeletstreet.org.uk, Shoreditch High St tube, ☎).

April

18 April

Shop 'til You Drop

Knightsbridge (SW3) is more than just a road; it also lends its name to an exclusive district in central London, famous as an ultra-expensive residential area and as the home of some seriously upmarket retail outlets. In fact, Knightsbridge has more than its fair share of exclusive stores – not just Harrods and Harvey Nichols, but also the flagship stores of many British and international fashion houses, including shoe designers Jimmy Choo and Manolo Blahnik and two branches of Prada.

If you have any money left after that lot, take the time to 'browse' the boutiques in Beauchamp Place (pronounced 'Beecham'), one of London's most famous and unique streets where royalty and celebrities shop, and one of the city's most exclusive addresses. Not surprisingly, the district is also home to private banks catering to the super rich (including Coutts, bankers to the Queen), some of London's most renowned restaurants, a wealth of exclusive hair and beauty salons, antiques dealers and fine art galleries, and chic bars and clubs.

Knightsbridge, SW1/SW3 (Knightsbridge tube).

Take some time out from shopping to have lunch or afternoon tea in Harvey Nicks Fifth Floor Restaurant (££, ☏), a perennial favourite with London's fashionistas.

Don't miss Harvey Nichols' flagship store in Knightsbridge, one of London's leading international luxury fashion destinations and a one-stop-shop for the world's most exclusive brands. Founded in 1831, when Benjamin Harvey opened a linen shop in a terraced house on the corner of Knightsbridge and Sloane Street, the current building was constructed in the 1880s. The store was purchased by Debenhams in 1919, but after having a number of corporate owners was returned to private ownership in 2003. Today Harvey Nicks' (to its fans) comprises eight floors of fashion, beauty and lifestyle collections, with the fifth floor dedicated to food and restaurants.

Harvey Nichols, 109-125 Knightsbridge, SW1X 7RJ (020-7201 8641, harveynichols.com/stores/london, Knightsbridge tube).

19 April

Go Down to the Woods Today...

Seek out the magnificent display of bluebells in Claybury Woods (Claybury Park) in the borough of Redbridge. The park extends to some 173 acres, containing an ancient area of oak and hornbeam woodland (44 acres) renowned for its carpet of woodland spring flowers, including bluebells, wood anemones and wild garlic, plus rare wild service trees, butcher's broom and broad-leaved helleborine orchids.

Claybury Woods, Claybury Park, Tomswood Hill/Manor Rd, Woodford Green, Ilford, IG8 8AJ (wildessex.net/sites/claybury park. htm, free, ⓘ).

Wander around the beautiful City of London Cemetery (Grade I listed), one of London's most interesting and attractive burial grounds. Opened in 1856, the 200-acre site is a picturesque parkland with glorious formal gardens and tree-lined avenues. The cemetery contains over 3,500 trees, a woodland area, water features, ponds and a nature area.

City of London Cemetery, Aldersbrook Rd, Manor Park, E12 5DQ (020-8530 2151, cityoflondon.gov.uk > Cemetery and Crematorium, Manor Park rail, free).

20 April

Boots & Other Clobber

Grab some bargain vintage threads on a Sunday at the Battersea Boot, established in 1999 and still going strong. Not your average car boot sale – for starters it doesn't start until noon, so you don't need to get up with the larks. It isn't the cheapest around, with designer goods, vintage, shabby chic, even antiques and collectables, alongside general tat, but is well worth a visit.

Battersea Boot, Battersea Park School, Battersea Park Rd, SW11 5AP (batteseaboot.com, Queenstown Rd rail).

If you have no luck at the car boot try the British Red Cross Chelsea shop – but not on a Sunday – Chelsea's most popular charity shop where the area's well-heeled residents off-load last season's wardrobe. It bills itself as a 'designer charity shop' (clothes, shoes, bags and accessories), with prices based on the original cost, so they aren't a steal but are still great value.

British Red Cross Chelsea, 69-71 Old Church St, SW3 5BS (020-7376 7300, redcross.org.uk, South Kensington tube).

21 April

Three Cheers for HRH!

See (and hear) Her Majesty The Queen's Birthday Gun Salute in Green Park, a spectacular show of pomp and ceremony. The Queen (born in 1926) celebrates her actual birthday (as opposed to her official birthday – celebrated in May/June with the Trooping the Colour ceremony) on 21st April privately, but the occasion is marked publicly by music from the Band of the Royal Artillery (around 11.30am) and a 41-gun royal salute at noon by the King's Troop Royal Horse Artillery.

Queen's Birthday Gun Salute, Green Park, SW1 (royal.gov.uk/ royaleventsandceremonies/gunsalutes/gunsalutes.aspx, Green Park tube, free).

March (smartly) along to the Household Calvary Museum, a unique living museum offering a rare 'behind-the-scenes' look at the ceremonial and operational roles of the Household Cavalry Regiment. You can see troopers working with their horses in the original 18th-century stables via a glazed wall.

Household Calvary Museum, Horse Guards, Whitehall, SW1A 2AX (020-7930 3070, householdcavalrymuseum.co.uk, Charing Cross tube).

22 April

House & Garden

Lambeth Palace

Step into the Garden Museum in Lambeth – the world's first museum dedicated to the history of gardening – which celebrates British gardens and gardening through its collection, temporary exhibitions, events, symposia and garden. The museum is based in the deconsecrated church of St Mary-at-Lambeth, dating from the 14th century (restored in 1850), which has a lovely, recreated 17th-century knot garden. Great café!

Garden Museum, St Mary-at-Lambeth, Lambeth Palace Rd, SE1 7LB (020-7401 8865, gardenmuseum.org.uk, Lambeth North tube).

Admire nearby Lambeth Palace, the official London residence of the Archbishops of Canterbury since 1200. It's one of the capital's oldest and most overlooked treasures, containing a number of London's few remaining Tudor buildings, some of which can be viewed from outside. It's possible to tour the palace (see website) but it must be booked well in advance.

Lambeth Palace, Lambeth Palace Rd, SE1 7JU (0844-248 5134, archbishopofcanterbury.org/pages/visit-lambeth-palace.html, Lambeth North tube).

23 April

Cry God for William, England & St George!

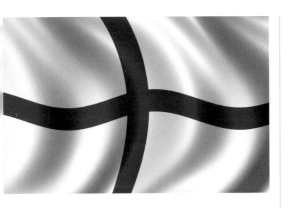

Celebrate St George's Day, which falls on this day, although the London celebrations in Trafalgar Square are held on the Saturday before or after the saint's day (assuming it doesn't fall on a Saturday), as the day itself isn't a national holiday. It's one of the few days when flag waving is actively encouraged (apart from England soccer matches) in recognition of England's dragon-slaying patron saint. There are live bands on the main stage and food stalls around Trafalgar Square.

William Shakespeare's birthday falls on the same date – 2014 is the 450th anniversary of the Bard's birth in Stratford-on-Avon in 1564 – and Shakespeare's Globe hosts its own celebrations to tie in with St George's Day, when workshops and interactive fun and games bring the Bard to life. (The largest celebrations are held in Stratford-on-Avon – see shakespearesbirthday.org.uk – a tradition dating back some 200 years.)

St George's Day (stgeorgesday.com) and Shakespeare's Globe, 21 New Globe Walk, SE1 9DT (020-7902 1400, shakespearesglobe.com, London Bridge tube, free).

Toast the achievements of George, Will and Joseph at **The Swan Bar & Chophouse** (New Globe Walk, SE1, 020-7928 9444, ££, ☏) at Shakespeare's Globe theatre, which offers sweeping views of the River Thames and St Paul's Cathedral. The elegant bar and restaurant serves everything from breakfast to dinner or you can just have a coffee, glass of wine or a cocktail. The bar also hosts live music and DJ sessions throughout the year.

Alternatively you could have a pint at the nearby 17th-century **George Inn** (77 Borough High St, SE1, £), the city's only remaining galleried coaching inn, where Shakespeare was reputedly a customer (along with Samuel Pepys, Samuel Johnston and Charles Dickens).

April

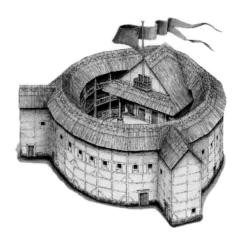

April 23rd is also the anniversary of the birth of Britain's greatest painter, Joseph Mallord William (JMW) Turner, who was born on this day in Covent Garden in 1775.

24 April

Designs for Life

View the nominations in the 'Designs of the Year' award at the Design Museum in Shad Thames (Bermondsey). The awards, 'the Oscars of the design world', showcase the most innovative and imaginative designs from around the world over the past year, spanning seven categories: Architecture, Digital, Fashion, Furniture, Graphics, Transport and Product.

Design Museum, 28 Shad Thames, SE1 2YD (020-7940 8790, designsoftheyear.com and designmuseum.org, Tower Hill tube).

Have lunch in the Design Museum's acclaimed Blueprint Café (free entry), while enjoying the panoramic views from its terrace, extending from Tower Bridge to Canary Wharf. Located on the first floor of the museum, the café occupies an enviable Thameside location, just a short stroll from London Bridge. Serves delicious modern European cuisine.

Blue Print Café, Design Museum, 28 Shad Thames, SE1 2YD (020-7378 7031, blueprintcafe.co.uk, Tower Hill tube, £).

25 April

Something Fishy in East London

Learn how to fillet fish and much more at the Billingsgate Seafood School, at Billingsgate Fish Market in East London (where it moved to from the City in 1982), the UK's largest inland fish market formally established in 1699. The School provides tailor-made courses and demonstrations in fish and shellfish recognition, knife skills, presentation, preparation, cooking and nutrition.

Billingsgate Seafood School, Billingsgate Market, Trafalgar Way, E14 5ST (020-7517 3548, seafoodtraining.org, Poplar DLR, 🚇).

Enjoy a fishy lunch or supper at Formans, a lovely riverside restaurant and bar overlooking the Olympic Stadium. The Forman family has been smoking fish since 1905 and their cured salmon can be found on all the best tables. The classic menu offers the best of seasonal British food and drink which (weather permitting) can be enjoyed on the terrace overlooking the Hertford Union Canal.

Formans, Stour Rd, Fish Island, E3 2NT (020-8525 2365, formans. co.uk/restaurant, Hackney Wick rail, ££, 🚇).

26 April

Marvellous Marylebone

Spend the day (or weekend) in Marylebone Village, one of London's loveliest neighbourhoods with a wealth of interesting independent shops, cafés and restaurants. On Saturday visit the delightful Cabbages and Frocks Market, where you can buy delicious artisan and organic foods and items from local designers and cottage industries, such as retro and vintage clothing, homewares, children's clothes, hand-blown glass and jewellery.

Cabbages and Frocks Market, St Marylebone Parish Church Grounds, Marylebone High St, W1U 5BA (020-7794 1636, cabbagesandfrocks.co.uk, Baker St tube).

On Sunday drop into Marylebone Farmers' Market (10am to 2pm) for some more shopping and eating. Even more than Cabbages and Frocks, the farmers' market was responsible for putting Marylebone Village on the London foodies' map. It usually has 30-40 stalls and heaves with locals and visitors from all over the capital, attracted by the wide range of organic cheeses and artisan bread, seasonal organic fruit and veg, delicious meats and charcuterie, fresh fish, honey, preserves, cut flowers, cakes and puddings (etc.) – with tasty snacks such as bangers, pies and burgers to sustain you.

While visiting the market, allow some time to see the Browning Chapel in the lovely St Marylebone Church (17 Marylebone Rd, free) – or perhaps attend a service – where poets Robert Browning and Elizabeth Barrett were secretly married in 1846 after exchanging 574 love letters! If you're lucky you may hear the superb Riegel organ and heavenly choir, both renowned for their excellence.

Marylebone Farmers' Market, Cramer St Car Park, Marylebone, 11U 4EW (lfm.org.uk/markets/marylebone, Baker St tube).

Enjoy a delicious meal in the Landmark Hotel's stunning Winter Garden restaurant, in the eight-storey glass atrium, a fabulous place to don your Sunday best and swank about like a Hollywood star. And if you stick to the set menu (££) it needn't break the bank.

April

27 April

Wake Up & Smell the Coffee

Sample some delicious brews at the London Coffee Festival in The Old Truman Brewery in Spitalfields. The festival was launched in 2011 to celebrate the upsurge of interest in artisan coffee from London's wealth of coffee enthusiasts, food lovers and professional baristas. There's also a tea garden, chocolate factory, street food, artisan market and a coffee roastery.

London Coffee Festival, The Old Truman Brewery, 91 Brick Ln, E1 6QL (020-7691 8836, londoncoffeefestival.com, Shoreditch High St rail, ⓵).

When you've had your fill of coffee and street food, feed your soul with some superb East London art. Check out the street art in Brick Lane which is famous for its graffiti, including artists such as Banksy, D*Face and Ben Eine. The area also contains a wealth of commercial galleries and is one of the city's most exciting neighbourhoods for cutting edge art.

Brick Lane, E1 6PU (visitbricklane.org, Shoreditch High St rail, free).

28 April

Cathedral of Ironwork

Marvel at the wonders of Victorian engineering at Crossness Pumping Station (1865), built by Sir Joseph William Bazalgette and architect Charles Henry Driver as part of Victorian London's main sewerage system. The Beam Engine House was constructed in Romanesque (Norman) style in gault (clay) brick, with considerable ornamentation, described as "a Victorian cathedral of ironwork" by architectural expert Nikolaus Pevsner.

Crossness Pumping Station, The Old Works, Crossness S.T.W., Belvedere Rd, Abbey Wood, SE2 9AQ (020-8311 3711, crossness. org.uk, Abbey Wood rail, ☏).

Take a walk in Lesnes Abbey Woods, 217 acres of broadleaved woodland on a hill overlooking the ruins of Lesnes Abbey (founded 1178). The lovely woods are rich in flora and fauna – with glorious spring displays of bluebells and daffodils – and trails leading through valleys with ancient hornbeam trees, wild flowers such as figwort and dogs mercury, open heath land and ornamental gardens.

Lesnes Abbey Woods, Abbey Rd, Belvedere, Bexley DA17 (Abbey Wood rail).

Lesnes Abbey ruins

April

29 April

Art Feast

Enjoy a smorgasbord of art at the Institute of Contemporary Arts and the Mall Galleries on The Mall. The Institute of Contemporary Arts (ICA) is one of London's leading artistic and cultural centres, where you can see cutting edge art, hear the latest bands and enjoy avant-garde classic films. The Mall Galleries next door is one of the city's coolest art venues and major contemporary art showcases.

Institute of Contemporary Arts, The Mall, SW1Y 5AH (020-7930 3647, ica.org.uk) and Mall Galleries, 7 Carlton House Terrace, The Mall, SW1Y 5BD (020-7930 6844, mallgalleries.org.uk). Charing Cross tube, free.

Refresh yourself at the ICA bar and café, tucked away inside London's coolest cultural centre. In keeping with the hip ICA, it's a modern, arty and effortlessly relaxed spot which has become something of a destination venue for the city's creative and fashion types in recent years.

ICA Bar & Café (020-7930 8619, peytonandbyrne.co.uk/ica-bar, £).

30 April

Bathing Beauty in Bayswater

Work up a storm or simply relax at the Porchester Centre in Bayswater, a beautiful Art Deco (Grade II listed) centre that opened in 1929. The centre offers a wide selection of facilities and activities (day passes available), including a 90-station gym, exercise studios, a 25m swimming pool, a teaching pool, a spa and meeting rooms.

Porchester Centre, Queensway, W2 5HS (020-7792 2919, better.org. uk/leisure/porchester-centre, Royal Oak tube).

———————

Have a well-deserved beer or 'gastro' meal at The Prince Bonaparte in Notting Hill, a gastropub that also manages to be a proper pub (with excellent ales) and doesn't make drinkers feel unwanted. It's a large, striking corner establishment, with high ceilings, bare brick, neutral colours, open fires and picture windows.

The Prince Bonaparte, 80 Chepstow Rd, W2 5BE (020-7313 9491, theprincebonapartew2.co.uk, Notting Hill Gate tube, ££, ☎).

April

May

1 May

Mayday! Mayday!

Celebrate May Day with a traditional fête at The Book Club in East London, one of London's quirkiest cultural venues. Held in the Leonard Street Car Park, the fête includes all the fun of the fair including a maypole, Morris dancers, music, town crier, fortune telling, games, food and drink – and a May Queen.

The Book Club, Leonard Street Car Park, Leonard St, EC2A 4RH (020-7684 8619, wearetbc.com, Shoreditch High St rail, free).

Indulge your senses at the eastern-themed spa at the May Fair Hotel in – you guessed it – Mayfair. The spa has seven treatment rooms, a luxurious mud bath and steam chamber, a herbal steam room and a tranquil relaxation room. A day pass includes use of the wet spa and relaxation facilities. Blissful!

May Fair Hotel, Stratton St, W1J 8LT (020-7915 2826, themayfairhotel.co.uk/spa, Green Park tube, ☎).

2 May

Batman or Fungi?

Go for an organised Bat Walk with the London Bat Group (londonbats.org.uk), a charity working throughout Greater London to protect and enhance the bat populations. The group organises a series of public bat walks and surveys, mainly during the summer months (see website for information). The website also contains a list of sites ('where to see bats') where bats can be seen feeding on summer evenings.

London Bat Group (londonbats.org.uk, ☎).

Go foraging for mushrooms with 'Fungi to be With' on Hampstead Heath, which organises educational walks (usually 3-4 hrs) and workshops in a number of locations around London. Walks take in some of the city's most beautiful spots, including fern covered woodlands, heather laden heaths and parks with ancient trees.

Fungi to be With (fungitobewith.org, ☎).

> **WARNING: If you forage for mushrooms on your own, always check with an expert before eating any!**

May

3 May

Busy Bees

Visit the Hive Honey Shop in Clapham to learn about beekeeping and buy honey and beeswax products. The Hive is a pioneer in the creation of health and medicinal lotions, potions, ointments and cosmetics using natural ingredients harvested from bee hives. Products sold in the shop include everything from beeswax candles and fresh royal jelly to honey mustard, mead and delicious honey.

Hive Honey Shop, 93 Northcote Rd, SW11 6PL (020-7924 6233, thehivehoneyshop.co.uk, Clapham Junction rail).

See the working windmill and museum on Wimbledon Common, built by Charles March in 1817, and a museum since 1976. Exhibits tell the story of the development and construction of windmills, explain how the windmill worked and how grain was milled to produce flour (children can try their hand at milling flour), plus a magnificent collection of millwright's tools.

Wimbledon Windmill & Museum, Windmill Rd, Wimbledon, SW19 5NR (020-8947 2825, *wimbledonwindmill.org.uk,* **Wimbledon tube).**

The Windmill Wimbledon

4 May

Watery Wonderland

Have a great family outing at the Canalway Cavalcade at Little Venice over the May Day holiday weekend. Organised by the Inland Waterways Association (IWA), it's a unique waterways and community festival held annually since 1983. The colourful gathering sees over 100 canal boats moored along the stretch of the Grand Union Canal at Little Venice, plus a range of attractions.

Canalway Cavalcade, Little Venice, Maida Vale, W2 1TH (waterways. org.uk/events_festivals, Warwick Ave tube, free, ⓘ).

Head to one of Little Venice's many excellent eateries for lunch, such as The Waterway (54 Formosa St, 020-7266 3557), a Scandinavian-inspired gastropub with a lovely terrace overlooking the canal, or The Summershouse (opp. 60 Blomfield Rd, 020-7286 6752) run by the same outfit. If you're feeling more adventurous you could try Kateh (5 Warwick Place, 020-7289 3393) for delicious Persian cuisine.

Little Venice, Maida Vale, W2 (Warwick Ave tube, ££, ☏).

May

5 May

On Your Marx!

Visit the Marx Memorial Library in Clerkenwell on the anniversary of the birth (in Trier, Germany) of Karl Heinrich Marx (1818-1883), German philosopher and revolutionary socialist who developed the socio-political theory of Marxism. Founded in 1933 on the 50th anniversary of Marx's death, the library is dedicated to the advancement of education, knowledge and learning relating to all aspects of the science of Marxism.

Marx Memorial Library, 37a Clerkenwell Green, EC1R 0DU (020-7253 1485, marx-memorial-library.org, Farringdon tube, free).

Admire the tomb of Karl Marx in Highgate's East Cemetery (Grade I listed, 1839), one of London's Magnificent Seven garden cemeteries. Among the prominent figures buried here – in addition to Marx – are the family of Charles Dickens, Michael Faraday, Christina Rossetti, Douglas Adams, George Eliot, Malcolm McLaren, Sir Ralph Richardson, Max Wall, John Galsworthy and Beryl Bainbridge.

Highgate Cemetery, Swains Ln, N6 6PJ (020-8340 1834, highgate-cemetery.org, Highgate tube, free).

6 May

Make it Snappy!

See stunning photography at the Sony World Photography Awards Exhibition at Somerset House on the Strand, which coincides with the World Photo London photography festival. The annual awards are one of the world's leading photographic competitions, showcasing the winners and shortlisted photographers from international contemporary photography in fashion, travel, wildlife, landscape, portraiture and current affairs.

Sony World Photography Awards Exhibition, Somerset House, Strand, WC2R 1LA (020-7845 4600, worldphoto.org/festivals-and-events/events/sony-world-photography-awards-exhibition, Temple tube, ⓘ).

Treat yourself to a meal at Tom's Kitchen, Somerset House, a modern brasserie serving British comfort food. Opened in 2010 by Tom Aiken, it has a rustic, informal style, serving lunch and dinner (Mon-Fri) and its famous brunch on weekends. It features everything from classic British fish and chips to some of Toms' signature dishes, such as seven-hour braised shoulder of lamb.

Tom's Kitchen, Somerset House, Strand, WC2R 1LA (020-7845 4646, tomskitchen.co.uk/somerset-house, Temple tube, ££, 🍽).

7 May

Ravishing Richmond Park

S pend a glorious day in Richmond Park, London's largest royal park and the second-largest urban park in Europe, extending to 2,360 acres. It's classified as a European Special Area of Conservation, a National Nature Reserve and a Site of Special Scientific Interest – with a plethora of flora and fauna – and is famous for its deer which number around 650. The park's royal connections date back to Edward I (1272-1307), who established a royal palace at the Manor of Shene (Sheen), which remained in royal ownership until 1851.

Be sure to visit the magical Isabella Plantation, a 42-acre ornamental woodland garden packed with exotic plants and designed to be interesting all year round. In spring there are camellias, magnolias, daffodils and bluebells, while the azaleas and rhododendrons flower in late April and early May. The Plantation has 15 varieties of deciduous azalea and houses the national collection of 50 Japanese Kurume azaleas, as well as 50 different species of rhododendron and 120 hybrids.

Richmond Park, Richmond, TW10 5HS (020-8948 3209, royalparks. org.uk/parks/richmond_park, Richmond tube, free).

───────────

T ake a detour to the White Lodge Museum and Ballet Resource Centre in Richmond Park, a fine example of Neoclassical English Palladian architecture. Formerly a royal residence (Prince Albert, the future George VI, lived here),

today it houses the Royal Ballet Lower School (for students aged 11-16) and is the first dedicated ballet museum in the UK. Visitors can learn about the daily life of students at The Royal Ballet School, the history and development of classical ballet, and the appealing story of White Lodge itself. Exhibits include Margot Fonteyn's ballet shoes, the death mask of Anna Pavlova and the school reports of famous alumni.

White Lodge Museum & Ballet Resource Centre, White Lodge, Richmond Park, Richmond TW10 5HR (020-8392 8440, royal-ballet-school.org.uk/wl_museum.php, Mortlake rail, ☎).

May

8 May

Green, Green Grass…

Chill out in Green Park, a lush pasture that's peaceful, relaxing and – as its name suggests – **very** green. It's a popular venue for picnics, sunbathing or just having a nap in a deck chair. Although there's no lake for wildlife, there are plenty of common birds such as blackbirds, starlings and tits and, in winter, migrant birds. In spring there's a magnificent display of thousands of daffodils.

Green Park, SW1A 2BJ (0300-061 2350, royalparks.org.uk/parks/green-park, Green Park tube).

Stroll over to St James's Park for lunch or a drink at Inn the Park, which offers beguiling vistas of the park's tinkling fountains and lovely flowerbeds. It's a gorgeous place to enjoy a leisurely (service can be slow) lunch or cocktail. On a rare, balmy summer evening with its floor-to-ceiling windows rolled back, it blends seamlessly into its surroundings.

Inn the Park, St James's Park, SW1A 2BJ (020-7451 9999, peytonandbyrne.co.uk/inn-the-park, Charing Cross tube, ££, ☎).

9 May

Free-Wheeling Fun

Hire an electric bike from Hertz and glide serenely around London. Forget Boris bikes and hire a bike which allows you to cruise under power, enabling you to see the city without working up a sweat. As easy to ride as a conventional bike, you receive a lock and a helmet (if you want one). Way to go!

Hertz, 35 Edgware Rd, W2 2JE (0843-309 3049, Marble Arch tube, ☎).

Enjoy an evening of song and dance at Cecil Sharp House with the English Folk Dance and Song Society, the national folk arts development organisation for England. The society hosts a variety of concerts, lectures, multi-media events and social dances, plus a comprehensive programme of classes, courses, workshops and talks about dance, music and song.

English Folk Dance & Song Society, Cecil Sharp House, 2 Regent's Park Rd, NW1 7AY (020-7485 2206, efdss.org, Camden Town tube, ☎).

May

10 May

Art Deco Delights

Take a deco at Dorich House Museum, the former home, studio and gallery of the sculptor Dora Gordine (1895-1991) and her husband the Hon. Richard Hare (1907-1966). Built in 1936, the house is a fine example of Art Deco design. However, it's the comprehensive collection of Gordine's bronzes, plaster sculptures, paintings and drawings that pulls in the visitors. Open on certain days only (see website).

Dorich House Museum, 67 Kingston Vale, Kingston-upon-Thames, SW15 3RN (020-8417 5515, dorichhousemuseum.org.uk, East Putney tube then bus, ⓘ).

Have a wander around Putney Village, one of London's most beautiful villages whose architecture is largely a mixture of Arts & Crafts and Art Deco, with a wealth of mansions and mansion blocks. The heathland has long been celebrated for its large open spaces and clean air, which Londoners have visited for generations to partake in games and sports.

Putney Village (putneyvillage.com, East Putney tube).

11 May

That's the Way to Do It!

Say Happy Birthday to Mr Punch at the May Fayre & Puppet Festival in Covent Garden. Held on the second Sunday in May on or near the date of Mr Punch's birthday, which is held to be 9th May. The annual May Fayre celebrates the red nosed, stick-wielding puppet, bringing together dozens of puppeteers in a colourful and entertaining day.

Covent Garden May Fayre & Puppet Festival, St Paul's Church, Bedford St, WC2E 9ED (punchandjudy.com/coventgarden.htm, Covent Garden tube, ⓘ).

Join in or support the MoonWalk (so called as it starts at 11pm) at Battersea Power Station, the world's only power walking marathon. The walk attracts some 15,000 participants and raises money for Walk the Walk, a breast cancer charity. Each year the event has a different theme (in 2013 it was 'Space'), with participants striding out in outrageous outfits.

MoonWalk, Battersea Power Station, 188 Kirtling St, SW8 5BP (01483-41430, walkthewalk.org/challenges, Vauxhall tube, ☎, ⓘ).

May

12 May

The Lady with the Lamp

Remember Florence Nightingale (1820-1910) on the anniversary of her birth by visiting the Florence Nightingale Museum at St Thomas' Hospital. It tells the engrossing story of one of Britain's greatest heroines, and exhibits some fascinating objects; from the slate she used in school to the Turkish lantern she carried during the Crimean War (she was dubbed The Lady with the Lamp after her habit of making rounds at night). Don't miss her pet owl, Athena, which she had stuffed after its death.

Florence was a visionary health reformer whose ideas completely changed society's approach to nursing, and her legacy remains strong to this day. Her theories, published in *Notes on Nursing* (1860), were hugely influential and her concerns for sanitation, military health and hospital planning established practices which are still in use today. The Nightingale Pledge taken by new nurses was named in her honour, and International Nurses Day is celebrated throughout the world on her birthday.

Florence Nightingale Museum, St Thomas' Hospital, 2 Lambeth Palace Rd, SE1 7EW (020-7620 0374, florence-nightingale.co.uk, Lambeth North tube).

Discover what surgery was like in the days before Florence Nightingale, as you explore the Old Operating Theatre in Southwark, one of the world's oldest surviving operating theatres (1822). The museum of surgical history is evocatively situated in the garret (roof space) of the now disused English Baroque church of St Thomas's (ca. 1703) on the original site of St Thomas's Hospital, which dates back to the 12th century when it was part of a monastery. The museum displays a collection of objects relating to medical history and that of St Thomas's and Guy's hospitals, many of which reveal the grisliness of medicine before the age of science.

Old Operating Theatre & Herb Garret, 9A St Thomas's St, Southwark, SE1 9RY (020-7188 2679, thegarret.org.uk, London Bridge tube).

13 May

A Different Perspective

See London from a different perspective from a speedboat on the Thames. London RIB Voyages offer Thames boat trips with a difference in a rigid-inflatable boat (RIB), a light-weight, high-performance speedboat (the fastest on the river). Departing from the London Eye Millennium Pier, the organisers promise that you'll go further, faster and see more than on any other sightseeing trip in London.

London RIB Voyages (020-7928 8933, londonribvoyages.com, Waterloo tube, ☏).

Get a bird's eye night view of London from the London Eye, a giant Ferris wheel situated on the banks of the River Thames. It's the tallest Ferris wheel in Europe – 443ft high and 394ft wide – and the most popular paid tourist attraction in the UK. A variety of unique night-time experiences are offered, including 'Wine and Tapas' and 'Nightcap'.

London Eye, Riverside Bldg, County Hall, Westminster Bridge Rd, SE1 7PB (0871-781 3000, londoneye.com, Waterloo tube, ☏).

14 May

Naughty But Nice

Enjoy some cheeky thrills by taking in a show during the London Burlesque Festival, held at a number of venues across the capital including Madame JoJos (West End) and Bush Hall (Shepherd's Bush). What was initially a weekend of glitz, vaudeville and striptease now extends to ten nights of raucous entertainment showcasing the best of British glamour and tastefully risqué entertainment, from avant-garde to erotic, sexy circus artists.

London Burlesque Festival (londonburlesquefest.com, ☏, ⓘ).

Plan a purrfect night on the tiles at the Black Cat Cabaret restaurant in Soho, one of London's hottest and most sensational shows. The Black Cat has transformed the Titanic Ballroom of the former Café de Paris into a bohemian den, drawing inspiration from the absinthe-soaked heyday of Montmartre's dark and daring cabaret underworld. It's a riot!

Black Cat Cabaret, Café de Paris, 3-4 Coventry St, W1D 6BL (020-7284 4700, theblackcat.info, Piccadilly Circus tube, ££, ☏).

May

15 May

Compelling City Charms

Enjoy a picnic in the magical St Dunstan-in-the-East garden in the City. St Dunstan's dates back to the 12th century but has been rebuilt many times, the last by Sir Christopher Wren in 1695-1701. It was largely destroyed in the Blitz of 1941, although Wren's tower and steeple survived intact. The spire was reconstructed in 1953 and the tower restored in 1970-1, but it was decided not to rebuild the church. The Corporation of London acquired the (Grade I listed) ruins in 1967, which, along with the former churchyard, were incorporated into the garden (opened in 1971).

St Dunstan-in-the-East Garden, St Dunstan's Hill, EC3 (cityoflondon. gov.uk > city gardens, Monument tube, free).

Tour the beautiful and historic Charterhouse – officially called Sutton's Hospital in Charterhouse – in the City of London. A Carthusian monastery was founded here in 1371 by Sir Walter de Mauny (Manny), one of Edward III's senior advisers; in 1535 the monks refused to conform to Henry VIII's Act of Supremacy, resulting in some being executed at Tyburn. It was subsequently given to Lord North who constructed a fine Tudor mansion, later sold to the fourth Duke of Norfolk, who further embellished it. In 1611, Norfolk's son, Thomas Howard, first Earl of Suffolk, sold the mansion to Thomas Sutton, who used his wealth to endow a charitable foundation to educate boys (Charterhouse School, founded in 1611, now situated in Godalming, Surrey) and an almshouse (a home for gentlemen pensioners, called 'brothers') – which it remains to this day.

It's possible to tour the beautiful Tudor Charterhouse, one of London's most fascinating buildings, which conveys a vivid impression of the large, rambling, 16th-century mansions that once existed throughout the city. See the website for information about tours.

Charterhouse, Sutton's Hospital, Charterhouse Sq, EC1M 6AN (020-7253 9503, thecharterhouse.org, Barbican tube, ☎).

May

16 May

Non-Potable!

Seek out the Cholera Pump and John Snow (1813-1858) memorial in Broadwick Street (Soho), which commemorates an outbreak of cholera in 1854 in which 616 people died. Snow noticed that the majority of deaths happened to people who used the Broad Street Pump, and when the handle of the pump was removed the outbreak stopped. It was later discovered that sewage in a cesspit was seeping into the channel which provided water for the pump.

Cholera Pump, Broadwick St, W1 (Oxford Circus tube).

Spend a night at a museum during the annual Museums at Night festival, a series of inspiring events taking place during the evening (and into the night). The after-hours opening of London's major museums and galleries has proved hugely successful, with visitors often amazed (and delighted) at the atmospheric party atmosphere.

Museums at Night (culture24.org.uk/places to go/museums at night, ⓘ).

17 May

Spend, Spend, Spend!

Go on a spending spree assisted by your own 'personal shopper' at Selfridges (Oxford St), the ultimate shopping experience for the lady (or man?) who feels daunted by the overwhelming choice at Selly's. A personal 'stylist' will help you find an extraordinary dress for a VIP event, a new season update or a total wardrobe makeover – and their advice is free. The only snag: the minimum spend is £2,000!

Selfridges Personal Shopping, 400 Oxford St, W1A 1AB (020-7318 3536, selfridges.com, Marble Arch tube, ☏).

If your budget is more cast-off than Chanel, try visiting some of London's wealth of charity, thrift, secondhand and vintage shops for a bargain. If you baulk at buying someone else's cast-offs and cannot afford fashion labels in the posh shops, try London's underground sample sales (see editer.com/sample-sale-diary), which sell excess stock, store samples or pieces with hardly noticeable flaws for a fraction of their original price.

May

18 May

Flower Power

Buy a bouquet for someone special at Columbia Road's Sunday flower market in Bethnal Green, London's only dedicated flower market. On Sundays the street is transformed into an oasis of foliage and flowers – everything from bedding plants to 10-foot banana trees – and the air is intense with the scent of flowers. Columbia Road's Victorian architecture is also home to over 50 independent shops.

Columbia Road Flower Market, Columbia Rd, E2 7RG (020-7613 0876, columbiaroad.info, Hoxton rail).

Have a right old knees up at Bethnal Green Working Men's Club, an old-fashioned working men's club that hasn't changed much since the '50s. Fortunately the entertainment has evolved, with regular weekly social events, some racy, others more cultured and refined, but mostly it's simply FUN! There's a restaurant serving delicious, inexpensive East End nosh, and, of course, a bar.

Bethnal Green Working Men's Club, 42-44 Pollard Row, E2 6NB (020-7739 7170, workersplaytime.net, Bethnal Green tube, £).

19 May

Gardeners' World

Treat the family to a day at Capel Manor Gardens, a stunning 30-acre estate surrounding a Georgian manor house and Victorian stables. It features a variety of richly-planted themed gardens, including the Old Manor House Gardens, the Family Friendly Garden, an Italianate maze, a Japanese garden, a 17-century walled garden and Sunflower Street. There are events throughout the year, a restaurant and a gift shop.

Capel Manor Gardens, Bullsmoor Ln, Enfield, EN1 4RQ (08456-122122, capelmanorgardens.co.uk, Turkey St rail).

Visit nearby Forty Hall Country Park, Enfield's 'Jewel in the Crown', extending to 260 acres, containing a walled garden, formal and informal gardens, a lime walk, lakes, lawns, woodland, meadows and a farm. Forty Hall (Grade I listed), one of England's finest historic houses built by Sir Nicholas Rainton (1569-1646) in 1632, is now home to Enfield's local history museum.

Forty Hall & Estate, Forty Hill, Enfield, EN2 9HA (020-8363 8196, fortyhallestate.co.uk, Turkey St rail, free).

Forty Hall

20 May

Wander the Wandle

Spend the day in magnificent Morden Hall Park, a watery, green oasis in the heart of suburbia, and one of the jewels in the crown of the National Trust (with no entrance fee). Covering over 125 acres of parkland in what was once rural Surrey, this tranquil former deer park is one of the few remaining estates of those which lined the River Wandle during its industrial heyday. The estate encompasses Morden Hall itself (currently unused), pretty Morden Cottage and many old farm buildings.

Morden Hall Park sits on the flood plain of the beautiful River Wandle and consists of three main habitats: meadowland, marshland and woodland. Water lies at the heart of the park, with the river, mill ponds and a lake. The lush wetlands, riverbanks and islands provide an ideal habitat for a wealth of plants, animals, insects and abundant birdlife, including wildfowl, herons and kingfishers. There's also a beautiful rose garden, laid out in 1922, containing some 2,000 roses, plus a café, shop, craft stalls and a demonstration kitchen garden.

Morden Hall Park, Morden Hall Rd, SM4 5JD (020-8545 6850, nationaltrust.org.uk/main/w-mordenhallpark-2, Morden tube, free).

Visit the Wandle Industrial Museum, a unique and remarkable museum established in 1983 to preserve and interpret the heritage and history of the industries and people of the Wandle Valley. The fast-flowing River Wandle has been used by people living along its banks since prehistoric times, first as a source of water and fish, and later for power to drive water wheels. In its heyday in the 18th and 19th centuries there were around 50 working mills on the Wandle, which at the time was the most industrialised river in the world.

Wandle Industrial Museum, The Vestry Hall Annex, London Rd, Mitcham, CR4 3UD (020-8648 0127, wandle.org, Mitcham Junction rail).

May

21 May

Cool Designs

Experience some of London's most cutting edge design during Clerkenwell Design Week, the UK's leading independent design festival. The annual three-day festival hosts an array of the world's most notable design, architectural and creative names, plus a comprehensive programme of workshops, presentations, product launches and debates. Clerkenwell is the UK's foremost design community, boasting **over** 60 showrooms and a wealth of creative businesses and architects.

Clerkenwell Design Week, Clerkenwell, EC1 (020-3225 5200, clerkenwelldesignweek.com, Farringdon tube, ☎, ⅈ).

Enjoy a pint and good music at The Betsey Trotwood (named after a character in Dickens's novel, *David Copperfield*), a large, characterful Victorian pub with good beer and friendly staff. The Betsey's main claim to fame, however, is its entertainment, usually staged in the cellar gig room, including indie bands, alternative country and folk, plus comedy, drama, readings and disco nights.

The Betsey Trotwood, 56 Farringdon Rd, EC1R 3BL (020-7253 4285, thebetsey.com, Farringdon tube, £).

22 May

Blooming Marvellous!

Buy, beg, borrow or steal a ticket to the RHS (Royal Horticultural Society) Chelsea Flower Show, the world's leading flower show. Founded in 1913 and attended by some 160,000 visitors annually, it's held in Ranelagh Gardens and the South Grounds of the Royal Hospital Chelsea in May. Highlights include avant-garde show gardens designed by leading international names, plus smaller artisan, fresh and generation gardens.

Chelsea Flower Show, Royal Hospital Chelsea, SW3 4SL (rhs.org. uk/ shows-events, Sloane Sq tube, ☎, ⅈ).

Relax over lunch or afternoon tea at The Orange in Pimlico, a welcoming gastropub (and boutique hotel) with excellent ales, food (wood-fired pizzas, oven roasts, fish, etc.) and service. Housed in a beautiful restored Georgian building, The Orange has a number of lovely light and airy rooms with an informal weathered interior bathed in natural sunlight.

The Orange, 37-39 Pimlico Rd, SW1W 8NE (020-7881 9844, theorange.co.uk, Sloane Sq tube, ££, ☎).

23 May

The Early Bird...

Bermondsey antiques market Square

Get up before dawn to hunt for bargains at Bermondsey Antiques Market (4am to 1pm) on a Friday. The market started in 1855 as a place to trade with impunity (i.e. stolen goods bought here didn't have to be returned) and is now a busy weekly antiques market. Following the redevelopment of Bermondsey Square, the ancient market flourishes in an expanded space, accommodating some 200 stalls.

Bermondsey Antiques Market, Bermondsey Sq, SE1 (London Bridge tube).

Rest up with a well-earned breakfast (and a pint?) at The Garrison gastropub, just a few minutes from Bermondsey Square. Opening at 8am, the Garrison offers one of the area's best breakfast menus, including smoked haddock kedgeree, porridge with fresh fruit, and buttermilk pancakes with maple syrup – there's even a vegetarian full English.

The Garrison, 99-101 Bermondsey St, SE1 3XB (020-7089 9355, thegarrison.co.uk, London Bridge tube, £).

24 May

Float On

Drift away at Floatworks in Bankside, one of the world's leading floatation centres, established in 1993. Floatation REST (Restricted Environmental Stimulation Therapy) involves floating on top of a 12in deep pool of heated salt water in a specially-

designed tank resembling a large enclosed bathtub, designed to eliminate all outside distractions such as sight, sound, tactile sensations and gravity.

Floatworks, 1 Thrale St, SE1 9HW (020-7357 0111, floatworks.com, London Bridge tube, 🚇).

Soak up the history in Shad Thames in Bermondsey, a historic, partly-cobbled street near Tower Bridge running along the south bank of the Thames, set back behind a row of converted warehouses. Shad Thames (also the informal name for the area) was regenerated in the '80s and '90s, when the disused but picturesque warehouses were converted into luxury flats, many with restaurants, bars and shops on the ground floor.

Shad Thames, Bermondsey, SE1 (Tower Hill or London Bridge tube).

May

25 May

Join the Tea (& Coffee) Set

Drink your fill at the Tea & Coffee Festival at the Southbank Centre, a three-day celebration of all things tea and coffee. As well as the drinks in their pure form, you can enjoy tea and coffee based cocktails, tea- and coffee-flavoured macaroons, churros with mocha sauce, coffee flavoured cheese cakes and much more. There are also tastings, masterclasses, talks and demonstrations, plus all the latest machines and paraphernalia.

Tea & Coffee Festival, Southbank Centre (teacoffeefestival.com, Waterloo tube, 🛈).

Had enough of tea/coffee? Drop into The Baltic bar and restaurant in Southwark for something a bit stronger. Located in a converted carriage works, it's a minimalist, sleek and achingly trendy establishment with a buzzy atmosphere. Vodka is the drink of choice at Baltic, including traditional, new and Baltic flavours, with a selection of Eastern European bar food to soak up the alcohol. *Okrzyki!*

The Baltic, 74 Blackfriars Rd, SE1 8HA (020-7928 1111, balticrestaurant.co.uk, Southwark tube, ££, ☎).

26 May

Take the Plunge

Learn to scuba dive with the London School of Diving, the Capital's premier dive school with its own dive training facility and purpose-built heated pool. The LSD is a PADI (Professional Association of Diving Instructors) 5* Career Development Centre and offers all PADI courses from try dives, initial open water to instructor level.

London School of Diving, 11 Power Rd, W4 5PT (020-8995 0002, londonschoolofdiving.com, Gunnersbury tube, ☎).

Make a fool of yourself (or practise for your *X Factor* audition) at The Source Below in Soho, one of London's original and coolest karaoke bars, equipped with a state-of-the-art touch screen karaoke system, professional sound equipment and an unrivalled choice of over 8,000 songs. The Source is available for private hire from Thursday to Sunday evenings for parties of up to 40.

The Source Below, 11 Lower John St, W1F 9TY (020-7060 3614, sourcebelow.com, Piccadilly Circus tube, ££, ☎).

27 May

18th-Century Motorways

Discover the absorbing story of the capital's canals at the London Canal Museum in Camden; from their early days as vital trade routes – long before motorised vehicles and motorways – through years of decline and abandonment, to their resurrection as today's corridors of leisure and urban greenery for boaters, walkers and cyclists.

The museum opened in 1992 in a former Victorian ice warehouse and features two floors of exhibits, including half a narrow boat, the *Coronis*, where visitors can experience the cramped conditions in which boatmen and their families lived from the 1840s until the 1950s. The museum tells the story of the building of Regent's Canal – built to link the Grand Junction Canal's Paddington Arm (which opened in 1801) with the Thames at Limehouse. You're given an excellent overview of the scope of London's waterways by the 'Big Map' which provides a detailed historical survey of the capital's canals and other navigations, including canals that were built and closed, those that were planned but never built, and those that survive today.

London Canal Museum, 12-13 New Wharf Rd, N1 9RT (020-7713 0836, canalmuseum.org.uk, King's Cross tube).

Take to the water for an enchanting trip back in time with a canal ride between bustling Camden Lock and picturesque Little Venice along the nine-mile historic Regent's Canal, one of London's best-kept secrets, meandering through the rich urban landscape of yesteryear. Travel on a traditional canal narrow boat along the historic Regent's Canal; slip quietly along the green and leafy fringes of Regents Park, past London Zoo, through the mysterious, murky Maida Hill tunnel to Browning's Pool at Little Venice, surrounded by elegant Regency architecture. No need to book, just turn up ten minutes before departure and pay on the boat. Magical!

London Waterbus Company (020-7482 2660, londonwaterbus.com, King's Cross tube for Camden Lock or Warwick Ave tube for Little Venice).

May

28 May

Hidden Treasure

Get a few mates or colleagues together for a themed treasure hunt, available at a wide range of locations throughout the city and with a variety of themes. It's an imaginative way to explore new parts of the city, while cracking the clues along the way and, hopefully, finding the pot of gold. A great way to get a group of people thinking, working and laughing together.

Treasure Hunts (0845-006 0606, treasurehunts.co.uk, ☏).

Get your hands on a gold bar at the Bank of England Museum, which tells the story of the bank from its foundation in 1694 to its role as the UK's central bank. Housed in a 20th-century replica of Sir John Soane's classic 18th-century building, the museum contains a collection of banknotes and coins, gold bars, documents, paintings, photographs, a silver collection, statues, furniture and other artefacts.

Bank of England Museum Threadneedle St, EC2R 8AH (020-7601 5545, bankofengland.co.uk/education/museum/index.htm, Bank tube, free).

29 May

A Real Page Turner

Rub shoulders with the literati at the London Literature Festival at the Southbank Centre, bringing together poets, authors, musicians and speakers from across the globe to celebrate all things literary. Enjoy a wealth of readings (including the Man International Booker Prize and the Women's Prize for Fiction), lectures, talks, discussions and interactive workshops.

London Literature Festival, Southbank Centre, Belvedere Rd, SE1 8XX (020-7960 4200, southbankcentre.co.uk, Waterloo tube, ☏, ⓘ).

Browse the shelves at Hatchards, London's oldest bookshop and the second-oldest in the UK. Founded by John Hatchard in 1797 on Piccadilly, from where it still trades today (over five floors), customers have included most of Britain's greatest political, royal, social and literary figures – from Queen Charlotte (it holds three Royal Warrants), Disraeli and Wellington, to Kipling, Wilde and Lord Byron. It also has a reputation for attracting famous authors for signings/readings.

Hatchards, 187 Piccadilly, W1J 9LE (020-7439 9921, hatchards. co.uk, Piccadilly Circus tube).

30 May

Row, Row, Row Your Boat…

Get out on the long and lovely Serpentine lake in Hyde Park, which gets its name from its sinuous shape, although only the eastern stretch is called the Serpentine (the western end beyond the bridge is the Long Water). The Serpentine offers a fleet of rowing and pedal boats, plus the UK's first Solarshuttle, powered only by the sun.

Hyde Park Boat House, W2 2UH (020-7262 1330, royalparks.org.uk/ parks/hyde-park/hyde-park-attractions/boating-in-hyde-park, Hyde Park Cnr tube).

Disembark for a delicious lunch at the Serpentine Bar and Kitchen in Patrick Gwynne's iconic '60s building, with uninterrupted views over the Serpentine from its floor-to-ceiling windows and terrace. The restaurant offers an all-day, seasonal dining menu based on modern English and traditional French cuisine, while on summer evenings barbecues and a 'pop-up' Citröen gin van are an added draw.

Serpentine Bar & Kitchen, Hyde Park, W2 2UH (serpentinebarandkitchen.com, Knightsbridge tube, ££, 🚇).

31 May

Hail & Arty

Hire an air-conditioned taxi for an exclusive personal tour of London's landmarks and historic buildings led by drivers who are also City of London guides. The tours are ideal for anyone who wants to see the city's major sights but has little time or who doesn't want the hassle of using the tube and buses, particularly if you have poor mobility or young children in tow.

London Taxi Tour (londontaxitour.com, 🚇).

Attend a performance at the Grade I listed Theatre Royal Haymarket, one of London's best-loved theatres, known originally as 'The Little Theatre in the Hay'. Designed and constructed by John Potter in 1720, the theatre seats almost 900 and is the third-oldest London playhouse still in use. Young people aged 17-30 can attend free Masterclasses (see masterclass.org.uk) during the day.

Theatre Royal Haymarket, 18 Suffolk St, SW1Y 4HT (020-7930 8890, trh.co.uk, Piccadilly Circus tube, 🚇).

May

June

1 June

Ode to Hampstead

most romantic in London and is planted to reflect its Regency heritage.

Keats House, 10 Keats Grove, Hampstead, NW3 2RR (020-7332 3868, cityoflondon.gov.uk/keatshousehampstead, Hampstead tube, ⒤).

Tuck into a late lunch or afternoon tea at Aubaine in Hampstead village, a small chain of all-day licensed café/ restaurants which are a seductive blend of cosmopolitan style and French cuisine. Difficult to pigeonhole, Aubaine is a combination of café, boulangerie, patisserie and brasserie, serving wonderful croissants and pastries, oven-fresh baguettes and a range of mouth-watering, Mediterranean-influenced seasonal dishes, from eggs royale to filet de boeuf. *Vive les Aubaine!*

Aubaine, 82 Hampstead High St, NW3 1RE (020-3432 9260, aubaine. co.uk/location/hampstead, Hampstead tube, £).

Celebrate the life and work of the English romantic poet John Keats (1795-1821) at the Keats House Summer Festival in Hampstead. The annual summer celebration gives literary lovers a chance to enjoy the great poet's work through readings, performances, music and creative workshops. Keats' former home (Grade I listed) was built between 1814 and 1816 and was originally two separate properties, where Keats lodged with his friend Charles Brown from December 1818 to September 1820, which although only a short period, was one of his most productive. In 1820 Keats travelled to Italy, where he died of tuberculosis aged just 25. (In 1838, the actress and one-time favourite of George IV, Eliza Jane Chester, purchased the houses and knocked them through to create one dwelling.)

Keats House contains a huge variety of Keats-related material, including books, paintings and the engagement ring he gave to Fanny Brawne (the girl next door). Various rooms in the house have been faithfully recreated as they would have been when occupied by Keats, Brown, the Brawnes and Eliza Chester. The garden – where Keats is said to have written *Ode to a Nightingale* – has been described as one of the

June

2 June

Viva Italia!

Celebrate Italy's Republic Day (*Festa della Repubblica*) at the Italian Cultural Institute in London, the official Italian governmental body dedicated to promoting Italian language and culture via its offices worldwide. The Institute promotes the image of Italy as a centre of production, conservation and diffusion of culture from the Classical age to today.

Italian Cultural Institute, 39 Belgrave Sq, SW1X 8NX (020-7235 1461, icilondon.esteri.it/iic_londra/menu/istituto, Hyde Park Cr tube, ☏).

Salute the Republic with a delicious Italian meal at E Pellicci, a beacon of Italian warmth and hospitality. Pellicci's is an East End institution, first opened in 1900 and still run by the same family. It's a throwback to a bygone golden age of caff culture with a wonderful Art Deco interior, a profusion of marquetry, stained glass, wood panelling and Formica tables. A gem.

E Pellicci, 332 Bethnal Green Rd, E2 0AG (020-7739 4873, Bethnal Green tube, £).

3 June

Cook up a Storm

One of London's leading cookery schools. Whether you want to just make a hamburger or a loaf of bread for your kids, or cook up a six-course cordon bleu meal, L'atelier can show the way. The school offers a wide range of classes, focussing on skill, cuisine and cooking techniques.

L'atelier des Chefs Cookery School, 19 Wigmore St, W1U 1PH (020-7499 6580, atelierdeschefs.co.uk, Bond St tube, ☏).

See how the experts do it at Mon Plaisir in Covent Garden, London's oldest French restaurant and purveyor of fine French cuisine for over half a century. From the pewter topped bar (from a Lyonnais brothel!), wealth of French artefacts and knickknacks, to the waiters' accents, this is as French a bistro as you're likely to find this side of *La Manche*.

Mon Plaisir, 19-21 Monmouth St, WC2H 9DD (020-7836 7243, monplaisir.co.uk, Covent Garden tube, ££, ☏).

June

4 June

Say Cheese!

See some fabulous photos at the Photographers' Gallery in Soho, the largest public gallery in London dedicated solely to photography, offering inspiration for everyone from phone snappers to professionals. From the latest emerging talent to historical archives and established artists, it's the place to see photography in all its forms. The gallery features three dedicated floors of gallery spaces; at the heart of the building is the studio floor which hosts a range of talks, events, workshops and courses, as well as a *camera obscura*, the study room and Touchstone – a changing display of a single photographic work. Complementing the exhibition and education floors are a bookshop, a print sales room and a café/bar, all at street level.

The Photographers' Gallery is the venue for the high-profile annual Deutsche Börse Photography Prize, worth £30,000, which is awarded to a living photographer who has made the most significant contribution (exhibition or publication) to the medium of photography in Europe during the previous year. The work of the nominated photographers is displayed in the gallery from April to June.

Photographers' Gallery, 16-18 Ramillies St, W1F 7LW (020-7087 9300, thephotographersgallery.org.uk, Oxford Circus tube, free).

Have a rave up at Pacha in Victoria (next to the station), a glamorous antidote to London's often gritty club scene. Pacha brings the hedonistic and sophisticated Ibiza (where Pacha began) experience to London, with top European DJs, thumping funky house music (from the bespoke Martin Audio passive sound system), delicious cocktails and an open-air roof terrace. It's one of London's few remaining super clubs with exciting club nights and a fashionable crowd – so dress to impress. Winner of Best Dance Club at the London Club & Bar Dance Awards 2013.

Pacha London, Terminus Place, SW1V 1JR (0845-371 4489, pachalondon.com, Victoria tube).

5 June

Connoisseurs' Collection

Laugh along with *The Laughing Cavalier*, a painting by Frans Hals at the Wallace Collection, housed in a lovely Georgian (1776) building in beautiful Manchester Square. One of London's – and the world's – best private art collections, with over 25 galleries of fine and decorative arts containing some 5,500 objects, including French 18th-century paintings and furniture, sculpture, miniatures, porcelain and glass, gold boxes, arms and armour.

Wallace Collection, Hertford House, Manchester Sq, W1U 3BN (020-7563 9500, wallacecollection.org, Bond St tube, free).

Relax in Paddington Street Gardens, a lovely park and haven in Marylebone, with many beautiful trees including cherry, laburnum, hawthorn and a monkey puzzle, shrubs, roses and seasonal bedding. In summer you can hire a deckchair and enjoy a concert. Don't miss the striking statue *Street Orderly Boy* by Milanese sculptor Donato Baraglia, installed in 1943.

Paddington Street Gardens, Paddington St, W1U 5QA (020-7641 5271, westminster.gov.uk > Parks and open spaces, Baker St tube, free).

6 June

Reflections on D-Day

March over to the National Army Museum in Chelsea on the anniversary of D-Day, the Western Allies' invasion of Normandy which ultimately led to victory in World War Two. Four main permanent exhibitions 'tell the ordinary and extraordinary stories of the men and women who served in Britain's armies across the globe and how they helped shape the world of today'.

National Army Museum, Royal Hospital Rd, SW3 4HT (020-7881 6606, nam.ac.uk, Sloane Sq tube, free).

Pay your respects to the forgotten victims of war at the *Animals in War* monument in Hyde Park. London has a wealth of war memorials, but none more powerful and moving than this tribute to the millions of animals (particularly horses) that served, suffered and died alongside British, Commonwealth and Allied forces in the wars and conflicts of the 20th century.

Animals in War, Hyde Park, Brook Gate/Upper Brook St, W1 (animalsinwar.org.uk, Marble Arch tube).

7 June

Antiques Roadshow

Enjoy the thrill of finding something special with a rummage in Alfies Antiques Market in Marylebone, London's largest indoor antiques emporium, with a bohemian chic atmosphere. For over 30 years Alfies Antique Market has been a London institution, attracting collectors, interior designers and international dealers to its Aladdin's cave of antiques, vintage fashion and collectibles.

Alfies Antiques Market, 13-25 Church St, NW8 8DT (020-7723 6066, alfiesantiques.com, Edgware Rd tube).

For those with deeper pockets, there's the Olympia International Art & Antiques Fair, London's premier art and antiques fair, which attracts dealers and buyers from around the world. Exhibits include everything from 18th- and 19th-century English furniture to Art Nouveau and Art Deco, from clocks and watches to ceramics and jewellery, Asian and tribal art to antiquities and contemporary art.

Olympia International Art & Antiques Fair, Olympia Exhibition Centre, Olympia Way, W14 8UX (0114-223 9811, olympia-art-antiques.com, Kensington Olympia tube, ⓘ).

8 June

Sport of Princes

Watch the sport of princes at Hurlingham Park, Fulham (home of the swanky private members Hurlingham Club), during MINT Polo in the Park. The three-day World Series event showcases a more accessible (i.e. affordable) version of polo, with teams taking part from around the world. There's also medieval jousting and an array of bars, shops and food stalls.

Polo in the Park, Hurlingham Park, SW6 3RH (0844-248 5069, polointheparklondon.com, Putney Bridge tube, ☎, ⓘ).

Have a drink or dinner at The Atlas, a notable gastropub secreted in a Fulham backstreet. Its menu is a trip around the Mediterranean, with Italian, Moroccan and Turkish influences, and the pub offers a choice of real ales and a serious wine list (the pub also hosts wine workshops). In short, a welcoming place to enjoy good food, beer and wine.

The Atlas, 16 Seagrove Rd, SW6 1RX (020-7385 9129, theatlaspub. co.uk, West Brompton tube, ££, ☎).

June

9 June

Anyone for Tennis?

Brush up your tennis technique before Wimbledon at Bush Hill Park in Enfield which has ten free tennis courts, making it one of the largest free tennis centres in London. In general you can simply turn up and play, with no booking or payment required, although courts are sometimes used for coaching sessions and by local tennis leagues, so it's advisable to check.

Bush Hill Park, Lincoln Rd, Enfield, EN1 1PS (tennisforfree.com, Bush Hill Park rail).

Take to the water at the Docklands Sailing & Watersports Centre at the west end of Millwall Outer Dock, in the heart of London's Docklands. The award-winning, purpose-built facility is a Royal Yachting Association recognised training centre offering courses in sailing, windsurfing and power-boating, plus British Canoe Union approved courses in paddlesports.

Docklands Sailing & Watersports Centre, 235a Westferry Rd, E14 3QS (020-7537 2626, dswc.org, South Quay DLR, 🖥).

10 June

Designs on Docklands

Seek out cutting edge art at Canary Wharf, which has one of the UK's largest collections of public art, including work by leading artists and designers, plus a year-round free temporary exhibition programme. Canary Wharf's public art collection numbers over 60 works of art, including stand-alone pieces and integrated artist-architectural works, executed by some of the world's leading artists, designers and craftsmen.

Canary Wharf, E14 (canarywharf.com/visitus/public--art/public--art, Canary Wharf tube).

Aeolus, Luke Jerram

Spend lunchtime in Spain at Camino Puerto del Canario, close to Canary Wharf Pier, one of an acclaimed chain of tapas restaurants. Camino takes you on a gastronomic tour of Spain's regions with a surfeit of delights, including all the usual tapas favourites plus more adventurous offerings. It's also serious about wine, with around 50 on offer, including cavas and sherries. *Delicioso!*

Camino, 28 Westferry Circus, E14 8RR (020-3589 4514, camino. uk.com/canarywharf, Canary Wharf tube, ££, 🖥).

June

11 June

Peonies & Puppets

Visit Clifton Nurseries, an oasis in west London, the city's oldest garden centre established in 1880 (but used to grown plants and flowers from around 1865), and probably the most famous nursery in the world. The nursery is an inspiring and beautiful place to visit, tucked down a side street in the heart of Little Venice, it's like stumbling upon a secret garden. It offers an extensive choice of shrubs, trees, plants and flowers, homewares and tools, and also has a gift shop and café. There's also a programme of events and workshops (see website for information).

Clifton Nurseries also offers a garden design service (since the '60s) and over the past 40 years has won numerous prizes for its design, construction and garden maintenance, including five gold medals at the prestigious RHS Chelsea Flower Show (the world's foremost flower show).

Clifton Nurseries, 5A Clifton Villas, W9 2PH (020-7289 6851, clifton. co.uk, Warwick Ave tube, free).

Treat the kids to a show on board the unique Puppet Barge moored on the Grand Union Canal in Little Venice. It's an established 55-seat theatre – now in its fourth decade – with comfortable seating and modern facilities, heated in winter and cool in summer. The charming Puppet Barge is rich in atmosphere and provides the ideal setting for the shows. It's ever-popular with families, but don't assume that it's just for children, as the cleverly-staged shows and intriguing puppets appeal just as much to adults. Performance times and dates are erratic and the barge isn't a permanent fixture, so book well in advance.

Puppet Barge, Little Venice, opp. 35 Blomfield Rd, W9 2PF (020-7249 6876, puppetbarge.com, Warwick Ave tube, ☎).

Have lunch in the Clifton Kitchen (£), the nursery's pretty café set amid the greenery and plants.

12 June

All Aboard!

See the sights from the top of an iconic red Routemaster bus. London's original Routemaster buses were decommissioned in 2005 but it's still possible to travel on the popular vehicles on two 'heritage routes' that serve the city. Route 9 (Kensington to Trafalgar Sq) and 15 (Tower Hill to Trafalgar Sq) buses travel during daytime hours and fares are the same as on regular bus services.

Transport for London (tfl.gov.uk/modalpages/2605.aspx).

Be stirred by the spectacular bands of the Household Division at 9pm on Horse Guards Parade in the heart of London. This pageant of military music, precision drill and colour takes place on two successive evenings in June when the massed bands of the Household Division (some 300 musicians, drummers and pipers) perform the Ceremony of Beating Retreat.

Ceremony of Beating Retreat, Horse Guards Parade, Whitehall, SW1A 2AX (royal.gov.uk/royaleventsandceremonies/beatingretreat/ beatingretreat.aspx, Charing Cross tube, ☎, ⓘ).

13 June

Night Owls

Join the night owls at London Zoo in Regent's Park on a Friday night during 'zoo lates', when the zoo is open from 6-10pm in June-July. A trip to the zoo is usually the quintessential family day out, but on Friday evenings it's an over 18s affair, with improvised comedy, twisted cabaret, roving performances, bars, street food and more – plus some 17,500 creatures.

Zoo Lates, ZSL London Zoo, Regent's Park, NW1 4RY (0844-225 1826, zsl.org/zsl-london-zoo/whats-on/zoo-lates, Regent's Park tube, ☎, ⓘ).

Finish off your night with a rave at The Underworld in Camden Town, one of north London's coolest live music venues with a long history of hosting big acts. Friday night is club night, when you can dance until 3am to the best pop of the last three decades – sign up online (www.facebook.com/ popitclub) and entry's free before midnight (£4 after).

The Underworld, 174 Camden High Street, NW1 0NE (020-7482 1932, theunderworldcamden.co.uk, Camden Town tube).

June

14 June

Pomp & Ceremony

See the magnificent Trooping the Colour ceremony on Horse Guards Parade, the display of pageantry to celebrate the Sovereign's Official Birthday (although the Queen was born on 21st April), which dates back to the 17th century. The ceremony is performed by troops of the Household Division (Foot Guards and Household Cavalry) and watched by HM the Queen, who takes the salute.

Trooping the Colour, Horse Guards Parade, Whitehall, SW1A 2AX (trooping-the-colour.co.uk, Charing Cross tube, ☏, ⓘ).

Take the opportunity to see some of London's secret gardens during Open Garden Squares Weekend, when community gardens and private squares throughout the city are thrown open to the public. Gardens range from historical private squares to contemporary roof gardens, prisons and barges. A single ticket (which includes a guide book) provides access to over 200 gardens over the weekend. Note that it's necessary to book to visit some gardens.

Open Garden Squares Weekend (opensquares.org, ⓘ).

15 June

Dad's Day

It's Father's Day, so treat the 'old man' to a day out at the Motorexpo at Canary Wharf, billed as 'the world's largest free motoring event', where you can see the latest vehicles from many of the world's leading motor manufacturers. For a week, London's premier business district is transformed into a vast showcase for vehicles positioned throughout the indoor and outdoor public spaces of the Canary Wharf estate.

Motor Expo, Canary Wharf (motorexpo.com, Canary Wharf DLR, free, ⓘ).

———————

Buy dad a nice juicy steak at Gaucho Canary Wharf, boasting a superb riverside location with a huge terrace for sunny days. One of a city-wide chain of sleek, slick Argentinean steakhouses, Gaucho is riding a crest of popularity in eating big juicy steaks – in this case pampas-reared, 'wet-aged' Argentinean beef, which waiters proudly parade on wooden boards.

Gaucho Canary Wharf, 29 Westferry Circus, London E14 8RR (020-7987 9494, gauchorestaurants.co.uk/restaurants/restaurant.php?id=canary, Canary Wharf DLR, £££, ☏).

16 June

Hampstead Haven

Hill Garden

Burgh House

Visit charming Hill Garden and the beautiful pergola (800ft in length) secreted within Hampstead Heath. The formal Arts & Crafts garden was created between 1906 and 1925 by celebrated landscape architect Thomas Mawson (1861-1933) for the soap magnate Lord Leverhulme (1851-1925). It's situated at the rear of Inverforth House, formerly The Hill, which Leverhulme purchased in 1904 for his London residence.

Mawson brought architectural treatment and formality to garden design, and the pergola and gardens are the best surviving examples of his work. The pergola was a magnificent Edwardian extravagance and became the setting for garden parties and summer evening strolls. In late spring and early summer the raised, covered pergola is festooned with fragrant flowers, including jasmine, buddleia, sage, honeysuckle, vines, clematis, kiwi, potato vine, lavender and wisteria. Visit during the early evening and you may even see roosting long-eared bats.

In contrast to the wild decadence of the pergola, Hill Garden is beautifully manicured and designed, and a slice of paradise; a delightful sanctuary and perfect antidote to the stresses of modern life, offering panoramic views over London.

Hill Garden & Pergola, Inverforth Close, off North End Way, NW3 7EX (cityoflondon.gov.uk > The Pergola and Hill Garden, Hampstead tube, free).

Take a detour to another Hampstead highlight: Burgh House, built in 1704 during Queen Anne's reign and one of the area's oldest buildings. Today it's home to the Hampstead Museum and an art gallery, with a permanent display of over 3,000 objects, many relating to social history, fine art and notable Hampstead residents, such as John Constable and John Keats. Have a drink or lunch in the lovely (licensed) Buttery Café (£), with its charming garden full of nooks and crannies.

Burgh House, New End Sq, Hampstead, NW3 1LT (020-7431 0144, burghhouse.org.uk, Hampstead tube, free).

Hill Garden pergola

June

17 June

Splendid Spitalfields

Marvel at Christ Church Spitalfields, Nicholas Hawksmoor's (1661-1736) Baroque masterpiece built between 1714 and 1729, and restored in 2004 at a cost of £10m. The church is famous for its beautiful stonework and pleasing geometry, with a volume half that of the nave of St Paul's. The splendid organ installed in 1735 was made by England's greatest Georgian organ builder, Richard Bridge (d 1758).

Christ Church Spitalfields, Commercial St, E1 6LY (020-7377 6793, christchurchspitalfields.org and ccspitalfields.org, Aldgate East tube, free).

Listen to a concert during the Spitalfields Music Summer Festival, which brings together world class artists and local people in Tower Hamlets. The summer festival includes small-scale classical, folk and contemporary performances held in a variety of contrasting venues, including classical concerts in Christ Church. The eclectic programme includes baroque, jazz and world music, plus a series of talks and debates, walks, visits and interactive workshops.

Spitalfields Music Summer Festival (020-7377 1362, spitalfieldsmusic.org.uk, 📞, ℹ️).

18 June

Visit the Iron Duke

Admire the home of one of England's greatest soldiers on Waterloo Day, the anniversary of the defeat of Napoleon at the Battle of Waterloo in 1815. Designed by Robert Adam (built 1771-1778), Apsley House was acquired by Arthur Wellesley, 1st Duke of Wellington in 1817. Now a museum and splendid art gallery, the dazzling interiors are a magnificent example of the Regency style.

Apsley House, 149 Piccadilly, Hyde Park Cnr, London W1J 7NT (020-7499 5676, english-heritage.org.uk/daysout/properties/apsley-house, Hyde Park Cnr tube).

Pop into The Wellington pub – named after the great man – on the Strand for a pint and a pie. This characterful Edwardian pub (1903) has an attractive neo-gothic exterior and striking, long wooden bar. There's also a large upstairs room, although the most prized tables are outside, where you can enjoy the usual Nicholson's fine selection of real ales.

The Wellington, 351 Strand, WC2R 0HS (020-7836 2789, nicholsonspubs.co.uk/thewellingtonstrandlondon, Temple tube, £).

June

19 June

Up, Up & Away!

Get a bird's eye view of the capital with a dawn balloon flight over London. The ultimate trip for high fliers, the sensation as you rise above the sights and sounds of London is unforgettable. Flights are available on weekday mornings from late April to mid-August, meeting shortly after dawn, with most launch sites within a few miles of the Tower of London or the Thames.

Adventure Balloons (01252-844222, adventureballoons.co.uk/london-balloon-flights, ☎).

After such an early start, grab 40 winks in a deckchair in Victoria Tower Gardens, a long strip of park beside the Thames close to the Palace of Westminster. The gardens are noted for their statues, including Auguste Rodin's *The Burghers of Calais* (1889), and one of the suffragette Emmeline Pankhurst (1858-1928) who endured many spells of imprisonment in order to win women the right to vote.

Victoria Tower Gardens, Millbank, SW1P 3SF (0300-061 2000, royalparks.org.uk, Westminster tube, free).

20 June

Dipping & Digging

Have a dip in the iconic Art Deco lido in Brockwell Park – opened in July 1937 and recently restored to its former glory. Brockwell Park is one of south London's best and most diverse public parks, incorporating ornamental ponds, wetlands, a wild meadow, open grassland, formal flower beds and a tranquil walled rose garden.

Brockwell Park Lido, Brockwell Park, Norwood Rd, SE24 9BJ (020-7926 9000, lambeth.gov.uk > parks and green spaces, brockwelllido.com, Brixton tube).

Learn some new skills at the Centre for Wildlife Gardening, an idyllic spot in Peckham, developed in the late '80s and operated by the London Wildlife Trust. What was once a council depot has been transformed into a Green Flag garden, with an award-winning visitor centre demonstrating innovative environmental building techniques. You can also buy plants and delicious 'Peckham' honey.

Centre for Wildlife Gardening, 28 Marsden Rd, SE15 4EE (020-7252 9186, wildlondon.org.uk, East Dulwich rail, free).

June

21 June

Regent's Park Blowout

Stuff yourself silly at the Taste of London food festival in Regent's Park, which is transformed in June into a foodie wonderland for four days of eating, drinking and entertainment. Savour the ultimate alfresco feast with forty of the city's best restaurants dishing up their finest dishes, while 200 artisan producers provide a bounty of the best food and beverages from around Britain and the world.

Taste Festivals (tastefestivals.com/london, Regent's Park tube, ⓘ).

Feast your eyes on the majestic Georgian crescents surrounding Regent's Park, where a stroll around the Outer Circle is an architectural treat. Between Gloucester Gate in the north-eastern corner and Hanover Gate to the west of the lake, there are ten fine terraces of elegantly proportioned white stucco houses designed by John Nash or one of his protégés. The longest and most famous is Chester Terrace, a row of 42 houses stretching for 920ft.

Regent's Park Crescents (Regent's Park tube).

22 June

Risen from the Ashes

Lose yourself in the 'secret' Phoenix Garden, a little oasis next to the Phoenix Theatre and the last survivor of Covent Garden's community gardens. Founded in 1984 on the site of the old St Giles Leper Hospital (1117-1539), this award-winning garden has an interesting history, having been the site of a charity school, a tragic World War II bombing and a car park.

Phoenix Garden, 21 Stacey St, WC2H 8DG (020-7379 3187, phoenixgarden.org, Tottenham Court Rd tube, free).

Head underground to a secret basement bar, The Cellar Door in Aldwych, tucked away in a converted Victorian loo. The house speciality is its signature cocktails, with names such as Starbucks Must Die and Dita von Tease, with entertainment provided by cabaret/burlesque singers, drag queens and snuff (tobacco) parties, giving it a pre-war New York speakeasy or '30s Berlin cabaret feel. Great fun!

The Cellar Door, Zero Aldwych, WC2E 7DN (020-7240 8848, cellardoor.biz, Covent Garden tube, ££).

23 June

Great Balls of Fire!

Climb the London Monument which commemorates the Great Fire of London (1666) and celebrates the subsequent rebuilding of the City. Designed by Sir Christopher Wren and his friend the scientist Dr Robert Hooke, it's a huge, fluted doric column of Portland stone, containing a 311-step cantilevered stone staircase leading to a viewing platform topped by a drum and a copper urn, from which flames once emerged symbolising the fire. Built between 1671 and 1677, the memorial is 202ft high (the world's tallest isolated stone column) – the exact distance between it and the site in Pudding Lane where the fire started. It also happens to be where the Roman bridge touched land on the north bank of the Thames, and is therefore close to where London itself began.

From the viewing gallery (160ft) you're treated to panoramic views of the City in all directions. It was also put to another, bleaker use: six people committed suicide by throwing themselves from the gallery, the last in 1842, after which it was enclosed in an iron cage. Be warned, climbing the steps isn't for the nervous or very unfit.

The Monument, junction of Monument St and Fish St Hill, EC3R 6DB (020-7626 2717, themonument.info, Monument tube).

PUDDING LANE EC3

CITY OF LONDON

Look for the plaque that marks the spot where the Great Fire of London started in Thomas Faryner's bakery in Pudding Lane in 1666, located off Eastcheap near London Bridge and the Monument. The street is named after the 'puddings' (a medieval word for entrails and organs) which fell from the carts coming down the lane from the butchers in Eastcheap, as they headed for the waste barges on the River Thames. The plaque was erected in 1986 by the Worshipful Company of Bakers to commemorate the 500th anniversary of their charter granted by Henry VII in 1486.

Pudding Lane, EC3R (Monument tube).

Monument staircase

24 June

Lovely Lincoln's Inn

Visit Lincoln's Inn Fields, London's largest garden square dating back to the 12th century, a former site of jousting, notorious duels and the occasional public execution. A municipal public garden since 1894, it consists of shrubberies, flower beds, tennis courts and an octagonal pavilion/bandstand. Visitors are welcome (Mon-Fri, 7am to 7pm) and can also take an organised tour (see website) of the Inn's buildings.

Lincoln's Inn Fields, *Lincoln's Inn*, **WC2A 3TL (lincolnsinn.org.uk/index.php/tours-and-visits, Holborn tube, free).**

Buy some treats from the Fleet River Bakery and have a picnic in Lincoln's Inn Fields. The Fleet serves superb coffee (from the Monmouth Coffee Company), iced latte, and delicious sandwiches, pastries and cakes. They also have a large seating area if you prefer something more substantial, such as quiche, frittata, toasties, mezze, quesadilla, bruschetta and antipasti – in addition they are licensed.

Fleet River Bakery, 71 Lincolns Inn Fields, WC2A 3JF (020-7691 1457, fleetriverbakery.com, Holborn tube, £).

25 June

Rollicking Riverside Rave-Up

Let your hair down at the Greenwich & Docklands International Festival, London's leading festival of free street performances, art and dancing. The 10-day celebration offers a programme of world-class theatre and dance, family entertainment, extraordinary spectacles and a traditional Greenwich Fair. Featuring over 150 performances by 30 national and international companies, it attracts over 80,000 people to events taking place across the local area.

Greenwich & Docklands International Festival (festival.org, Cutty Sark DLR, ☎, ⓘ).

Stroll under the Thames via the Greenwich Foot Tunnel from Cutty Sark Gardens to Island Gardens on the Isle of Dogs. Once there, have a pint or lunch in one of the Dogs' many excellent pubs, such as The Gun (ten minutes' walk from Island Gardens), an 18th-century, Thameside gastropub serving award-winning modern British cuisine (and allegedly the love nest of Admiral Nelson and Lady Hamilton).

The Gun, 27 Coldharbour, E14 9NS (020-7515 5222, thegundocklands.com, Blackwall DLR, ££, ☎).

Royal Naval College

26 June

Relax in Richmond

Have lunch at The Roebuck pub on top of Richmond Hill, overlooking the River Thames and the surrounding countryside. The panoramic views from the beer garden have inspired writers and painters, from William Wordsworth to JMW Turner, and can turn the Roebuck's fine (Taylor Walker) ales and solid pub grub into ambrosia.

The Roebuck, 130 Richmond Hill, TW10 6RN (020-8948 2329, taylor-walker.co.uk/pub/roebuck-richmond/s5628, Richmond tube, ££, ☎).

Spend an enjoyable evening at the **Orange Tree Theatre** in Richmond, an intimate 172-seat theatre-in-the-round which creates a powerful intimacy between audience and performer. It's an actors' theatre committed to encouraging new and 'undiscovered' writing from the UK and abroad, and making live theatre more accessible and less expensive. There's a bar that opens 45 minutes before each performance.

Orange Tree Theatre, 1 Clarence St, Richmond, TW9 2SA (020-8940 3633, orangetreetheatre.co.uk, Richmond tube, ☎).

27 June

Stars in Your Eyes

Duke & Duchess of Cambridge

Meet the famous faces at Madame Tussauds, London's world-famous wax museum established (as the Baker Street Bazaar) in 1835, moving to its current site in 1884. The museum allows you to get up close and personal with royalty, A-list celebrities, sporting legends, political heavyweights, historical icons and even the infamous. Kitsch – and, let's face it, a bit tacky – but nevertheless interesting.

Madame Tussauds, Marylebone Rd, NW1 5LR (madametussauds. com/london, Baker St tube).

Eat what you're given at Le Relais de Venise L'Entrecôte in Marylebone, a classic Parisian-style brasserie with a difference – there's no menu! The starter is a green salad followed by steak and frites – your only decision is how you want your steak cooked. There's also a small choice of wines, a choice of cheeses and a dessert list. Enjoyable and a bargain.

Le Relais de Venise, 120 Marylebone Ln, W1U 2QG (020-7486 0878, relaisdevenise.com/marylebone, Bond St tube, £, ☎).

June

28 June

Trees Company

Hug a tree (or two) in Highgate Wood, a majestic preserved segment of the ancient Forest of Middlesex which once covered much of London and is mentioned in the *Domesday Book*. The wood covers 70 acres and is rich in oak, holly and hornbeam, plus the rare wild service tree – an indication of ancient woodland. It's also home to over 50 other tree and shrub species and rich in wildlife, including five species of bat, over 70 bird species and some 250 types of moth.

Excavations show that Romano-Britons were producing pottery from local materials here between AD 50-100, and there are ancient earthworks that may have formed part of an enclosure for deer during the medieval period, when the Bishop of London owned the wood. Between the 16th and 18th centuries the wood was leased to various tenants who managed (coppiced) the wood and produced timber (particularly oak) for the Crown to construct ships and for church buildings. In 1886, the City of London Corporation acquired the wood for public use and renamed it Highgate Wood. There's a children's playground, an information centre and a superb café.

Highgate Wood, Muswell Hill Rd, N10 3JN (020-8444 6129, cityoflondon.gov.uk > green spaces, Highgate tube, free).

Enjoy an alfresco lunch at the beautiful Pavilion Café in Highgate Wood, housed in an old cricket pavilion; a quintessential English idyll set in a clearing surrounded by a picket fence and ancient forest. With its large, wisteria- and rose-clad terrace and sea of outdoor tables (with umbrellas) and benches, the café is the perfect spot for a drink or lunch on a sunny day; or it would be if it wasn't for the like-minded hordes of families, joggers and walkers who descend upon it in summer.

Pavilion Café, Highgate Wood, Muswell Hill Rd, N10 3JN (020-8444 4777, Highgate tube, £).

June

29 June

Big Boys' Toys

Launch a model boat on the Round Pond in Kensington Gardens or just sit back and watch the experts. It's the home of Britain's oldest model yacht clubs, the Model Yacht Sailing Association (mysa.org.uk, est. 1876) and the London Model Yacht Club (est. 1884). To have a go, all you need do is turn up at the pond on a Sunday morning at 11am – all are welcome and no experience is required.

Round Pond, Kensington Gardens (Queensway tube).

Visit the Serpentine Gallery Pavilion, an annual programme of temporary structures by internationally acclaimed architects and designers, and an important site for architectural experimentation. The unique series showcases the work of an international architect (or design team) who hasn't completed a building in England at the time of the invitation. The pavilion is sited on the gallery's lawn during the summer months.

Serpentine Gallery Pavilion, Kensington Gardens, W2 3XA (020-7402 6075, serpentinegallery.org, Lancaster Gate tube, free).

30 June

Super Scoop

Enjoy free entertainment at The Scoop, a sunken, open-air amphitheatre (seating 800) next to the Thames beside City Hall. Throughout the summer months, The Scoop regularly hosts a variety of free events, from music concerts, theatre and films to local community events and activities (even keep-fit classes). While you're in the area, you might also wish to take a look inside the iconic City Hall.

The Scoop, Queen's Walk, More London, SE1 2DB (morelondon.com/scoop.html, London Bridge tube, free).

———————————

Have a game of pool at the Number 1 Bar near London Bridge, the only venue in the area that offers a nightclub (Thu-Sat), a sports bar, restaurant (grill and steak house), pool tables, dance floors, a smoking balcony and even VIP rooms, under the same roof – and it's open until 6am. There's even free parking after 6.30pm (Mon-Sat and all day Sun).

Number 1 Bar 1 Duke St Hill, SE1 2SW (020-7407 6420, n1bar.com, London Bridge tube, ££).

June

July

1 July

We are Sailing…

Set sail on a tall ship from Woolwich with Sail Royal Greenwich. This spectacular cruise lasts two hours and takes you from the Royal Arsenal Pier, along the River Thames past the O2 Arena, Canary Wharf, the Cutty Sark, the Old Royal Naval College and the Royal Observatory. It also passes through the Thames Barrier and crosses the Greenwich Meridian Line.

Sail Royal Greenwich, 10th Floor, 6 Mitre Passage, Greenwich, SE10 0ER (020-3040 2350, sailroyalgreenwich.co.uk, ☎).

Drop into The Dial Arch gastropub, housed in what was once the gatehouse of the Woolwich Arsenal munitions factory. This beautifully-renovated building dates back to 1720 and has exposed brickwork, chandeliers, wood and stone flooring, original artwork and a huge terrace (heated when necessary). The British seasonal menu contains all the usual pub favourites, including Sunday roast.

The Dial Arch, Major Draper St, Royal Arsenal, SE18 6GH (020-3130 0700, dialarch.com, Woolwich Arsenal DLR, ££, ☎).

2 July

Do the Strand

Walk the Thames from Kew Bridge along Strand-on-the-Green in Chiswick, one of London's most picturesque stretches of waterfront. Among the lovely old buildings is a group of almshouses, originally built in 1658 and replaced in the 1720s. The footpath along the river bank is fronted by some imposing 18th-century houses – home to many famous residents over the centuries – and quaint pubs. The downside is that being on the tideway, it's regularly flooded!

Strand-on-the-Green, Chiswick, W4 (Gunnersbury tube).

Stop for lunch at The Bull's Head, which has an enviable position overlooking the Thames just along from Kew Bridge. The rambling Grade I listed Chef & Brewer pub oozes history – its licence dates back to 1722 – with low ceilings, exposed beams and creaking floorboards. The Bull's Head serves reasonable pub grub, cask ales and lagers, plus keenly priced house wines.

The Bull's Head, 15 Strand on the Green, W4 3PQ (020-8994 1204, chefandbrewer.com/pub/bulls-head-chiswick-london/c6789, Gunnersbury tube, ££, ☎).

3 July

Riding Rotten Row

Ride out in style along Hyde Park's Rotten Row. You can hire a horse at Hyde Park Stables or Ross Nye Stables; both offer group horse riding at all skill levels, as well as semi-private riding for couples or small groups and private tuition. Hyde Park also has a dedicated horse-riding arena and two designated bridlepaths.

Hyde Park Stables, 63 Bathurst Mews, W2 2SB (020-7723 2813) or Ross Nye Stables, 8 Bathurst Mews (020-7262 3791, Lancaster Gate tube, ☎).

See the Queen's horses and carriages at the Royal Mews, designed by John Nash in 1825 as part of George IV's upgrade of Buckingham Palace. It was built to accommodate 54 horses, although Queen Victoria had as many as 200, while Prince Albert kept dairy cows here! Many eye-catching royal carriages are housed at the Mews, including the Gold State Coach.

Royal Mews, Buckingham Palace, SW1W 1QH (020-7766 7302, royalcollection.org.uk/visit/royalmews, Victoria tube).

4 July

Murray Mania

Cheer on the players at the Wimbledon Tennis Championships. Most tickets are sold by ballot well in advance, but some Centre Court tickets are available via Ticketmaster for the following day's play. Admission to the grounds – and 'Murray Mound' – plus a limited number of tickets for Centre, No.1 and No.2 Courts can be purchased each day at the turnstiles.

The All England Lawn Tennis Club, Church Rd, Wimbledon, SW19 5AE (020-8944 1066/01543-250239, wimbledon.com, Wimbledon Park tube, ☎, ⓘ).

Enjoy a play or show at the New Wimbledon Theatre. Built in 1910 by J B Mulholland, it has a beautiful Edwardian auditorium with three levels of seating for over 1,600, making it one of London's largest theatres. Nowadays it stages touring productions of musicals, ballets, operas and plays, as well as a Christmas pantomime.

New Wimbledon Theatre, 93 The Broadway, SW19 1QG (0844-871 7646, atgtickets.com/venues/new-wimbledon-theatre, Wimbledon tube, ☎).

July

5 July

Islington Idyll

Take a stroll along the New River Walk from Canonbury Square to Newington Green (4mi) – a section of the 28mi New River Path, a delightful linear public park and tranquil wildlife oasis. Commissioned in 1613 by Sir Hugh Myddleton (1560-1631), the New River was originally an aqueduct to bring drinking water to central London.

New River Walk, Canonbury Grove, N1 (020-7527 2000, islington. gov.uk > parks and green spaces, Highbury & Islington tube).

See stunning modern Italian art at the Estorick Collection – named after the collector Eric Estorick (1913-1993) – a hidden gem housed in a handsome 19th-century house. It isn't just Britain's only gallery devoted to modern Italian art, but is also one of the world's best collections of early 20th-century Italian art, particularly the Futurism movement. There's also an excellent café.

Estorick Collection, 39A Canonbury Sq, N1 2AN (020-7704 9522, estorickcollection.com, Highbury & Islington tube).

6 July

Commune with Nature

Watch the birds at the London Wetland Centre in Barnes, covering over 100 acres and probably Europe's best urban wildlife viewing area. The Centre was the brainchild of Sir Peter Scott (1909-1989), founder of the World Wide Fund for Nature and the Wildfowl and Wetlands Trust. In 2012 it was voted Britain's Favourite Nature Reserve by readers of *Countryfile* magazine.

London Wetland Centre, Queen Elizabeth's Walk, Barnes, SW13 9WT (020-8409 4400, www.wwt.org.uk/visit-us/london, Barnes rail).

Mandarin duck

Feed the ducks (and yourself) at The Sun Inn in Barnes village, a large, rambling establishment occupying a striking, whitewashed building. The inexpensive daily menu has a gastro edge, with Saturday brunch and Sunday roast options. The pub's terrace is a popular spot in fine weather – or you can take your pint over the road to the duck pond.

The Sun Inn, 7 Church Rd, SW13 9HE (020-8876 5256, thesuninnbarnes.co.uk, Barnes Bridge rail, £, ✆).

7 July

New Sensations

Learn the art of mime at the Theatre de l'Ange Fou in Finsbury. Created in Paris in 1984 and relocated to London in 1995, the school is devoted to the development of the technique, growing repertoire and dramaturgy of corporeal mime, and offers a full range of professional training programmes.

Theatre de l'Ange Fou & International School of Corporeal Mime, Unit 207, Belgravia Workshops, 157-163 Marlborough Rd, N19 4NF (020-7263 9339, angefou.co.uk, Archway tube, ☎).

Try an unusual eating experience at Dans le Noir restaurant, where you eat entirely in the dark! You can choose between four menus – chef surprise (exotic and unusual), fish and seafood, meat or vegetarian – which are served in a 'dark room' by blind guides. The experience is designed to make you more aware of your other senses, such as taste and smell.

Dans le Noir, 30-31 Clerkenwell Green, EC1R 0DU (020-7253 1100, london.danslenoir.com, Farringdon tube, ££, ☎).

8 July

Chill Out in the City

Seafood and eat it at The Angler restaurant, in the City's South Place Hotel. The long, elegant dining room has stunning floor-to-ceiling windows and an expansive terrace, offering spectacular views of landmarks such as the Gherkin and Tower 42 (weather permitting). A quintessentially British seafood restaurant, the menu focuses on seafood and shellfish from around the UK.

The Angler, South Place Hotel, 3 South Place, EC2M 2AF (020-3215 1260, southplacehotel.com/restaurants-and-bars/angler-restaurant, Moorgate tube, £££, ☎).

Have a blast at The Old Blue Last in Shoreditch, one of London's coolest pubs with great live music and a fantastic juke box, brought to you by *Vice* magazine (vice.com). The décor is Victorian gin palace but the music is very much of the moment, with the best hip bands and DJs seven nights a week – and entry is usually free.

The Old Blue Last, 38 Great Eastern St, EC2 (020-7739 7033, theoldbluelast.com, Old St tube, £).

July

9 July

Heavenly Holland Park

Treat yourself to lunch at the Belvedere restaurant in lovely Holland Park, an affluent, fashionable part of west London, dotted with large Victorian townhouses and upmarket restaurants and shops. The elegant Belvedere occupies the former Summer Ballroom of Holland House, surrounded by flower gardens and lawns – a glorious location at the heart of what many consider to be London's most peaceful and romantic park. The menu is classic French, but includes a few British favourites, such as fish and chips and a Sunday roast.

Although one of the capital's smallest public parks (54 acres), Holland Park is also one of the most interesting and has plenty to offer. A Green Flag winner since 2001, its treasures include beautiful views, glorious gardens, striking statuary, galleries, sports facilities, an ecology centre, some of London's best children's play facilities, a café, large areas of woodland, a pride of free-roaming peacocks and a stunning Japanese (Kyoto) garden.

Belvedere Restaurant, Holland Park, Abbotsbury Rd, W8 6LU (020-7602 1238, belvedererestaurant.co.uk, Holland Park tube, £££, ☎).

Enjoy opera in Holland Park, where the magical atmosphere of the productions owes a lot to the verdant surroundings. The productions change each year but include many of the most popular operas from the world's greatest composers such as Bizet's *Carmen*, Puccini's *Madame Butterfly* and Verdi's *Aida*. What's more, it doesn't cost a fortune – there are subsidised and even some free tickets available through Opera Holland Park's 'Inspire' scheme. You could even be onstage as an unpaid extra (see website) in some of the productions. In the words of *The Independent on Sunday*: 'For inclusivity, accessibility, bonhomie and sheer ebullience, Opera Holland Park takes some beating.'

Opera Holland Park, Holland Park, Stable Yard, W8 6LU (0300-999 1000, operahollandpark.com, Holland Park tube, ☎, ⓘ).

10 July

Fragrant Hampton Court

Breathe in the floral scents at the Hampton Court Palace Flower Show, which is combined with the Hampton Court Palace Festival, a musical extravaganza featuring a series of concerts by international names. The Royal Horticultural Society HCP Flower Show is second only to Chelsea in prestige and importance, and is the world's largest flower show. Tickets sell fast, so get yours well in advance.

If you want to avoid the crowds (and who doesn't?), grab a ticket to the exclusive preview evening the day before the show opens to the public, which not only allows you to explore the wonderful gardens and floral displays in comfort and style, but includes a range of dining options. Roaming musicians and live bands add to the party atmosphere throughout the evening, which culminates in a spectacular fireworks display.

While you're here, take the opportunity to see the spectacular Hampton Court Palace gardens, featuring sparkling fountains and glorious displays of over 200,000 flowering bulbs.

Hampton Court Palace Flower Show, Hampton Court Palace, East Molesey, KT8 9AU (0844-338 0338, *rhs.org.uk/hampton-flower-show and hamptoncourtpalacefestival.com,* **Hampton Court rail,** ✆, ⓘ**).**

Get lost in Hampton Court maze – the most famous maze in the world – with a convoluted series of twists and turns covering a third of an acre. Designed by George London and Henry Wise and commissioned around 1700 by William III, it has been baffling visitors for centuries. Mental dexterity is required to escape, but a soothing sound installation integrated into the structure is designed to prevent the process becoming too stressful.

Hampton Court Palace, East Molesey, KT8 9AU (0844-482 7777/020-3166 6000, hrp.org.uk/hamptoncourtpalace, Hampton Court rail).

Stop for refreshments at the King's Arms Hotel (020-8977 1729), a 300-year-old inn perched on the palace's Lions Gate, rich in atmosphere, décor and history.

July

11 July

Get a Tat Like Becks

Get a tattoo like David Beckham's at Good Times, a stylish tattoo emporium in bohemian Shoreditch. The antithesis of your usual tattoo shop, Good Times is a co-operative or group practice, where a number of London's top tattoo artists practise under the same roof. They offer an eclectic mix of styles, including western traditional, Japanese and Tibetan – with a feminine edge.

Good Times, First Floor, 147 Curtain Rd, EC2A 3QE (020-7739 2438, ilovegoodtimes.co.uk, Shoreditch High St tube, ☏).

Enjoy an outstanding meal at Otto's, an unassuming French restaurant with lovely '50s kitsch décor, moderate prices, splendid service and delectable food. Moreover, the fine French wines are an oenophile's delight and Otto's has one of the lowest mark-ups in town, allowing you try superior wines at bargain prices. *Superbe!*

Otto's Restaurant, 182 Grays Inn Rd, WC1X 8EW (020-7713 0107, ottos-restaurant.com, Chancery Ln tube, ££, ☏).

12 July

Voluptuous Vicky Park

Try your hand at lawn bowls in Victoria Park in East London, the city's oldest public park. Founded in 1845 to provide essential green space for working folk, it soon became famous as a centre for political meetings and rallies. The park boasts delightful open parkland with shrubs and trees, wide tree-lined carriageways, a deer park, lakes, leisure gardens and ornate bridges over canals.

Victoria Park, Grove Rd, Bow, E3 5SN (020-7364 2494, towerhamlets. gov.uk/default.aspx?page=12670, Mile End tube, free).

Bite into a bacon butty at the excellent Pavilion Café in Victoria Park, widely acknowledged as one of London's best park cafés. The domed Pavilion overlooking the lake is an idyllic spot and serves one of the capital's most celebrated breakfasts, plus excellent coffee and cakes. Its locally-sourced, organic menu also makes it a popular spot for an alfresco lunch.

Pavilion Café, Victoria Park, Grove Rd, Bow, E9 7DE (020-8980 0030, the-pavilion-cafe.com, Mile End tube, £).

13 July

Masters at Work

Listen to some lovely music at St James's church on Piccadilly. Consecrated in 1684, it's one of Sir Christopher Wren's masterpieces, with a font, organ case and reredos by England's finest wood carver, Grinling Gibbons. St James's has an impressive music programme, with free lunchtime recitals and regular paid evening concerts. There's also an arts & crafts market in the courtyard (Wed-Sat, 10am to 6pm).

St James's Church, 197 Piccadilly, W1J 9LL (020-7734 4511, sjp.org. uk, Piccadilly Circus tube, free).

Dine to a backdrop of mellow jazz at Le Caprice, a Green Park institution since 1947 and a perennial favourite among well-heeled Londoners. It offers house jazz on the second and last Sunday of the month (7-11pm), as well as a Saturday jazz brunch twice a month, featuring the musical styling of Dom Pipkin.

Le Caprice, Arlington House, Arlington St, SW1A 1RJ (020-7629 2239, le-caprice.co.uk, Green Park tube, £££, ☏).

14 July

Off With His Head!

Join London's flourishing French community **to** celebrate Bastille Day, with a Gallic extravaganza at the free Bastille Festival in Bankside. Celebrating French food and culture, the festival hosts a feast of culinary delights (with Borough Market's French traders joining in the celebrations) including a French-themed demonstration kitchen, plus wandering performance artists, musicians, a traditional waiters' race, pétanque, story-telling, face painting and screenings of gastronomic-themed films.

Bastille Festival, Borough Market, Bankside, SE1 9SP (bastillefestival.co.uk, London Bridge tube, free).

Chill out with a game of pétanque and a glass of (French) wine at Balls Brothers Wine Bar in Hays Galleria, a striking shopping and entertainment centre in Southwark. Balls Brothers isn't just a great place to have a drink or meal, but also has one of London's only pétanque pitches during the summer months – there's even an annual lunchtime tournament.

Balls Brothers Wine Bar, Hay's Galleria, Tooley St, SE1 2HD (020-7407 4301, ballsbrothers.co.uk, London Bridge tube, ££, ☏).

15 July

Visual & Edible Art

See some fine art at the Royal Academy (RA) Summer Exhibition (June to August), an annual exhibition 'open to all artists of distinguished merit' to finance the training of young artists in the Academy's Schools. The Exhibition is the highlight of the Academy's year, attracting thousands of applications, and is an opportunity for unknown artists to display their work alongside current Academicians.

Summer Exhibition, Royal Academy of Arts, Burlington House, Piccadilly, W1J 0BD (020-7300 8000, royalacademy.org.uk, Green Park tube).

Tuck into good-value, traditional French cuisine at Brasserie Zedel, a Parisian bar and brasserie from the prolific partnership of Chris Corbin and Jeremy King. The vast subterranean dining room is a vision of La Belle Époque, and has the ambience of an ocean liner during the pre-war golden era of transatlantic travel. There's also a café, bar, and glitzy cabaret and night club.

Brasserie Zedel, 20 Sherwood St, W1F 7ED (020-7734 4888, brasseriezedel.com, Piccadilly Circus tube, ££, ☏).

16 July

Messing About on the River

Watch the historic Thames Doggett's Coat & Badge Race, rowed over a 4.5-mile course between London Bridge and Cadogan Pier (Chelsea) on a Friday in July. The race – founded in 1715 – is named after Thomas Doggett, who created the Coat and Badge prize in honour of the House of Hanover, to commemorate George I's accession to the Throne. It's the oldest rowing race in the world.

Doggetts Coat & Badge Race, London Bridge (doggettsrace.org.uk, London Bridge tube, free, ⓘ).

Paddle your canoe at the Pirate Castle on the Regents Canal in Camden. The experienced crew welcomes participants of all ages to take part in water-based activities, and provides training on canoes, kayaks and canal boats. Pirate Castle also offers a wide range of other activities, from comedy and theatre workshops to dance, yoga and taekwondo.

Pirate Castle, Oval Rd, NW1 7EA (020-7267 6605, thepiratecastle. org, Camden Town tube, ☏).

Doggett's Coat & Badge winners

17 July

Marianne & Music

Visit the Marianne North Gallery at the Royal Botanic Gardens in Kew. Recently restored, the gallery opened in 1882 and is the only permanent solo exhibition by a female artist in Britain. Marianne North (1830-1890) – naturalist and botanical artist – was a remarkable Victorian who travelled the globe to satisfy her passion for recording the world's flora with her paint brush. Intriguing and inspiring.

Marianne North Gallery, Royal Botanic Gardens, Kew, TW9 3AB (020-8332 5655, kew.org/collections/art-images/marianne-north, Kew Gardens tube).

Listen to some great music in Kew Gardens during the Kew the Music festival, one of the summer's most popular picnic concert series attracting a wealth of star names. You can also order a picnic hamper, enjoy a BBQ in the beautiful surroundings of the Pavilion Restaurant or reserve your place for dinner in the Marianne North Gallery.

Kew the Music, Royal Botanic Gardens, Kew, TW9 3AB (020-8332 5655, kew.org/visit-kew-gardens/whats-on/kew-the-music, Kew Gardens tube, ☎, ⓘ).

18 July

Thyme Out

Discover the Culpeper Community Garden, a green oasis in the midst of Islington's inner-city bustle, serving both as a city park and an environmental community project. Named after the famous 17th-century herbalist Nicholas Culpeper (1616-1654), it's a beautiful place to explore and admire the wealth of plants, lend a hand (volunteers welcome), enjoy a picnic or simply relax.

Culpeper Community Garden, 1 Cloudesley Rd, N1 0EG (020-7833 3951, culpeper.org.uk, Angel tube, free).

Go in search of good beer and great music at The Lexington pub, which has a ground floor bar and an upstairs music venue. The latter specialises in indie music – live bands and DJ sounds – while the bar is in the retro American lounge style, with décor described as 'bordello baroque': red curtains, plush upholstery, mood lamps, flock wallpaper and cows' skulls.

The Lexington, 96-98 Pentonville Rd, N1 9JB (020-7837 5371, thelexington.co.uk, Angel tube, £).

July

19 July

Let Roses Grow on You

Explore the exquisite Garden of St John's Lodge, built in 1817-19 by architect John Raffield for Charles Augustus Tulk, MP. This quintessential English garden offers fine views of the imposing lodge, which was the first house to be built in Regent's Park.

In 1892, a new garden 'fit for meditation' was designed (for the third Marquess of Bute). Incorporating formal areas, a fountain pond, Doric temple, lovely statues, a stone portico and partly sunken chapel, it reflects the Arts & Crafts ideas in vogue at the time, and the revival of interest in the classical.

In order to enjoy this haven of calm and beauty, you first have to find it! From the Inner Circle, proceed anti-clockwise past Chester Road on your right, and some 200 yds further on you'll find the (hidden) entrance gate to St John's Lodge Gardens – if you pass the Lodge itself you've gone too far.

Garden of St John's Lodge, Inner Circle, Regent's Park, NW1 4NX (londongardensonline.org.uk/gardens-online-record.asp?id=wst108, Regent's Park tube, free).

Take in a performance at the Open Air Theatre in Regent's Park's Inner Circle, situated within Queen Mary's Gardens, London's largest and best formal rose garden (the aroma on warm evenings is heavenly). The theatre is a summer fixture (now in its 80th year) with a three- to four-month season, typically including a production of *A Midsummer Night's Dream*, a second Shakespeare play, a musical and a children's show, performed in rotation.

The theatre boasts one of the longest bars of any 'theatre' in London, stretching the entire length of the seating, and also serves full meals from an hour and a half before performances begin as well as during the interval. Other food options include a buffet, a BBQ and a picnic lawn with tables, where you can enjoy your own food.

Open Air Theatre, Queen Mary's Gardens, Inner Circle, Regent's Park, NW1 (0844-826 4242, openairtheatre.org, Regent's Park tube, 🎭).

20 July

Hampstead Hideaway

Affluent, leafy Hampstead is full of sizeable, attractive properties and 17th-century Fenton House is one of the earliest, largest and most architecturally important: a charming Queen Anne-style merchant's house, built around 1686, that's virtually unaltered during 300 years of continuous occupation. Today, the house is home to a rare collection of early keyboard instruments, fine old masters, world-class porcelain, 17th-century needlework and lovely Georgian furniture.

Fenton House, Hampstead Grove, Hampstead, NW3 6SP (01494-755 563, nationaltrust.org.uk/fenton-house, Hampstead tube).

See a play or film at the Tricycle Theatre in Kilburn, one of London's best small fringe theatres, noted for its innovative presentations. Originally an old music and dance hall, it opened in 1980 and quickly established a reputation as a powerhouse for political theatre. Today, the Tricycle presents the highest quality British and international work, reflecting the diversity of the local community.

Tricycle Theatre, 269 Kilburn High Rd, NW6 7JR (020-7328 1000, tricycle.co.uk, Brondesbury tube, ✆).

21 July

Swanning Around

See the ceremony of Swan Upping, the annual census of the mute swan population on the Thames. The historic census dates from the 12th century, when the crown claimed ownership of all mute swans, which were regarded as a delicious dish at banquets and feasts. Nowadays it plays an important role in the conservation of the swan population, with the Queen's Swan Warden collecting data and assessing the health of young cygnets.

Swan Upping (royal.gov.uk/royaleventsandceremonies/swanupping/swanupping.aspx and royalswan.co.uk, free, ℹ).

———————

Glide along to The White Swan, an attractive gastropub combining a traditional downstairs bar and curved mezzanine, with a bright, Art Deco-style upstairs dining room. The Swan offers a good choice of ales and wines, but the emphasis is very much on hearty British fare. The set-price lunch is good value, although the bar menu offers enough to keep most people happy.

The White Swan, 108 Fetter Ln, EC4A 1ES (020-7242 9696, thewhiteswanlondon.com, Chancery Ln tube, ££, ✆).

July

22 July

Eureka!

Discover the 18th century at the Enlightenment Gallery, housed in George III's former library in the British Museum. The Enlightenment was an age of reason and learning that flourished across Europe and America from 1680 to 1820. The gallery comprises seven sections – religion and ritual; trade and discovery; the birth of archaeology; art history; classification; the decipherment of ancient scripts; and natural history.

British Museum, Great Russell St, WC1B 3DG (020-7323 8299, britishmuseum.org/explore/galleries/themes/room_1_enlightenment.aspx, Tottenham Court Rd tube, free).

Take afternoon tea with Bea in Bloomsbury, the original and best of this celebrated chain. Bea's is famous for its heavenly cakes and pastries, including cupcakes, loaf cakes, scones, cookies, brownies, marshmallows, meringues and much more. Note that bookings are necessary for full afternoon tea (noon to 7pm) on Sat-Sun – with optional Champagne.

Bea's of Bloomsbury, 44 Theobalds Rd, WC1X 8NW (020-7242 8330, beasofbloomsbury.com/pages/bloomsbury-1, Chancery Ln tube, £, ☎).

23 July

Follow in Wiggo's Tracks

Try your hand (legs?) at track riding at the Herne Hill Velodrome in south London, where (Sir) Bradley Wiggins began his career. The iconic, open-air cycle track has a rich history; first built in 1891, it hosted cycling events at the 1948 Olympic Games. Today it's run by cyclists for cyclists, competitive and non-competitive, and its lack of steep banking makes it ideal for beginners.

Herne Hill Velodrome, 104 Burbage Rd, SE249HE (020-7737 4647, hernehillvelodrome.com, North Dulwich rail, ☎).

Order award-winning fish and chips at Olley's Fish Experience in Herne Hill, which has been earning accolades for two decades. Olley's offers over 20 species of fish, including halibut and mahi mahi, plus fishy starters such as mussels and king prawns (eat in or take away). It's licensed, so you can enjoy a beer or glass of wine with your fish supper.

Olley's Fish Experience, 65-69 Norwood Rd, SE24 9AA (020-8671 8259, olleys.info, North Dulwich rail, £).

24 July

South of the River

Take a magical tour around Nunhead Cemetery, consecrated in 1840 and one of seven large Victorian cemeteries – known as the Magnificent Seven – built in a ring around London's outskirts. Nunhead contains many examples of the magnificent monuments erected in memory of the most prominent citizens of the day, which contrast sharply with the small, simple headstones marking common or public burials. Its formal avenue of towering limes and the Gothic gloom of the original Victorian planting give way to paths recalling the country lanes of yesteryear.

Much of the cemetery is mysterious and overgrown, which many people see as fundamental to its charm; weathered gravestones, tumbling statuary poking through extravagant overgrowth and weed-choked paths. Not surprisingly, it's a haven for flora and fauna and is also a local nature reserve.

Nunhead Cemetery, Linden Grove, SE15 3LP (020-7525 2000, southwark.gov.uk and fonc.org.uk, Nunhead rail, free).

Admire the art at the South London Gallery in Camberwell, an elegant art space displaying a publicly-funded collection of contemporary art. Founded in 1891, it occupied various locations until moving to its current, purpose-built home, constructed of Portland stone and hand-made pressed bricks, much favoured by the Arts & Crafts tradition of the time. The gallery's popularity has grown in recent years and it has staged exhibitions by internationally acclaimed artists such as Tracey Emin and Gavin Turk. In 2010, the gallery opened additional buildings that provide new small-scale galleries, plus an acclaimed café, gardens, and an education and events studio.

South London Gallery, 65-67 Peckham Rd, SE5 8UH (020-7703 6120, southlondongallery.org, Peckham Rye rail, free).

> Don't miss the excellent Café No 67 in the South London Gallery. It serves as a café from 8am, Mon-Fri (10am weekends), serving home-made cakes and lunches, while at night it becomes a bistro-style restaurant (£).

July

25 July

Quacking Good Fun

Take a Duck Tour around central London, a combination road and river adventure that appeals to all ages, employing amphibious DUKW vehicles, affectionately called ducks. Famously used in the D-Day landings in 1944, the duck's route takes in major London landmarks such as Buckingham Palace, the Houses of Parliament and Trafalgar Square, before a dramatic launch into the River Thames from the slipway at the MI6 building.

London Duck Tours, Chicheley St, SE1 7PY (londonducktours. co.uk, Waterloo tube).

Enjoy great entertainment at the City of London Festival, founded in 1962 and firmly established as one of Britain's leading arts events. The programme of over 100 (mostly free) events includes music, visual arts, film, walks and talks, which take place during June and July across a number of historic venues and outdoor spaces. One unique 'event' in 2012 involved pianos left in random spots in the capital for anyone to play.

City of London Festival (colf.org, ☎).

City of London Festival

26 July

Pulsating Portobello

Browse the stalls at Portobello Road market in west London – the world's largest antiques market on one of London's most atmospheric streets. It's really several markets rolled into one. In addition to the famous Saturday antiques market, check out the Portobello Green fashion market for vintage and designer fashion (Fri-Sun), and Golborne Road market for produce, household and second-hand goods, and bric-a-brac.

Portobello Road Market, Portobello Rd, W11 (portobelloroad.co.uk, Notting Hill Gate tube).

Snapped up a bargain? Celebrate with lunch at the 2-Michelin starred **Ledbury** restaurant, one of London's most acclaimed eateries. If you can't get a table, there's always **Osteria Basilico**, a popular Italian restaurant established in 1992 (or one of its sister restaurants, Mediterraneo and Essenza, in the same street).

The Ledbury, 127 Ledbury Rd, W11 2AQ (020-7792 9090, theledbury. com, Westbourne Park tube, £££, ☎). Osteria Basilico, 29 Kensington Park Rd, W11 2EU (020-7727 9957, osteriabasilico. co.uk, Ladbroke Grove tube, ££, ☎).

27 July

Bishop to Queen...

Discover Fulham Palace, one of London's oldest and most historically significant buildings, the country home of the Bishops of London from at least the 11th century and their main residence from the 18th century until 1975. Much of the surviving palace dates from 1495. Fulham Palace includes a museum that records the site's long history, plus a contemporary art gallery and a café.

Fulham Palace, Bishop's Ave, SW6 6EA (020-7736 3233, fulhampalace.org, Putney Bridge tube, free).

Play giant outdoor chess on the lawn at Fulham Palace, a game which would have been played by the Bishops of London. The lovely Palace gardens are an unexpected  haven occupying a tranquil Thameside location; an ideal picnic spot, with lawns, an orchard, unusual tree species, a wisteria-draped pergola and an 18th-century walled herb garden. The gardens also host regular displays of sculpture and other art.

Giant Chess, Fulham Palace, SW6 (fulhampalace.org/fulham-palace-giant-chess-on-the-lawn, Putney Bridge tube, free).

28 July

Breaking the Fast

Celebrate the feast of Eid-al-Fitr with food and fun in Trafalgar Square. Eid marks the end of the Muslims' holy fasting month of Ramadan and is traditionally celebrated in the UK on the first day of Shawwal in the Islamic calendar and actually begins at sundown the day before. The date falls earlier each year, according to the lunar calendar – it's 28th July in 2014, 18th July in 2015 and so forth.

Eid in the Square, Trafalgar Sq, WC2N 5DS (Charing Cross tube, free, ⓘ).

Break the fast with a delicious meal at Adiva in Spitalfields, an affordable (unlicensed) restaurant serving a fusion of Lebanese and Turkish cuisine. The menu is influenced by food from the ancient Arab Persian and Turkish Ottoman empires, culminating in unique fare, including classic mezzes and traditional meat, fish and vegetarian dishes prepared with authentic herbs and spices.

Adiva, 43A Commercial St, E1 6BD (020-7247 7181, adivarestaurant. com, Aldgate East tube, £, 🍴).

29 July

Croquet & Cake

Try your hand at croquet on Hampstead Heath (near the West Heath Avenue entrance to Golders Hill Park), site of the only fully public croquet lawns in London and a good option if you just fancy a casual game. The club was formed in 2008 to enable players of all ages and abilities to enjoy a challenging and relaxing game in pleasant surroundings.

Hampstead Heath Croquet Club, West Heath Ave, NW11 7QL (07943-658 242, hampsteadheathcroquetclub.org.uk, Golders Green tube, ☏).

Take afternoon tea at the café in Golders Hill Park – owner Tony Pazienti calls it the Refreshment House but everyone knows it as 'Tony's Café' – which serves delicious home-made cakes and ice cream (in summer). It's a lovely place to have an alfresco drink or meal, overlooking the park zoo with flamingos, deer, pheasants and goats (there's also a butterfly house).

Refreshment House, Golders Hill Park, West Heath Ave, NW11 7QP (020-7332 3511, cityoflondon.gov.uk, Golders Green tube, £).

30 July

Hidden Highgate

Take a peek at Holly Village, a small self-contained hamlet of houses in Highgate built in 1865 by Baroness Burdett-Coutts and designed by Henry Astley Darbishire. Step through the elaborate gatehouse arch and you're plunged into a 19th-century Gothic kingdom of turrets, spires and gables. Holly Village has both architectural and historical significance, being the first example of a gated housing development, built in an elaborate Gothic style.

Holly Village, Swains Ln, N6 6QJ (Archway tube).

———————

Dine in style at The Bull & Last, a gastropub situated close to Hampstead Heath. The cooking is a particular highlight, with separate lunch, dinner and Sunday menus – the *Observer* Food Monthly has awarded the pub its 'Best Sunday Lunch' gong. The Bull is popular and invariably full, so booking is essential.

The Bull & Last, 168 Highgate Rd, NW5 1QS (020-7267 3641, thebullandlast.co.uk, Kentish Town tube, ££, ☏).

July

31 July

Sophisticated Syon

Devote a day to the splendours of Syon House in west London and its 200-acre park, one of England's finest estates and the London home of the Dukes of Northumberland for over 400 years. The name derives from Syon Abbey (named after Mount Zion in the Holy Land), a medieval monastery of the Bridgettine Order founded nearby in 1415 and dissolved in 1539. In 1594, Henry Percy, 9th Earl of Northumberland, acquired Syon House through marriage to Dorothy Devereux, and the Percy family have lived there ever since.

In 1761, architect and interior designer Robert Adam (1728-1792) and landscape designer Lancelot 'Capability' Brown (1716-1783) were commissioned to redesign the house and estate respectively. Adam's Neo-classical designs have been praised as his early English masterpiece and are the finest surviving evidence of his revolutionary use of colour. The house also contains a sumptuous collection of period furniture and paintings.

Syon Park includes 40 acres of gardens and an ornamental lake, and is famous for its extensive collection of rare trees and plants, although its crowning glory is the Great Conservatory, designed by Charles Fowler (1792-1867) and completed in 1830. There's also an excellent café.

Syon House, Syon Park, Brentford, TW8 8JF (020-8560 0882, syonpark.co.uk, Syon Ln rail).

Enjoy a pint and some good food at The Botanist Brewery & Kitchen near Kew Bridge, an airy, light, bar and restaurant resembling one of the glasshouses at nearby Kew Gardens. The in-house microbrewery is a major draw, producing the bar's own craft beer, and there's also an extensive range of British, American and continental bottled beers and lagers, a good wine list and creative cocktails. Food consists of bar snacks, sharing boards and more substantial dishes.

The Botanist Brewery & Kitchen, 3-5 Kew Green, TW9 3AA (020-8948 4838, thebotanistkew.com, Kew Gardens tube, ££, ☎).

August

1 August

The Tudors in Eltham

Admire elegant Eltham Palace, which was given to Edward II in 1305 and remained a royal residence until the 16th century (Henry VIII lived here as a young prince). The current building dates mainly from the '30s, when Sir Stephen and Lady Virginia Courtauld were granted a lease. They restored the Great Hall, which boasts England's third-largest hammer-beam roof, gave it a minstrels' gallery and incorporated it into a sumptuous home with a striking interior in a variety of Art Deco styles.

The stunning circular entrance hall, designed by Swede Rolf Engströmer, boasts an impressive glazed dome that floods it with light, highlighting the lush, figurative parquetry. The red brick and Bath stone exterior is modelled on Wren's work at Hampton Court Palace, while the extensive gardens feature a 15th-century bridge spanning a 14th-century moat planted with lilies.

Eltham Palace, Court Yard, Eltham, SE9 5QE (020-8294 2548, english-heritage.org.uk/daysout/properties/eltham-palace-and-gardens, Eltham rail).

Eat like a king at the Tudor Barn in Well Hall Pleasaunce (Eltham), a lovely 11-acre park of landscaped gardens dating back to the 13th century. It contains many historical elements, including an original Tudor barn and a moat with a 16th-century bridge. Formal gardens, including an Italian garden displaying glorious colour, sit adjacent to natural gardens, which along with the park are a haven for flora and fauna.

The Tudor Barn (Grade II* listed) has been restored and the stunning oak roof construction exposed, along with stained glass windows depicting paintings (by Holbein) of the family of former occupant Sir Thomas More, ill-fated Lord Chancellor to Henry VIII. Today the barn houses an atmospheric bar and fine restaurant, offering panoramic views over the parkland and moat from two lovely alfresco dining areas.

Well Hall Pleasaunce & Tudor Barn Eltham, Well Hall Rd, SE9 6SZ (0845-459 2351, tudorbarneltham.com, Eltham rail, ££, ☎).

2 August

Lie Low at the Lido

Cool down with a dip at the Serpentine Lido in Hyde Park, the second-largest of central London's superb royal parks. The Serpentine was created in 1733 by Charles Bridgeman (1690-1738), who dammed the Westbourne stream that flowed down from Hampstead. The Lido and children's paddling pool are open daily from June to mid-September (plus weekends in May).

Serpentine Lido, Hyde Park, W2 2UH (020-7706 7098, royalparks. org.uk/parks/hyde-park/sport-in-hyde-park/serpentine-lido, Hyde Park Cnr tube).

Lunch at the Lido Café in Hyde Park, rated one of London's best park cafés, situated on the south bank of the Serpentine with outdoor seating for several hundred people. The changing menu includes everything from a full English breakfast and porridge to coffee and pastries, fish and chips and salads to pizzas and organic ice cream. There's also a licensed bar.

Lido Café, Hyde Park, W2 2UH (companyofcooks.com/locations/ our-locations/hyde-park, Hyde Park Cnr tube, £).

3 August

Splash Out in Brixton

Have a ball at Brixton Splash, a free community street festival held on the first Sunday in August to celebrate the area's diversity and progress, and the fusion of the numerous ethnic groups that call Brixton home. It's a celebration of peaceful relations, vibrant living in Brixton and the area's contribution to London's wider culture. The music encompasses everything from reggae and rocksteady to dubstep and jungle.

Brixton Splash, Coldharbour Ln, Brixton, SW9 (brixtonsplash.org, Brixton tube, free, 1).

If Caribbean food's not your thing, try Upstairs Restaurant, a trendy, understated restaurant tucked away in a Victorian corner house on Brixton's Acre Lane. With soft colours, open fires, reclaimed wooden floors and leather banquettes, it has the ambience of an intimate local supper club, while the short, Francophile menu has been awarded a Michelin Bib Gourmand.

Upstairs Restaurant, 89B Acre Ln, SW2 5TN (020-7733 8855, upstairslondon.com, Brixton tube, £, ⌂).

August

August

4 August

Chin Up in Camden

Chill out with an unusual ice cream at Chin Chin Laboratorists in Camden, the first ice cream parlour in Europe to use liquid nitrogen to fast-freeze ice cream. It's an amusing gimmick, complete with billowing clouds of white 'smoke', but it also leaves the mixture luxuriously rich and smooth. The ever-changing menu features exotic flavours such as watermelon and dill – scrummy!

Chin Chin Laboratorists, 49-50 Camden Lock Place, Camden, NW1 8AF (07885-604284, chinchinlabs.com, Camden Town tube).

Be amused, outraged and entertained at the Camden Fringe, a four-week festival bringing together comedy, theatre, poetry, dance and much more – some 700 performances in various venues across the borough of Camden. It's been described by the *Metro* newspaper as: 'A dizzying alternative to the Edinburgh Festival extravaganza… frequently weird, sometimes wonderful and always unpredictable.'

Camden Fringe (camdenfringe.com, ☏, ⓘ).

5 August

Ham it Up in Hampstead

Swim with the ducks in one of a chain of historic ponds that lie along the eastern perimeter of Hampstead Heath. The men's and ladies' ponds – dating from the 1890s and 1925 respectively – are unique in the UK for being the only life-guarded, open-water swimming facilities open all year round. The third (mixed) bathing pond is available in summer only.

Hampstead Heath, NW5 1QR (020-7485 3873, cityoflondon.gov.uk > green spaces > swimming, Hampstead Heath tube).

Enjoy an evening of entertainment at Hampstead Theatre, which has been graced by many of the world's most famous actors over the last 50 years. It's noted for its robust, resonant and enriching plays, working with some of the industry's most talented theatre professionals to create productions of the highest standard. There's also a café bar with a lovely terrace overlooking Swiss Cottage park.

Hampstead Theatre, Eton Ave, Swiss Cottage, NW3 3EU (020-7722 9301, hampsteadtheatre.com, Swiss Cottage tube, ☏).

6 August

Ally Pally Playtime

Spend a day in Alexandra Park – named after Alexandra of Denmark, the wife of Edward VII – a sweeping 196-acre public park created in 1863. The park is best known as the site of Alexandra Palace (built in 1873 and dubbed the 'People's Palace'), but it has much more to offer and is one of London's most beloved green spaces – a delightful mixture of informal woodland, open grassland, formal gardens and attractions.

The park's nature reserve is a favourite with twitchers and attracts numerous common woodland and parkland birds, both residents and visitors. The park is also home to many ancient trees, particularly oak, and has a rose garden, a lake and a large fallow deer enclosure. There's also a wide range of recreation and sports facilities, including an ice-skating rink (open year round), various eateries, a children's play area, skate boarding park, pitch and putt golf course, fishing and boating, and soccer and cricket pitches. It also hosts a farmers' market on Sundays.

Alexandra Park, Alexandra Palace Way, N22 7AY (020-8365 2121, alexandrapalace.com and friendsofalexandrapark.org, Wood Green tube, free).

Step out along the Parkland Walk, a 4.5-mile linear green walkway that follows the course of the old railway line that ran between Alexandra Park and Finsbury Park (the line was closed in 1970, but you can still see 'ghost' stations along the route). The walk is London's longest Local Nature Reserve, supporting a remarkable variety of habitats and wildlife. Over 200 species of wild flower have been recorded here and it's one of the few places in London where orchids rub shoulders with dandelions and ivy clambers up fig trees. Hedgehogs, foxes, butterflies and a vast array of birds can regularly be seen, and if you're lucky, the rare and elusive muntjac deer. A map can be downloaded from the website.

Parkland Walk (parkland-walk.org.uk).

August

7 August

Tea with Her Majesty

See stunning art in the Queen's Gallery, one of the major draws at Buckingham Palace. The Royal Collection is one of the most important in the world, containing over 7,000 paintings, 40,000 watercolours and drawings, some 150,000 prints, plus photographs, tapestries, furniture, ceramics and other works of art. The gallery can only display some 450 items at a time, therefore is worth visiting frequently.

Queen's Gallery, Buckingham Palace, Buckingham Palace Rd, SW1A 1AA (020-7766 7301, royalcollection.org.uk/visit/ queensgallerylondon, Victoria tube, ☏).

———————

Admire the State Rooms at Buckingham Palace, the official London residence of the British monarch since 1837. The palace contains 775 rooms, including 19 state rooms, 52 royal and guest bedrooms, 188 staff bedrooms, 92 offices and 78 bathrooms. The magnificent state rooms (where guests and dignitaries are received) have been opened to the public since 1993. There's also a lovely Garden Café.

State Rooms, Buckingham Palace, SW1A 1AA (020-7766 7300, royalcollection.org.uk/visit/buckinghampalace, Victoria tube, ☏, ℹ).

Queen's Gallery

8 August

Meet Prince Albert, Peter Pan, et al

Albert Memorial

Explore the statuary and monuments in Kensington Gardens, one of London's most beautiful parks. Most people know that the gardens are home to the imposing Albert Memorial, the grand high-Victorian Gothic extravaganza facing the Royal Albert Hall, but there's much more to admire. Look out for the famous *Peter Pan* statue; the bronze of *Edward Jenner* (1749-1823), pioneer of the smallpox vaccine; *Physical Energy* by George Frederick Watts, which commemorates Sir Cecil Rhodes, founder of Rhodesia (now Zimbabwe); *The Arch*, donated by Henry Moore; and the magical *Elfin Oak*.

Kensington Gardens, W2 2UH (0300-061 2000, royalparks.org.uk/ parks/kensington-gardens, Queensway tube).

———————

Enjoy afternoon tea in the tranquil splendour of the elegant Orangery Restaurant, set in Queen Anne's former 'greenhouse' alongside Kensington Palace. It offers wholesome breakfasts, tasty lunches and decadent afternoon teas (with pink champagne) in a unique English palace garden setting.

Orangery Restaurant, Kensington Gardens, W2 2UH (0300-061 2000, hrp.org.uk/kensingtonpalace/foodanddrink/orangery, Queensway tube, ££, ☏).

9 August

Fiesta Fantástico!

Have a fabulous fun family day out at the Carnaval del Pueblo in East London, Europe's largest Latin American celebration including a carnival procession, stages featuring live music and dance acts, bars and marquees with a variety of Latin-American, Caribbean and western food and drink. An explosion of colour, music, dance and Latin flavours.

Carnaval del Pueblo, London Pleasure Gardens, Royal Victoria Docks, E16 2BS (020-7928 4277, carnavaldelpueblo.com, Pontoon Dock DLR, ⓵).

See how tomorrow's cities might look by visiting The Crystal in East London's Royal Victoria Docks, a sustainable cities initiative by Siemens which explores how we can create a better future for city dwellers. Housed in London's newest landmark building, it's the world's first centre dedicated to improving our knowledge of urban sustainability. Guided tours are available.

The Crystal, One Siemens Brothers Way, Royal Victoria Docks, E16 1GB (020-7055 6400, thecrystal.org, Royal Victoria DLR, free).

10 August

War & Peace

See the first phase of the remodelled Imperial War Museum in Southwark, which re-opened in summer 2013 with new atrium and terrace displays, shops and a café opening directly onto Geraldine Mary Harmsworth Park. The new First World War Galleries are a major part of the museum's contribution to the centenary of the start of the First World War in 2014.

Imperial War Museum London, Lambeth Rd, SE1 6HZ (020-7416 5000, iwm.org.uk/visits/iwm-london, Elephant & Castle tube, free).

Relax in the Tibetan Peace Garden, a tranquil spot incongruously sited in the shadow of the Imperial War Museum. The garden was consecrated in 1999 by His Holiness the Dalai Lama and honours one of his principal teachings: the need to create understanding between different cultures and to establish places of peace and harmony in the world.

Tibetan Peace Garden, Geraldine Mary Harmsworth Park, St George's Rd, SE1 6ER (tibet-foundation.org/page/peace_garden, Elephant & Castle tube, free).

August

11 August

Kensal Greenery

Lose yourself in Kensal Green Cemetery, one of the capital's most beautiful and distinguished burial grounds. The first of the Victorians' Magnificent Seven garden cemeteries, it pays just to wander aimlessly, getting slightly lost while stumbling across a wealth of visual and architectural treats. As well as mature shrubs and trees, there's a lovely rose garden and an adjoining canal.

Kensal Green Cemetery. Harrow Rd, Kensal Green, W10 4RA (020-8969 0152, kensalgreencemetery.com, Kensal Green tube, free).

Drop into Books for Cooks, Notting Hill's famous cook book shop. Crammed with thousands of tasty titles, it's equipped with a comfortable sofa for aspiring cooks seeking inspiration. The lovely shop also 'cooks the books' – not literally – but the staff do put recipes to the test in their kitchen at the back of the shop and sell the results in their charming café.

Books for Cooks, 4 Blenheim Crescent, W11 1NN (020-7221 1992, booksforcooks.com, Ladbroke Grove, £).

12 August

Corridors of Power

Take a tour of the magnificent Palace of Westminster, better known as the Houses of Parliament. UK residents can tour the building for free – book through your MP – while overseas visitors can buy tickets on most Saturdays throughout the year, and Tue-Sat during the summer opening period (see website). There are no tours on Sundays or Bank Holidays.

Houses of Parliament, Westminster, SW1A 0AA (020-7219 3000, parliament.uk/visiting, Westminster tube, 🚇).

Try a classy curry at the splendid Cinnamon Club, a prestigious Indian restaurant and bar, occupying a former library. The acclaimed restaurant holds 'Wine and Spice' events where individual dishes and wines are matched, while other food 'specials' are light years away from the high street curry house experience. There are also two bars serving superb cocktails.

The Cinnamon Club, 30-32 Great Smith St, SW1P 3BU (020-7222 2555, cinnamonclub.com, St James's Park tube, £££, 🚇).

13 August

Upstairs Downstairs

Go ghost-hunting in Ham House, a rare surviving example of a 17th-century house overlooking the Thames in Richmond. It's one of London's architectural and horticultural gems, built in 1610 for Sir Thomas Vavasour, Knight Marshal to James I. It was extended and refurbished as a palatial villa under the ownership of Elizabeth, Lady Dysart. and remained in her family until the National Trust assumed control in 1948. It's said to be haunted by the ghosts of Lady Dysart and her dog.

Ham House contains rooms of sumptuous splendour, including walls hung with tapestries and rococo mirrors, plus spectacular collections of furniture and paintings. The house also has original 17th-century formal gardens. Most were later replaced by more fashionable natural landscapes, but Ham's gardens have changed little in over 300 years and include Britain's oldest orangery and a lovely trellised cherry garden.

Ham House & Gardens, Ham St, Ham, Richmond-upon-Thames, TW10 7RS (020-8940 1950, nationaltrust.org.uk/ham-house, Twickenham rail).

Take Hammerton's Ferry (pedestrians only) from Ham House to Marble Hill House and gardens, built in 1724-1729 for Henrietta Howard, mistress of George II, who entertained guests such as Jonathan Swift and Alexander Pope. The Palladian villa on the north bank of the Thames is the last to remain intact from the lovely villas and gardens that lined the river between Richmond and Hampton Court in the 18th century. Now owned by English Heritage, the grand interiors have been beautifully restored and contain a collection of early Georgian furniture, Chinoiserie and some fine paintings, and conjure up a splendid vision of fashionable Georgian life.

The grounds, sloping gently down to the Thames, were laid out in the early 18th century, with terraced lawns, avenues of chestnuts, plus an ice house and two grottos, one of which remains.

Marble Hill House, Richmond Rd, Twickenham, TW1 2NL (020-8892 5115, english-heritage.org.uk/daysout/properties/marble-hill-house, St Margarets rail).

August

14 August

Hang Out with the East Enders

Sample delicious coffee and artisan grub at Allpress Espresso, a popular artisan roastery café in buzzy Shoreditch. Allpress was established in New Zealand in 1986 by Kiwi Michael Allpress, who teamed up with Sydney chef Tony Papas to oversee the café's delicious, gourmet home-made food. You can watch the coffee roasting on some days or even attend a roasting class.

Allpress Espresso, 58 Redchurch St, E2 7DP (020-7749 1780, uk.allpressespresso.com, Shoreditch High St, £).

Enjoy an (almost) private screening at the Aubin Cinema, a tiny cinema in the basement of the trendy Aubin & Wills store in Shoreditch. The Aubin seats up to 45 people and shows a variety of mainstream blockbusters and indie art-house films. It provides an unrivalled level of comfort and style, with a choice of plush seats or velvet two-seater sofas, complete with footstools.

Aubin Cinema, Aubin & Wills, 64-66 Redchurch St, E2 7DP (0845-604 8486, aubincinema.com, Shoreditch High St, 🎬).

15 August

The Real (Ale) Deal

Enjoy a pint (or two) of amber nectar at The Great British Beer Festival at Olympia. Join over 50,000 like-minded people for a celebration of our national drink, featuring over 800 real ales, ciders, perries and beers from around the world. Tutored tastings are offered for those who wish to learn the nuances of what makes a great beer.

The Great British Beer Festival, Olympia Exhibition Centre, Hammersmith Rd, W14 8UX (0844-412 4640, gbbf.org.uk, Kensington Olympia tube, 🚇).

Enjoy some fine food (and beer) at The Havelock Tavern in Shepherd's Bush, one of London's first gastropubs – a pub serving food rather than a restaurant with beer. The food isn't cheap but has won awards and recommendations from *Michelin* and the *Good Pub Guide*, so is worth pushing the boat out for. There's also a good wine list.

The Havelock Tavern, 57 Masbro Rd, W14 0LS (020-7603 5374, havelocktavern.com, Kensington Olympia tube, ££, 🎬).

16 August

Glastonbury for Teenyboppers

Take the kids to 'Glastonbury for the under-10s' with a trip to the LolliBop Festival in Queen Elizabeth Olympic Park (venue of the 2012 Olympics). Now into its fifth year, it's the UK's largest festival for children, featuring live music, fairground rides, a circus, appearances by kids' favourite characters, plus a wealth of workshops, arts & crafts.

LolliBop Festival, Queen Elizabeth Olympic Park, Stratford, E20 2ST (lollibopfestival.co.uk, Stratford tube, ⓘ).

Discover the history of London's docks at the Museum of London Docklands, one of the city's most absorbing museums. It records 2,000 years of history, from the first Roman 'port' to the docks' closure in the '70s and subsequent redevelopment, and traces how the Thames became an international gateway, bringing invaders, merchants and immigrants to London.

Museum of London Docklands, West India Quay, Canary Wharf, E14 4AL (020-7001 9844, museumoflondon.org.uk/docklands, Canary Wharf tube, free).

17 August

Bravo for Battersea!

Tempt your taste buds at Feast at Battersea Park organised by *Foodie* magazine, where you can meet Michelin-starred chefs, see live demonstrations and taste food from around the world. Enjoy demos by top chefs and sample signature dishes from famous London restaurants, washed down with posh fizz from Veuve Clicquot. A wonderful alfresco day of scoffing and slurping. *Bon appétit!*

Feast at Battersea Park, Battersea Park, Albert Bridge Rd, SW11 4NJ (0844-995 1111, foodiesfestival.com, Queenstown Rd rail, ⓘ).

Chill out at The Magic Garden in Battersea, a gastropub with vibrant live music and a lovely beer garden. It's famous for its eclectic selection of lesser-known artists and bands, ranging from acoustic music on Wednesdays and blues on Thursdays, to buzzing festival bands and DJs at weekends, when the atmosphere is more house party than local pub.

The Magic Garden, 231 Battersea Park Rd, SW11 4LG (020-622 4844, magicgardenpub.com, Queenstown Rd rail, £).

August

18 August

Musical Interlude

Promenade along to a concert during the BBC Proms. The Proms were inaugurated in 1895 and are the world's longest-running and largest music festival, presenting daily classical music events over eight weeks each summer. It includes over 70 concerts in the Royal Albert Hall, plus chamber concerts at Cadogan Hall. There are additional Proms in the Park events across the UK on the famous Last Night of the Proms.

BBC Proms (bbc.co.uk/proms, ☎).

Enjoy music with your meal at the elegant Piano Kensington bar and restaurant, as you dine to the accompaniment of pianist Bazz Norton (and guests) and his historic Collard & Collard grand piano. The reasonably priced food is pretty good, too, but the Piano is all about the music, including live jazz on Sunday evenings. A grand place to spend an evening.

Piano Kensington, 106 Kensington High St, W8 4SG (020-7938 4664, pianokensington.com, High St Kensington tube, £, ☎).

19 August

Regal Regent's Park

Get fit in Regent's Park which boasts some 400 acres of parkland and is home to London's largest outdoor sports facility. As well as outdoor exercise classes and children's activities, it maintains pitches for soccer, rugby, lacrosse, softball and cricket. The park is also popular with cyclists who ride around the Outer Circle (the local cycling club is the Regent's Park Rouleurs).

Regent's Park, NW1 4NR (0300-061 2300, royalparks.org.uk/parks/the-regents-park, Regent's Park tube).

Cool down with lunch or afternoon tea in the lovely Garden Café in Queen Mary's Gardens. The Garden Café was built in 1964, although the current building is a new one reflecting the original architectural style. The result is a simple, stylish, open plan space full of colour and beautiful natural light. The licensed café serves beverages and snacks, lunch, afternoon tea and summer suppers.

Garden Café, Queen Mary's Gardens, Inner Circle, NW1 4NU (020-7935 5729, Regent's Park tube, £).

20 August

Perfection in Petersham

Visit Petersham Nurseries and enjoy a gourmet lunch in its highly acclaimed café. Petersham Nurseries offers a huge selection of plants, tools, gifts and antiques in a beautiful, tranquil country location. However, it's most famous for its splendid licensed café which offers delicious, produce-led cooking – including edible flowers and herbs from the Petersham House kitchen garden – in a beautiful, convivial setting at antique tables dotted around the main glasshouse. Open for lunch six days a week (Tue-Sun, noon to 2.45pm), the celebrated café is a member of the international Slow Food Supporters Scheme (see slowfood.org.uk) which supports nutritional, sustainable and locally-produced food.

The ravishing garden of nearby Petersham House – the home of the owners of Petersham Nurseries – is open to the public once a year under the National Gardens Scheme (see ngs.org.uk, ⓘ). The 'secret' garden has an air of calm and tranquillity, with extensive yew hedges and lovely red brick walls.

Petersham Nurseries, Petersham Rd, Richmond, TW10 7AG (020-8940 5230, petershamnurseries.com, Richmond tube, ££, ☏).

Take a stroll around Petersham Village, one of south London's most architecturally interesting areas. The village is next to the River Thames between Richmond and Ham and is also noted for its picturesque landscape – which includes Petersham Meadows, once part of the Ham House estate – as well as the many famous people who lived here.

The main street is lined with magnificent 17th- and 18th-century mansions, built predominately of brick with elegant classical proportions and detailing, set in generous grounds with mature trees, behind high brick walls with fine ironwork railings and gates. In contrast, the west side of Petersham Road has an eclectic mix of closely-packed detached or terraced houses and cottages dating from the 18th and 19th centuries.

Petersham Village, Petersham, Richmond, TW10 (petershamvillage. org, Richmond tube).

Petersham House

21 August

Luxuriate in Little Venice

Relax in Rembrandt Gardens, a peaceful spot with splendid views over Little Venice. The gardens are quite formal, consisting of lawns, shrubs and bedding displays, with beech, rowan and silver birch trees, plus a raised terrace and pathways leading down to the towpath. There are also wildlife areas, and on summer evenings you may see bats flitting about.

Rembrandt Gardens, Warwick Ave, W2 1XB (020-7641 5271, westminster.gov.uk > parks and open spaces, Warwick Ave tube, free).

See the world's longest-running live comedy show at the Canal Café Theatre, perched on the edge of the canal in Little Venice (above the Bridge House pub). *NewsRevue* has been running since 1979 and is a mix of sketches and songs that propels you through world news and current events at breakneck speed. It's performed Thu-Sat at 9.30pm and Sundays at 9pm.

Canal Café Theatre, Delamere Terrace, Little Venice, W2 6ND (020-7289 6054, canalcafetheatre.com, Warwick Ave tube, ☎).

22 August

Kensington House Wine

Go back in time at Linley Sambourne House in Kensington, one of London's hidden gems: a unique, beautifully-preserved late Victorian townhouse, classical Italianate in style, with most of its original décor and furnishings. For 35 years it was home to Edward Linley Sambourne (1844-1910) – photographer, book illustrator and political cartoonist – and was preserved in its original style and opened to the public in 1980.

Linley Sambourne House, 18 Stafford Terrace, W8 7BH (020-7602 3316, rbkc.gov.uk/subsites/museums/18staffordterrace.aspx, High St Kensington tube).

Repair to The Kensington Wine Rooms, a stylish, inviting wine bar. The dining space serves Mediterranean and French-influenced food, with recommended wines for each dish, while there are bar plates featuring British cheeses and Spanish charcuterie if you just want something to complement the wine.

The Kensington Wine Rooms, 127-9 Kensington Church St, W8 7LP (020-7727 8142, greatwinesbytheglass.com, Notting Hill Gate tube, ££, ☎).

23 August

Howzat!

Watch a first class cricket match at Lord's in St John's Wood. Lord's is home to the Marylebone Cricket Club – usually referred to by its initials MCC – founded in 1787 and the world's oldest and most famous club. It's now the home ground of Middlesex County Cricket Club (middlesexccc.com) and also stages international matches. It also has an excellent museum.

Lord's Cricket Ground, St John's Wood, NW8 8QN (020-7616 8656, lords.org, St John's Wood tube, ☎, ⓘ).

Join cricket fans for a pint in The Lord's Tavern at Lord's Cricket Ground, a popular destination for cricket buffs and locals alike. The pub is closed to the public on match days, when it hosts posh corporate events, but most of the time it's a friendly local serving excellent Marston beers and good food.

The Lord's Tavern, Lord's Cricket Ground, St John's Wood, NW8 8QN (020-7616 8689, lords.org/lords/things-to-do/lords-tavern, St John's Wood tube, £).

24 August

Picture (Picnic) Perfect

Spread your picnic rug on the grass at Kenwood House during 'Live by the Lake', an eclectic series of world class gigs in a breathtaking location. In 2013 events included concerts by indie gods Suede and rock giants Keane, an epic Choral Greats concert (with fireworks), a stunning outdoor screening of *Singin' in the Rain* and an evening of music by Gershwin.

Live by the Lake, Kenwood House, Hampstead Ln, NW3 7JR (020-7154 5854, livebythelake.co.uk, Highgate tube, ☎, ⓘ).

August

Stop at the splendid Brewhouse Café in Kenwood House for lunch or tea. Formerly the estate's brewery, the café has flagstone floors, high ceilings, and a tiered and sheltered terrace. It serves sandwiches, salads, pastries, soups and stews, plus veggie and children's options, while in summer there's an outside stand selling ice cream and Pimm's.

Brewhouse Café, Kenwood House, Hampstead Ln, NW3 7JR (020-7154 5854, livebythelake.co.uk, Highgate tube, £).

25 August

August

Rio Comes to Notting Hill

Join the party at the Notting Hill Carnival, the largest street festival in Europe, when the streets are ablaze with extravagantly costumed dancers and decorated floats, and echo to the sound of calypso music and giant sound systems. Carnival takes place on the Sunday and Monday of August bank holiday weekend and attracts well over a million revellers. Sunday is Children's Day, when the parade takes place over a shorter route and the costume prizes are awarded, while Monday hosts the main cavalcade.

Carnival began in the early '60s as a small local event where west London's homesick Afro-Caribbean communities could celebrate their cultures and traditions, but has since become a major event on the capital's calendar. It has its roots in the Caribbean carnivals of the early 19th century – a particularly strong tradition in Trinidad – which celebrated the abolition of slavery.

Music is at the heart of the Notting Hill Carnival, with traditional and contemporary sounds filling the air for miles around. Historically, steel (pan) bands, soca and calypso music dominated the soundtrack, although in recent years these have been overtaken by the static sound systems playing anything from reggae to R&B, funk, house and much more. Live stages also feature local bands, top international artists and world music.

Note that it's advisable to use public transport to get to Carnival, as most local roads are for pedestrian use only and parking is virtually impossible.

——————

Eat your way around Carnival. Just as irresistible as the music is the Caribbean food whose wonderful aromas permeate the excited atmosphere. Notting Hill is the perfect place to sample jerk chicken, gumbo, callaloo, patties, goat curry, fried plantain, rum punch and other delicacies, served up at numerous street stalls.

Notting Hill Carnival, Notting Hill, W11 (thenottinghillcarnival.com, Notting Hill, Notting Hill Gate tube, free, ⓘ).

26 August

Naked Ambition

Get your kit off – and maybe make a few quid at the same time – by becoming a life drawing model. The Register of Artists' Models (RAM), which provides models to London's reputable art colleges, holds auditions at the Islington Arts Factory. Sounds easy? Most people find it cold and uncomfortable work, not just being scrutinised by strangers, but holding the same pose for hours on end.

Register of Artists Models (modelreg.co.uk, ☎).

If you'd rather be the artist than the model, why not try out life drawing… in a bar? The social club in Shoreditch offers informal life drawing classes on Saturday afternoons for a modest fee. The Book Club is a cultural revolution on the East End social scene, offering an eclectic programme of events and social activities, plus a good bar/restaurant.

The Book Club, Leonard St, EC2A 4RH (020-7684 8619, wearetbc.com, Old St tube, ☎).

27 August

Cable Street Capers

Admire the Cable Street Mural which celebrates a 'victory' against fascism on 4th October 1936, when people in the East End of London stopped Oswald Mosley and his British Union of Fascists marching through Cable Street, then mainly a Jewish area. The ensuing clash became known as the 'Battle of Cable Street'. The mural is a symbolic reminder of anti-fascism in the East End.

Cable Street Mural, 236 Cable St, E1 0BL (battleofcablestreet.co.uk, Shadwell tube station).

Listen to some top sounds at atmospheric Jamboree, one of East London's best music venues, harking back to 1900s vaudeville or Paris in the '30s. Offering music from across the globe, you could be greeted with Celtic folk, Costa Rican strings, country classics or travelling swing – every night is unique. Bohemian, hip Jamboree is one of the city's most original nightspots.

Jamboree, Cable Street Studios, 566 Cable St, E1W 3HB (020-7790 1309, jamboreevenue.co.uk, Limehouses DLR, £).

August

28 August

Old School Ties

Take a tour of splendid historic Harrow School, an independent school for boys founded in 1572 under Elizabeth I. The school has many claims to fame, from the straw Harrow hat that its pupils wear to the unique form of Harrow football played, plus a long line of famous alumni. Tours can be organised on weekdays in term time or by arrangement during school holidays.

Harrow School, 5 High St, Harrow-on-the-Hill, HA1 3HP (020-8872 8205, harrowschool.org.uk, Harrow-on-the-Hill tube, ☎).

Sample the flavours of southern Italy at award-winning (and inexpensive) Incanto, just a stone's throw from Harrow School. Occupying the former post office, the front room is a delicatessen-cum-café, while the main room at the rear is a stylish space, with simply-laid tables and leather banquettes beneath a long skylight and beamed ceiling.

Incanto, The Old Post Office, 41 High St, Harrow-on-the-Hill, HA1 3HT (020-8426 6767, incanto.co.uk, Harrow-on-the-Hill tube, £, ☎).

29 August

Food for Thought

Browse the shops in Neal's Yard, a small alley in Covent Garden between Shorts Gardens and Monmouth Street. Named after its 17th-century developer Thomas Neale, it's one of London's most colourful streets (the buildings are painted in bright colours). Among the many famous shops here are Neal's Yard Remedies (natural health and beauty products), Neal's Yard Dairy (a celebrated cheese maker) and the Wild Food Café.

Neal's Yard, Covent Garden, WC2H (Covent Garden tube).

Take your lover to lunch at Clos Maggiore, an oasis of calm in Covent Garden serving delicious contemporary Provençal-inspired cuisine. One of London's most romantic restaurants, it has a lovely conservatory with a fully retractable glass roof, creating a bright and airy alfresco dining space that's transformed at night by candles and starlight (and a roaring log fire in winter).

Clos Maggiore, 33 King St, WC2E 8JD (020-7379 9696, closmaggiore.com, Covent Garden tube, ££, ☎).

30 August

Dinosaurs & Other Creatures

Discover dinosaurs at Crystal Palace Park, originally home to the Crystal Palace erected in Hyde Park by Sir Joseph Paxton to house the Great Exhibition of 1851. It was relocated here in 1854 and the famous model dinosaurs, created by Benjamin Waterhouse Hawkins, were unveiled the same year. The palace burnt down in 1936, but the dinosaurs live on.

Crystal Palace Park, Crystal Palace Park Rd, *SE20 8DT* (020-3236 0078, bromley.gov.uk > parks and open spaces, Crystal Palace rail, free).

See more modern creatures at Crystal Palace Park Farm, a model farm opened in 2006 by Capel Manor College to provide education for children, and training in animal care, horticulture and arboriculture. The farm (noon to 4pm daily, except Wednesdays) has pigs, goats, rabbits, rodents, poultry and exotica in the form of lizards, snakes and spiders.

Crystal Palace Park Farm, Ledrington Rd, SE19 2BS (020-8659 2557, capel.ac.uk/crystal-palace-park-farm.html, Crystal Palace rail, free).

31 August

Made in Heaven

Marvel at the BAPS Shri Swaminarayan Mandir in Neasden (or Neasden Temple), one of the wonders of the modern world. Europe's first traditional Hindu temple and reportedly the largest of its kind outside India, it covers 1.5 acres and is 70ft high, topped by several pinnacles and five domes. The assembly hall can hold up to 5,000 worshippers. A modern masterpiece.

Neasden Temple, 105-119 Brentfield Rd, Neasden, NW10 8LD (020-8965 2651, londonmandir.baps.org, Neasden tube, free).

Sample splendid Indian vegetarian food at Neasden Temple's Shayona restaurant, one of London's best vegetarian restaurants (alcohol free!). A contemporary, authentic Indian vegetarian restaurant, Shayona offers a wide range of cuisine faithful to the best culinary traditions of the Indian sub-continent, from the Punjab and Rajasthan to Mumbai and southern India – its Gujarati buffet on weekday afternoons is a real treat.

Shayona, 54-62 Meadow Garth, Neasden, NW10 8HD (020-8965 3365, shayonarestaurants.com, Neasden tube, £, ☏).

August

September

1 September

A Pint & Ping Pong

For a relaxed lunch visit The Pembroke, a stylish pub in Earl's Court with a 60-seater dining room, function room and roof terrace. There's a good choice of real ales and a daily-changing seasonal menu offering traditional pub grub with a twist, including rare breed

Angus cheese burger, beer-battered haddock, pan roasted salmon and potato gnocchi primavera.

The Pembroke, 261 Old Brompton Rd, SW5 9JA (020-7373 8337, thepembrokesw5.co.uk, Earl's Court tube, ££, 🍴).

Have a game of ping pong (table tennis) at Ping, a restaurant, bar and games room in Earl's Court which opens from 6 to 11pm (2am, Thu-Sat). Ping is a cavernous, shabby-chic, funky venue specialising in Italian fare (e.g. pizzas) and cocktails, which is fairly relaxed on Monday to Wednesdays but livens up considerably later in the week. Table tennis pros should turn up on Tournament Tuesdays.

Ping, 180-184 Earl's Court Rd, SW5 9QG (020-7370 5358, weloveping.com, Earl's Court tube, £).

2 September

Casino Royale

Enjoy London's best martini (shaken not stirred, of course) at The American Bar in the Savoy Hotel. This famous bar evokes the atmosphere of the '20s, the so-called golden era of cocktails, with understated Art Deco styling, elegant curves, a white ceiling and Terry O'Neill photographic portraits on the walls, while a tuxedoed pianist plays American jazz.

The American Bar, Savoy Hotel, 100 Strand, WC2R 0EU (020-7836 4343, fairmont.com/savoy-london/dining/americanbar, Charing Cross tube, ££).

Enjoy a game of Baccarat (à la Bond) at the Casino at the Empire, a glitzy gambling den housed in the former Empire Ballroom (originally a Victorian music hall) on Leicester Square. Spanning over 55,000ft², the casino has some 30 gaming tables and numerous slot machines, plus four bars (each with a different theme), two restaurants and showgirls on Thu-Sat nights.

The Casino at the Empire, 5-6 Leicester St, WC2H 7NA (020-3014 1000, thecasinolsq.com/casino, Leicester Sq tube, ££).

3 September

Tate to Tate

Appreciate the works of Joseph Mallord William 'JMW' Turner (1775-1851) – considered by many to be Britain's greatest ever painter – at Tate Britain. This is the original Tate gallery, first opened in 1897. A rebranding in 2000 saw its modern art moved down the Thames to the Tate Modern at Bankside (see below) while Tate Britain, as it's now known, majors in historic and contemporary art. The gallery's permanent collection dates from 1500 to the present day, and is one of the most comprehensive of its kind in the world, including a priceless display of works by Turner (most are on display in the Clore Gallery), Gainsborough, Hogarth, Constable, Stubbs, Bacon, Moore, Hockney and many more.

Tate Britain, Millbank, SW1P 4RG (020-7887 8888, tate.org.uk/visit/tate-britain, Pimlico tube, free).

> Enjoy lunch at Tate Britain's excellent Rex Whistler Restaurant (££, ☎), while admiring Whistler's massive mural, *The Expedition in Pursuit of Rare Meats*.

Tate Modern

Venice, Bridge of Sighs, JMW Turner

Whizz down the Thames from Tate Britain to Tate Modern in just 16 minutes aboard a high-speed boat (tate.org.uk/visit/tate-boat). Tate Modern is one of the runaway success stories of the British arts scene. Created to show off the Tate's burgeoning collection of 20th-century art – from Matisse and Picasso to Warhol and Damien Hirst – and opened in 2000, it's now the most-visited modern art gallery in the world.

Housed in the former Bankside power station, the building is as visually arresting as the art inside. It's the perfect space in which to display installations and live art, which have become almost as important as traditional painting and sculpture, and is constantly evolving to meet demand. In 2009, Tate Modern began a new project which will include a separate extension and tower that's expected to be completed in 2016.

Tate Modern, Bankside, SE1 9TG (020-7887 8888, tate.org.uk/visit/tate-modern, Southwark tube, free).

September

4 September

Stunning Southwark

Take a self-guided tour around some of Southwark's many small parks, garden squares, churchyards and other green spaces, which reflect the area's rich industrial, ecclesiastical, literary and medical history. Starting and ending at Borough tube station, there are three separate walks – which can be combined to form a single walk lasting up to four hours – taking in Red Cross Garden, the Drapers' Almshouses and Guy's Hospital. Download a map and instructions from the website.

Southwark Walk (londongardenstrust.org/guides/guide. php?tour=southwark, Borough tube).

Have fun for nothing at the Southbank Centre, a complex of artistic venues on the Thames that hosts regular free events, performances and exhibitions. Live music is a big attraction on Friday evenings when musicians perform everything from jazz and blues to folk, or drop in to the Central Bar at the Royal Festival Hall (Fri and Sun) for a free lunchtime gig.

Southbank Centre, Belvedere Rd, SE1 8XX (020-7960 4200, southbankcentre.co.uk, Waterloo tube, free).

5 September

It Takes Two…

Learn how to tango at the Tango Fever dance school in Farringdon's Exmouth Market Centre (adjacent to the Holy Redeemer Church). The school offers Argentine tango classes, catering for all ages and standards, from absolute beginners to intermediate. Learning this sultry South American dance is a super way to stay fit and meet new people – and it's fun. ¡Hasta pronto!

Tango Fever, 24 Exmouth Market, EC1R 4QE (07530-493826, tango-fever.com, Farringdon tube, ☏).

Fuel your footwork with a delicious meal at Caravan, a cool, trendy restaurant, bar and coffee roastery in Exmouth Market. The restaurant has three menus – breakfast (weekdays), brunch (weekends) and an all-day lunch and dinner menu offering small and large sharing plates – using seasonal ingredients to create dishes featuring flavours from around the world.

Caravan, 11-13 Exmouth Market, EC1R 4QD (020-7833 8115, caravanonexmouth.co.uk, Farringdon tube, ££, ☏).

6 September

Feast on Modern Art

Compare the Serpentine and Sackler Galleries in Hyde Park. Opened in 1970 in a classical '30s tea pavilion, the Serpentine is one of London's most important contemporary art galleries, showcasing work by the world's finest artists. In 2013 it was joined by its sister gallery, the Serpentine Sackler, housed in a Grade II listed building designed by Zaha Hadid. It's well worth visiting both.

Serpentine & Sackler Galleries, Kensington Gardens, W2 3XA (020-7402 6075, serpentinegallery.org, Lancaster Gate tube, free).

Sample an authentic Neapolitan pizza at Da Mario, an Italian restaurant that could have been made for art lovers. It's housed in a beautiful 120-year-old building – a combination of Venetian and Gothic styles – where the eclectic array of objects, statues and paintings on display may make you wonder whether you've stumbled on a private art gallery.

Da Mario, 5 Gloucester Rd, SW7 4PP (020-7584 9078, damario.co.uk, Gloucester Rd tube, ££, ☎).

7 September

Lazy, Lazy Sunday

Start the day with a relaxing brunch at The Modern Pantry café and restaurant in Clerkenwell. There's more to the menu than bacon and eggs, as experimental chef Anna Hansen puts her own spin on British classics, to the delight of her clientele. It's also a great venue for alfresco dining.

The Modern Pantry, 48 St John's Sq, Clerkenwell EC1V 4JJ (020-7553 9210, themodernpantry.co.uk, Farringdon tube, ££, ☎).

Listen to a concert at Wigmore Hall, built in 1901 by the German piano firm Bechstein next door to its showrooms. The hall stages over 400 events each season and, in addition to being a platform for the world's most celebrated soloists and chamber musicians, it also fosters the careers of talented young artists. Many artists make their first professional appearance in London here.

Wigmore Hall, 36 Wigmore St, W1U 2BP (020-7258 820, wigmore-hall.org.uk, Bond St tube, ☎).

September

September

8 September

Fish for Your Supper

Cast your line in one of London's ponds and waterways; from Hampstead Heath to Walthamstow Reservoirs, the capital offers plenty of places for keen anglers to get their fix. In addition to a wealth of lakes and ponds, the Thames offers opportunities to catch both freshwater and sea fish throughout the year. And because the section of the Thames running through London is tidal, there's no need to seek permission to fish (though you'll need a rod licence).

Go Fish (go-fish.co.uk/london.htm).

Fish not biting? You won't starve, as London offers a wealth of places to enjoy a fish supper, including the award-winning Wright Brothers Oyster & Porter House in Borough Market. Although the speciality is oysters, a wide range of fresh fish is available from sustainable stocks, mostly caught by small Cornish day boats.

Wright Brothers, 11 Stoney St, Borough Market, SE1 9AD (020-7403 9554, thewrightbrothers.co.uk/restaurants/oyster_porter_house, London Bridge tube, ££, ☎).

9 September

Boris's Bash

Party down with Old Father Thames at the (London) Mayor's Thames Festival (i.e. Boris Johnson, not the Lord Mayor of London). Held over ten days in September, it's the capital's largest outdoor arts festival and one of the most spectacular events of the year. It celebrates London's iconic river, through art, music, dance, street entertainment, river races and educational events, both on the water and along its banks and bridges.

The Mayor's Thames Festival (thamesfestival.org, free, ⓘ).

Beard Boris in his den at City Hall, one of London's most iconic modern buildings. The striking ten-storey building was designed by celebrated architect Norman Foster at a cost of £65m and opened in 2002. A 1,640ft helical walkway ascends the interior and at the top there's an open viewing deck. There's also a free art gallery and a café.

City Hall, The Queen's Walk, SE1 2AA (020-7983 4000, london.gov. uk/city-hall, London Bridge tube, free).

10 September

Cabinet of Curiosities

On Tuesdays there are atmospheric candlelit evenings – a wonderful experience if you can cope with the crowds and queues.

Sir John Soane's Museum, 13 Lincoln's Inn Fields, WC2A 3BP (020-7440 4263, soane.org, Holborn tube, free).

V isit Sir John Soane's grave in St Pancras Old Church cemetery, one of the city's most attractive churchyards. This rare and lovely C of E parish church (Grade II* listed) is dedicated to the Roman martyr St Pancras, after which the surrounding area is named, and is believed to be one of the oldest sites of Christian worship in England. Soane's self-designed mausoleum (Grade I listed) reputedly inspired Sir Giles Gilbert Scott to design the iconic red telephone box.

St Pancras Old Church & Churchyard, 191 Pancras Way, NW1 1UL (020-7424 0724, oldstpancrasteam.wordpress.com/old-st-pancras, St Pancras tube, free).

September

H onour the birthday of one of London's greatest architects with a visit to Sir John Soane's Museum on the anniversary of his birth. Soane (1753-1837) lived in Holborn and his former home is now one of the city's most unusual and rewarding museums, displaying everything from masterpieces by Canaletto and Hogarth to a human skeleton.

Soane was born a bricklayer's son but became an innovative architect, noted for his designs of the Bank of England and the Dulwich Picture Gallery. He was also an avid collector, and designed his house to accommodate his antiquities and works of art. He amassed such a huge collection that at one stage he and his family were living in just two small rooms!

Exhibits include pieces from the classical, medieval, Renaissance and Oriental periods, from Roman cremation urns and the alabaster sarcophagus of Seti I to furniture, plus timepieces, stained glass, paintings, sculpture, jewellery, architectural drawings, historical volumes and historical architectural models. Look out for the marble tomb of Soane's favourite dog.

11 September

Chez De Morgan & Bruce

Step back in time at the splendid De Morgan Centre in Wandsworth which houses the world's largest collection of the work of William De Morgan (1839-1917) – the most important ceramic artist, potter and tile designer of the Arts & Crafts Movement – and his wife, the painter Evelyn De Morgan (1855-1919).

De Morgan Centre, 38 West Hill, SW18 1RX (020-8871 1144, demorgan.org.uk, East Putney tube).

Relish a magnificent meal at Michelin-starred Chez Bruce, which in an earlier incarnation was Marco Pierre White's first restaurant, Harvey's. Although it's now almost two decades since Bruce Poole and Nigel Platts-Martin took over the restaurant from the enfant terrible of celebrity chefs, it remains one of London's very best places to eat; *Harden's London Restaurants* guide voted it the city's favourite restaurant five years running. The set lunch and dinner are a steal for food of this quality – go!

Chez Bruce, 2 Bellevue Rd, SW17 7EG (020-8672 0114, chezbruce. co.uk, Wandsworth Common rail, ££, ☎).

12 September

Roll 'n Rock

Get your skates on and join the London Friday Night Skate (LFNS), a weekly marshalled street skate of up to 15 miles that departs from Hyde Park Corner each Friday at 8pm. A slightly more relaxed affair is the Sunday Stroll departing at 2pm. Both events are open to all skaters who can stop, turn and control their speed on hills, and both depend on the weather, so check the website first.

London Friday Night Skate (lfns.co.uk, free, ⓘ).

Looking for more fun on four wheels? Rock along to The Renaissance Rooms roller disco in Vauxhall (Thu to Sat) where you're sure to have a good time. Whether your musical taste leans towards classic disco and funk or R&B and house, there's something for everyone – from pro skaters to absolute beginners. The entry fee includes skate hire.

The Renaissance Rooms, Miles St, SW8 1RZ (020-7720 9140, rollerdisco.com, Vauxhall tube).

13 September

Bargain Hunt

Look for a bargain at Camden Passage antiques market, hidden down an 18th-century alleyway behind Upper Street in Islington, with an atmosphere that reeks of days gone by. Whether you're a dealer, an interior designer, a collector or just curious, you'll find Camden Passage intriguing. The market trades on Wednesdays and Saturdays, while the larger antique shops also open on other days or by appointment.

Camden Passage Antiques Market, Camden Passage, N1 8EE (camdenpassageislington.co.uk, Angel tube, free).

Even if the bargains elude you, you can enjoy a good value, fixed-price lunch at Frederick's, another stalwart of Camden Passage. Built in 1789 as The Gun public house, it was rebuilt in 1834 and renamed The Duke of Sussex in honour of Prince Augustus Frederick. It has two lovely dining rooms, including a light and airy 'garden' room, serving modern British cuisine.

Frederick's, 106 Camden Passage, N1 8EG (020-7359 2888, fredericks.co.uk, Angel tube, ££, ☎).

14 September

Temples of Desire

Seek peace and quiet in King's College Chapel on the Strand, a magnificent example of Victorian architecture designed by the eminent architect George Gilbert Scott (1811-1878) and completed in 1864. Beautifully restored in 2001 – including the venerable organ by Henry Willis – it's open to everyone for prayer and quiet reflection. A wonderful, spiritual building which perfectly reflects the college's motto: *Sancte et Sapienter* (with holiness and wisdom).

King's College Chapel, King's College, Strand, WC2R 2LS (020-7836 5454, kcl.ac.uk/aboutkings/principal/dean/chaplaincy/strand/chapel/index.aspx, Temple tube, free).

Treat yourself to a fine roast dinner at the landmark (est. 1828) Simpsons-in-the-Strand restaurant. Using the finest seasonal ingredients, Simpsons offers a wide range of classical dishes, including some of the best roast beef and lamb in Britain, plus game in season. It also serves its famous Great British Breakfast on weekdays, as well as cocktails in the lovely Art Deco Knight's Bar.

Simpson's-in-the-Strand, 100 Strand, WC2R 0EW (020-7836 9112, simpsonsinthestrand.co.uk, Temple tube, £££, ☎).

King's College Chapel

September

15 September

See You Inn Court!

See the glorious, historic gardens of the Inner and Middle Temples, two of the City's famous Inns of Court. Overlooking the Thames, these lovely gardens are thought to date back to the 12th century. They're open from Easter to September (12.30-3pm) and on special 'open' days (see website).

Inner Temple Gardens, Inner Temple, EC4Y 7HL (020-7797 8243, innertemple.org.uk > About > The Inner Temple Garden) and Middle Temple Gardens, Middle Temple Ln, EC4Y 9AT (020-7427 4820, middletemplehall.org.uk/gardens.html). Temple tube, free.

Middle Temple Gardens

Eat with the lawyers in the magnificent Middle Temple Hall, the centre of life for the Inn. Built between 1562 and 1573 and virtually unchanged, it remains the finest example of an Elizabethan hall. Bench, bar and students meet here daily for lunch – and you can join them on weekdays. Booking essential.

Middle Temple Hall, Middle Temple Ln, EC4Y 9AT (020-7427 4820, middletemple.org.uk, events@middletemple.org.uk, Temple tube, ££, ☎).

16 September

Ladies' Fashion Day

Watch a catwalk show at Somerset House during London Fashion Week. Along with the New York, Paris and Milan shows, this is one of fashion's premier showcase events, and features over 200 of the industry's most creative designers and businesses, both British and international, with catwalk shows, exhibitions and award ceremonies. Don't despair if you can't get a ticket for Somerset House, as there are public events across the city.

London Fashion Week (londonfashionweek.co.uk, ☎, ⅰ).

Sartorially inspired, get down to Oxford Street or Bond Street – depending on your budget – and shop 'til you drop! The heart of London fashion is bustling Oxford Street with over 300 shops, designer outlets and landmark stores, including the legendary Selfridges. For something a bit less frenetic, try St Christopher's Place (stchristophersplace.com), which offers boutique-style shopping – or blow your budget in Bond Street, home to Armani, Dior and Prada.

Oxford Street (oxfordstreet.co.uk) and Bond Street (bondstreet. co.uk). Bond St tube.

17 September

Salute Real Heroes

Pay homage to the 'ordinary' heroes remembered in Postman's Park, the City's most poignant park. The intriguingly titled space – its name reflects its popularity with workers from the nearby old Post Office HQ – has been a public garden since 1880, but is best known for its Memorial to Heroic Self Sacrifice, the brainchild of George Frederic Watts (1817-1904).

Postman's Park, King Edward St, EC1A 4AS (020-7606 3030, cityoflondon.gov.uk > Green spaces > City Gardens, St Paul's tube, free).

LEIGH PITT,
REPROGRAPHIC OPERATOR,
AGED 30, SAVED A DROWNING
BOY FROM THE CANAL AT
THAMESMEAD, BUT SADLY
WAS UNABLE TO SAVE
HIMSELF··JUNE·7·2007

Tuck into imaginative cuisine from Gascony in southwest France at the Michelin-starred Club Gascon, a Mecca for lovers of fine French food and wine. Pascal Aussignac's glorious restaurant has received numerous accolades and is one of London's most lauded eating houses. Although not cheap, the set menus are a bargain for food of this quality. *Parfait!*

Club Gascon, 59 West Smithfield, EC1A 9DS (020-7600 6144, clubgascon.com, Farringdon tube, ££, 🍴).

18 September

Tired of London…

Take a tour around Dr Samuel Johnson's house on the anniversary of his birth in 1709 (Lichfield). It was lexicographer Samuel Johnson who memorably said 'when a man is tired of London he is tired of life, for there is in London all that life can afford', a sentiment which many believe is even more relevant today than when Johnson said it in 1777.

Dr Johnson's House, 17 Gough Sq, EC4A 3DE (020-7353 3745, drjohnsonshouse.org, Blackfriars tube).

***

Drink a toast to Dr Johnson at his local, Ye Olde Cheshire Cheese, one of London's most historic pubs, dating back to the 1660s, and somewhere the great man would certainly have supped a few pints. Other regulars/visitors are said to have included Charles Dickens, David Garrick, Thomas Carlyle, WM Thackeray, Mark Twain, Arthur Conan Doyle, GK Chesterton and WB Yeats.

Ye Olde Cheshire Cheese, 146 Fleet St, EC4A 2BU (020-7353 6170, Temple tube, £).

September

19 September

Magical Music

Treat your eyes and your ears at Colourscape, one of the UK's most unusual music festivals, combining visual art with contemporary music. Taking place on Clapham Common in September, the festival runs for a week, with concerts at weekends and colour and music workshops throughout the week. See the website for details.

Colourscape Music Festival, Windmill Drive, Clapham Common, SW4 9DE (020-8673 5398, eyemusic.org.uk/Colourscape/colourscape.html, Clapham Common tube, ☎, ⓘ).

Put on your dancing shoes and shuffle along to the Clapham Grand, one of south London's best live music venues. Originally opened as a music hall in 1900, the Grand has previously served as a cinema, bingo hall, nightclub and theatre – where a wealth of music stars performed. Now resurrected after a painstaking refurbishment, the iconic Grand is rockin' them in the aisles once again.

Clapham Grand, 21-25 St John's Hill, SW11 1TT (020-7223 6523, claphamgrand.com, Clapham Junction rail).

20 September

Through the Keyhole

Step inside some of London's most exciting buildings during London Open House weekend, which celebrates all that's best about the capital's buildings, places and neighbourhoods. Each September it offers a unique opportunity to get under the skin of London's amazing architecture, with over 700 buildings of all kinds opening their doors – all for free. See the website for details and opening times.

London Open House (londonopenhouse.org, ☎, ⓘ).

Discover how London is being transformed at the Building Centre, the hub for New London Architecture (NLA) which focuses on architecture, planning, development and construction in the capital. The NLA's public galleries are free and tell the story of London's development, through a giant scale model and displays of major development activity across the city's 33 boroughs, as well as regularly changing exhibitions.

New London Architecture, The Building Centre, 26 Store St, WC1E 7BT (020-7636 4044, newlondonarchitecture.org, Goodge St tube, free).

21 September

Horsing Around

Trot off to Hyde Park to see a cavalcade of magnificent horses parading on Horseman's Sunday, which celebrates horse riding in the capital. It takes place on the penultimate Sunday in September, and at noon a parade of over 100 horses and riders gathers for a blessing at the church of St John's Hyde Park. The vicar is on horseback as well!

Horseman's Sunday, St John's Hyde Park, Hyde Park Crescent, W2 2QD (stjohns-hydepark.com, Marble Arch tube, ⓘ).

Hire a horse and carriage and see London in style. A horse-drawn sightseeing tour takes in all the city's famous landmarks from the Tower of London to Buckingham Palace, and can include a break for lunch or even a picnic in Hyde Park. Alternatively, be the envy of your friends and arrive like Her Majesty for a special occasion such as an anniversary party or wedding.

Adra Parc Carriages (horsedrawncarriageslondon.co.uk) and Westways Carriage Horses (westwayscarriagehorses.co.uk, ☎).

22 September

Go Wild in London

Spend a day communing with nature with the London Wildlife Trust, which manages over 40 nature reserves across the capital, covering a range of habitats from woodland to wetlands. The Trust's aim is to preserve and protect London's wildlife and wild spaces, as well as making them safe and enjoyable places to visit. Among its many London sites are Camley Street Natural Park (NW1) and the East Reservoir Community Garden (N4).

Wild London (wildlondon.org.uk, free).

Discover one of London's 'secret' gardens, the Natural History Museum's Wildlife Garden, a little-known space behind a hugely popular museum. Created in 1995, this one-acre space was the museum's first living exhibition, designed to show the potential for wildlife conservation in the inner city. A variety of wildlife lives in or visits the garden, which is buzzing with life throughout the year.

Natural History Museum Wildlife Garden, Cromwell Rd, SW7 5BD (020-7942 5011, nhm.ac.uk/visit-us/whats-on/wildlife-garden-whatson, South Kensington tube, free).

September

23 September

The Last Samurai

September

Learn the fascinating art of Japanese swordsmanship known as Battodo Fudokan, the practise of which brings increased awareness, strength, flexibility, coordination and vitality. 'Batto' means to draw and strike with the sword, while 'Do' refers to a path of training aimed at the complete development of the practitioner. The Fudokan School in London teaches complete Japanese swordsmanship at all levels (in Bethnal Green and Islington).

Battodo Fudokan London (020-8533 555, battodo-fudokan.co.uk, ☏).

Wind down with a drink at the sexy, subterranean Shochu Lounge. The speciality at this Japanese bar is Shochu, a spirit not dissimilar to vodka, usually distilled from barley, sweet potatoes or rice, and flavoured with various fruits and herbs. The Shochu Lounge is chic, intimate and sumptuous, with Japanese-influenced décor, including dark wood, red velvet and a rustic-style bar.

The Shochu Lounge, 37 Charlotte St, W1T 1RR (020-7580 6464, shochulounge.com, Goodge St tube, ££, ☏).

24 September

Yummy Mummies

Tutankhamun's death mask

See the splendid collection of ancient Egyptian artefacts at the British Museum, the largest collection of Egyptian antiquities outside Cairo. Room 4 contains the blockbuster sculptures, including the authoritative bust of Ramesses II (1250 BC), the Sarcophagus of Nectanebo II (360 to 343 BC) and the famous Rosetta Stone – featuring writing in Greek, everyday Egyptian and hieroglyphics – which enabled linguists to decipher the hieroglyphic code.

British Museum, Great Russell St, WC1B 3DG (020-7323 8299, britishmuseum.org/explore/cultures/africa/ancient_egypt.asp, Russell Sq tube, free).

Avoid the crowds with a visit to the Petrie Museum, a spectacular collection of around 80,000 Egyptian (and Sudanese) artefacts, covering life in the Nile Valley from prehistory through to the Coptic and Islamic periods. The Petrie focuses on the minutiae and provides a vivid picture of everyday life through a wealth of personal objects.

Petrie Museum of Egyptian Archaeology, Malet Place, WC1E 6BT (020-7679 2884, ucl.ac.uk/museums/petrie, Euston Sq tube, free).

25 September

Gratifying Gabriel's Wharf

Check out Gabriel's Wharf (and neighbouring OXO Tower Wharf), a popular riverside destination redeveloped in the '90s and now home to designers, artists, cafés, restaurants, bars and salons. A unique feature of the wharf is its concentration of retail studios for contemporary designers, where you can watch artisans at work and buy a wide variety of original products including fashion, fine art, textiles, jewellery, ceramics and glass.

Gabriel's Wharf, Upper Ground, SE1 (coinstreet.org/developments/gabrielswharf.html, Waterloo tube, free).

Have afternoon tea with a difference at The OXO Tower Brasserie at the top of the iconic 19th-century OXO Tower. The Brasserie offers an original afternoon tea – confusingly called 'Not Afternoon Tea' – the difference being that the cakes and pastries are accompanied by cocktails and champagne rather than tea!

The OXO Tower Brasserie, OXO Tower Wharf, Barge House St, SE1 9PH (020-7803 3888, harveynichols.com/restaurants/oxo-tower-london, Waterloo tube, ££, ☎).

26 September

Harvest Festival

Have a bite (or two) to eat at the Real Food Festival at the Southbank Centre, a three-day foodie fiesta that champions small specialist producers. In addition to sampling food from producers chosen for their high standards, sustainability and ethical production, there's also a wealth of street food, demos by top chefs, a mini farm and live music.

Real Food Festival, Southbank Centre Sq, Belvedere Rd, SE1 8XX (realfoodfestival.co.uk, Waterloo tube, ⓘ).

Surrender to your carnivorous cravings at Mark Hix's Tramshed restaurant in Shoreditch. It was voted London's best meat restaurant in 2012 by Time Out, and the menu couldn't be simpler: roast chicken or steak. The vast space – a Grade II listed 1905 tram shed building – features artwork by Damien Hirst of a cow and a cockerel.

Tramshed, 32 Rivington St, EC2A 3EQ (020-7749 0478, chickenandsteak.co.uk, Old St tube, ££, ☎).

September

27 September

Old Father Thames

Cheer on the oarsmen (and women) in the Great River Race, London's water marathon that's contested over a 21-mile course on the Thames, from Millwall Dock to Ham House. The race attracts over 300 crews (more than 2,000 competitors) from around the globe and is the largest and most prestigious event of its kind in Europe, appealing to every level of competitor from fancy-dressed charity fund-raisers to serious sporting types.

Great River Race (greatriverrace.co.uk, free, ⓘ).

Enjoy a relaxing dinner cruise along the Thames, taking in such sights as the Houses of Parliament, Tower Bridge and the Millennium Dome (O2 Arena) while you dine. There are a number of packages, which generally include live entertainment. It's not the cheapest way to eat but a fun way to celebrate a birthday, anniversary or any special occasion.

Bateaux London (bateauxlondon.com) or Thames Dinner Cruise (thamesdinnercruise.co.uk, ££, ☎).

28 September

East End Royalty

See London's Pearly Kings and Queens in all their majesty – Smother suits covered in pearl buttons, badges and glitter – during their annual Harvest Festival Parade. The celebrations start around 1pm with traditional entertainments at Guildhall Yard (EC2, Bank tube), before a parade to St Mary-le-Bow church for the Harvest Festival service. The parade includes mayors, donkey carts, marching bands and, of course, the Pearly Kings and Queens – an unforgettable sight.

The Pearly Society (pearlysociety.co.uk, ⓘ).

Eat like Pearly royalty at G. Kelly's famous eel & pie shop in Bow, East London, established in 1915. Along with jellied eels, pie and mash is also traditional East End fare, and Kelly's pies (made fresh daily on the premises) are to die for – try the beef pie followed by home-made apple or cherry pie. Real food!

G. Kelly's Eel & Pie Shop, 526 Roman Rd, E3 5ES (020-8980 3165, gkellypieandmash.co.uk, Bow Rd tube, £).

29 September

Arriba RIBA!

Admire the striking Royal Institute of British Architects (RIBA) building on Portland Place, an impressive example of early '30s (1934) Art Deco architecture designed by George Grey Wornum, with sculptures by Edward Bainbridge Copnall and James Woodford. The RIBA building houses a public gallery showcasing its world-class collections, an extensive library, bookshop, restaurant, café and bar.

Royal Institute of British Architects, 66 Portland Place, W1B 1AD (020-7580 5533, architecture.com, Regent's Park tube, free).

Have lunch at the RIBA Florence Hall restaurant. A well-kept secret, it's one of London's most peaceful places to eat and serves creative seasonal British food. The light and airy dining room has a stunning wood and marble floor and comfortable semi-circular banquettes, while on sunny days you can dine alfresco on the terrace.

Florence Hall Restaurant, Royal Institute of British Architects (020-7631 0467, restaurant@inst.riba.org, ££, ☎).

30 September

Shoot Out in Greenwich

Target your friends or workmates at Bunker 51, a decommissioned Cold War nuclear bunker a stone's throw from the O2 Arena in North Greenwich. This state of the art facility takes laser tag and paintball to a whole new level – below ground level – as you take part in a real-life video game. Both paintball and laser tag sessions last for two hours with a 30-minute mission briefing beforehand.

Bunker 51, 3 Herringham Rd, SE7 8NJ (0845-617 0685, ultimaterecreation.co.uk/bunker51/bunker-51-paintball-lasertag.asp, Charlton rail, ☎).

Debrief over a well-deserved beer at The Greenwich Union, the first pub opened (in 2001) by the Meantime Brewing Company, a microbrewery based in Greenwich. The Union – the name comes from Meantime's Union beer – focuses on the brewery's own beers, craft lagers, rarities, specials and seasonal brews, although it also stocks 60 beers from around the world. Cheers!

The Greenwich Union, 56 Royal Hill, SE10 8RT (020-8692 6258, greenwichunion.com, Greenwich DLR/rail, £).

September

October

October

1 October

Where all that Glitters *is* Gold

Buy a loved one a special present at the Goldsmiths' Fair in splendid Goldsmiths' Hall. The Goldsmiths' Company is one of the Twelve Great Livery Companies of the City of London, which received its royal charter in 1327. Established in 1983, the fair has grown in stature to become the most important and prestigious event of its kind in Europe.

Goldsmiths' Fair, Goldsmiths' Hall, 13 Foster Ln, EC2V 6BN (020-7606 3030, thegoldsmiths.co.uk, St Paul's tube, free, ⓘ).

Munch mixed meze at Haz, an acclaimed Turkish restaurant close to St Paul's. Sample the best of Turkish cuisine – renowned for its use of fresh ingredients – in a large, light and airy room, with communal tables and a long bar. The meze lunch, featuring several small dishes, is a great way to explore Turkish food.

Haz, 34 Foster Ln, EC2V 6HD (020-7600 4172, hazrestaurant.co.uk, St Paul's tube, ££, ☏).

2 October

Skiing – in October?

Learn to ski – or get in some practice – at the Sandown Ski Centre in Esher in Surrey on the southwest fringes of London. You can join in group lessons aimed at beginners or more experienced skiers/snowboarders, or opt for private lessons if you want a more sedate or intensive form of instruction. The ski slope is also open for recreational skiing and snowboarding.

Sandown Ski Centre, More Ln, Esher, KT10 8AN (01372-467132, sandownsports.co.uk/ski, Esher rail, ☏).

Although it's too early for 'real' skiing (in Europe at least), get some mates together and enjoy some early 'après-ski' practice at the Tiroler Hut in Notting Hill, one of London's best Austrian restaurants. Expect a boisterous evening of music, yodelling and the irresistible 'Tirolean cow bell cabaret', interspersed with 'a few' beers and some good food. *Zum Wohl!*

Tiroler Hut, 27 Westbourne Grove, W2 4UA (020-7727 3981, tirolerhut.co.uk, Bayswater tube, ££, ☏).

The
Tiroler Hut
Restaurant

3 October

Bountiful Bankside

Feed your soul at the Merge Festival in Bankside, an annual month-long festival of exhibitions, performances, events and happenings which draw on the rich heritage and contemporary culture of this up-and-coming area of Southwark. The festival brings together artists, performers, art organisations and collectives in experimental partnerships, often in unusual venues (such as 'lost' buildings prior to their regeneration). It also promotes and nurtures emerging talent, giving young artists the opportunity to display their work.

Merge Festival, Bankside (mergefestival.co.uk, free, ⓘ).

Merge Festival

For more traditional art, visit the Bankside Gallery – home to the Royal Watercolour Society and the Royal Society of Painter-Printmakers – where there's a changing programme of exhibitions, including contemporary watercolours and original prints. Many works are available for sale, including a large range of unframed prints and watercolours. The Bookshop stocks books, materials and cards for discerning art lovers.

Bankside Gallery, 48 Hopton St, SE1 9JH (020-7928 7521, banksidegallery.com, Southwark tube, free).

4 October

Bavaria Comes to Town

Enjoy the atmosphere – and beer – of Bavaria at the London Oktoberfest, celebrated over a number of weekends in September and October (two venues – see website). All the fun of the world's greatest beer festival – but without the Germans – with authentic 'schlager' music played by Bavarian bands, very large beers served by buxom wenches and an abundance of tasty wurst. *Prost!*

London Oktoberfest (london-oktoberfest.co.uk), Kennington Park, SE11 4BE (Oval tube) and Millwall Park, E14 3AY (Canary Wharf DLR, ⓘ).

Adopt an animal, visit a zoo or maybe feed the ducks in the park on World Animal Day. Inaugurated in Florence in 1931, this special day celebrates life in all its forms, with events  planned throughout the world – previous years' happenings in London have included special walks, and open days at animal charities. October 4th is also the feast day of Francis of Assisi (1182-1226), patron saint of animals and the environment.

World Animal Day (worldanimalday.org.uk).

October

5 October

Rutting in Richmond

Experience the power and drama of the deer rut in Richmond Park, London's largest royal park with a herd of around 650 red and fallow deer. The rut takes place in the autumn breeding season when the stags and bucks compete for females, with the large males barking and clashing their antlers to attract females and fight off rivals. **Don't get too close and leave the dog at home.**

Richmond Park, Richmond, TW10 5HS (0300-061 2200, royalparks. org.uk/parks/richmond-park, Richmond tube, free).

Relax over a superb lunch or dinner at The Petersham hotel in Richmond, which has a lovely restaurant overlooking the River Thames with a relaxed ambience and discreet, friendly service. Head chef Alex Bentley's award-winning menu offers fine British cooking using fresh and seasonal ingredients to create perfectly balanced flavours. The restaurant also offers a delicious afternoon tea.

The Petersham, Nightingale Ln, Richmond, TW10 6UZ (020-8940 7471, petershamhotel.co.uk/richmond_restaurant.aspx, Richmond tube, ££, ☎).

6 October

All Hail All Hallows

Breathe in the history at All Hallows-by-the-Tower, London's oldest church, overlooking the Tower of London. Established in 675 by the Saxon Abbey at Barking, the church was built on the site of a Roman building, of which there are traces in the crypt (now a museum). All Hallows survived the Great Fire in 1666 and is deservedly Grade I listed.

All Hallows-by-the-Tower, Byward St, EC3R 5BJ (020-7481 2928, ahbtt.org.uk, Tower Hill tube, free).

Pop next door to All Hallows-by-the-Tower for coffee or lunch at The Kitchen@Tower café. A welcome oasis on the edge of the City, the café has a bright interior with eclectic décor and a relaxing ambience, plus a peaceful garden with outdoor seating for warm days. The Kitchen is licensed and serves traditional British food, including full English breakfast, snacks, lunch and afternoon tea.

The Kitchen@Tower, Byward St, EC3R 5BJ (020-7481 3533, thekitchenattower.com, Tower Hill tube, £).

7 October

Art & Ale Fest

Take in two of north London's most innovative contemporary art galleries – the Parasol Unit and the Victoria Miro Gallery – which stand side by side just off the City Road.

The **Parasol Unit Foundation for Contemporary Art** (to give it its full name) was founded in 2004 and is a registered educational charity. Housed in an old warehouse building with 5,000ft² of exhibition space, the gallery has an impressive minimalist design by Italian architect Claudio Silvestrin. The Parasol features exciting multi-disciplinary exhibitions and is internationally recognised for its forward-thinking and challenging exhibition programme.

Victoria Miro opened her first gallery in Cork Street in 1985 and is one of the *grandes dames* of the Britart scene, gaining widespread acclaim for nurturing the careers of young British artists and showcasing the work of established and emerging artists from Europe, Asia and the US. The gallery – in a converted furniture factory – has a massive 9,000ft² of exhibition space (one of London's largest). It's also rare in having its own garden, a beautiful landscaped area overlooking the Regent's Canal, used for installations.

Parasol Unit, 14 Wharf Rd, N1 7RW (020-7490 7373, parasol-unit. org) and Victoria Miro Gallery, 16 Wharf Rd, N1 7RW (020-7336 8109, victoria-miro.com). Old St tube, free.

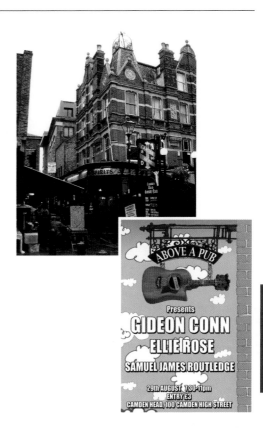

Raise a glass at The Camden Head, tucked away in Islington's antiques' quarter. Dating from 1849, this well-preserved Victorian gin palace has high ceilings, a striking red bar top, lovely glass work and mirrors, beautiful tiles and original wooden features which add warmth to the interior in winter. The large beer garden is a big draw in summer. The Head has music hall connections – celebrated in some of the decoration – and the tradition of entertainment continues to this day with free comedy evenings three times a week.

The Camden Head, 2 Camden Walk, N1 8DY (020-7359 0851, camden-head.co.uk, Angel tube, £).

October

8 October

Cycle Chukkas

Who needs a pony when you can play polo on a pushbike? Hardcourt bike polo is fun and easy to learn, and the London Hardcourt Bike Polo Association welcomes newbies. All you need to take part is a bicycle and any bike will do (although you can buy purpose-built polo bikes). It's usually possible to borrow a mallet and ball, but padded gloves are essential to cushion the inevitable falls.

London Hardcourt Bike Polo Association (lhbpa.org, ☎).

Spend cocktail hour at the highly-acclaimed Crazy Bear in Fitzrovia, one of London's smartest bar/restaurants. The stylish interior – including a super-cool basement bar specialising in award-winning cocktails – is Art Deco inspired, while the menu is a fusion of Asian cuisines (Chinese, Japanese and Thai), taking in sushi, sashimi and dim sum as well as curries and stir fries.

The Crazy Bear, 26-28 Whitfield St, W1T 2RG (020-7631 0088, crazybeargroup.co.uk/fitzrovia, Tottenham Court Rd tube, ££, ☎).

9 October

Walk On By

Explore the capital on foot with the oldest urban walking tour company in the world. Founded some 50 years ago, London Walks is widely recognised as London's most reliable walking company, with the city's best guides and an astonishing variety of routes (see the website for information). Walks take place every day and there's no need to book – just turn up at the designated tube station. Most walks last around two hours.

London Walks (020-7624 3978, walks.com).

Take a break for coffee and cake at Nude Espresso in Soho, winner of 'Independent Café of the Year UK' in 2010 and 2013, awarded by the Café Society. Like an increasing number of the city's cafés, Nude Espresso has its own roaster, based at its East London branch, which not only ensures the freshness and quality of its coffee but also its exclusivity.

Nude Espresso, 19 Soho Sq, W1D 3QN (nudeespresso.com/cafes/soho-square, Tottenham Court Rd tube, £).

10 October

Back to the Future

Relive the golden age of Rock 'n' Roll at Jukebox London in Islington, one of London's leading retailers of vintage jukeboxes. Visiting its showroom is like stepping back in time – there are models from Ami, Rock-ola, Seeburg and Wurlitzer, dating from around 1946 to 1962. Some still play old vinyl 45s while others use compact discs, iPod docking and even touch-screen technology.

Jukebox London, 16 Colebrooke Row, N1 8DB (020-7713 7668, jukeboxlondon.co.uk, Angel tube, 🖥).

Be a pinball wizard at the vibrant Pipeline Bar, which serves up jukebox music, DJs, pool, pinball, table football and darts, and (according to the website) is 'home to hot chicks, bums, punks, hipsters, bohemians, rockabilly greasers and regular Joes.' Guaranteed techno-free, the Pipeline is an unreconstructed, chaotic rocker's sanctuary, with a backdrop of legendary rock photos and cool drinks. Closed Sundays.

The Pipeline Bar, 94 Middlesex St, E1 7DA (020-7377 6860, thepipelinebar.co.uk, Liverpool St tube, £).

11 October

No Big Macs Here

Stock up on organic produce at the Whole Foods Market in the former Barkers department store, an Art Deco landmark in Kensington. Everything in this food emporium is organic and/

or locally sourced; free from artificial preservatives, colours, flavourings, sweeteners and hydrogenated fats. The market also has a number of places to eat, from salad bars to sushi.

Whole Foods Market, The Barkers Building, 63-97 Kensington High St, W8 5SE (020-7368 4500, wholefoodsmarket.com/stores/kensington, High St Kensington tube).

Discover that there's more to vegan food than brown rice and lentils by visiting Vitao in Soho. The restaurant promotes 'living food' – healthy organic ingredients served lightly cooked or raw, but without compromising on taste. Sample a range of tapas-style dishes at the bar, try the buffet on weekdays or order a healthy a la carte option from the Living Gourmet menu.

Vitao, 74 Wardour St, W1F 0TE (020-7734 8986, vitao.co.uk, Leicester Sq tube, ££, 🖥).

October

12 October

Centurions to City Traders

Roman Wall

October

route through the galleries. The museum underwent a £20m redesign in 2010, breathing new life into the permanent displays and increasing the space by a quarter, allowing a further 7,000 objects to be exhibited.

Museum of London, 150 London Wall, EC2Y 5HN (020-7001 9844, museumoflondon.org.uk, Barbican tube, free).

––––––––––––

Spend a day at the Museum of London in the heart of the City, the largest urban history museum in the world, which brings London's 2,000-year history to life. The saga begins before you even enter the museum – fragments of Hadrian's London wall (ca. 300AD) are visible outside – and once inside your journey takes you along a timeline from Neanderthal man to City slicker.

The Museum of London opened in 1976, and is a merger of two earlier museums: the Guildhall Museum, founded in 1826, and the London Museum (1912). The architects came up with an innovative plan whereby there's just one chronological

Discover the Barber-Surgeons' Hall Garden, tucked into a defensive bastion of the London wall in the shadow of the Museum of London, which dates back to the days when herbs were an essential part of the surgeon's stock-in-trade. There has been a garden here since the 1550s and this one, created in 1987, contains the Worshipful Company of Barbers' physic garden, with some 50 different species of plants used to treat wounds, bruises and burns, some of which have an application in modern medicine. The fragrant garden also contains a number of commemorative trees, including a yellow magnolia planted for the Queen's Golden Jubilee in 2002.

Barber-Surgeons' Hall Garden, off London Wall/Wood St, EC2 (barberscompany.org, Barbican tube, free).

Barber-Surgeons' Hall Garden

13 October

Viva España!

Take a Spanish lesson or attend a cultural event at the Instituto Cervantes to celebrate both Spanish National Day (*Fiesta Nacional de España*) and Columbus Day. A non-profit organisation founded by the Spanish Government in 1991, the mission of the Instituto Cervantes is to promote Spanish language teaching as well as that of Spain's co-official languages, such as Basque and Catalan.

Instituto Cervantes, 102 Eaton Sq, SW1W 9AN (020-7235 0353, londres.cervantes.es/en, Victoria tube, ☎).

Tuck into tapas and a glass of sherry at Barrafina in Soho, the yardstick by which other tapas bars are measured. The menu includes favourite morsels, such as delicious Ibérico ham, salty Manchego cheese and wedges of *tortilla*, but also gives a nod to British tastes with grilled quail (with alioli), ribeye steak with *piquillo* peppers and rump of lamb.

Barrafina, 54 Frith St, W1D 4S (020-7813 8016, barrafina.co.uk, Tottenham Court Rd tube, ££, ☎).

14 October

Strictly Kosher

Step inside Bevis Marks Synagogue (Grade I listed), the flagship synagogue of Anglo-Jewry. The oldest synagogue in Britain, it's the only one in Europe to have held services continuously for over 300 years. Completed in 1701, the interior is modelled on the great Portuguese Synagogue in Amsterdam (1677). There's also an acclaimed Kosher restaurant (££).

Bevis Marks Synagogue, 4 Heneage Ln, EC3A 5DQ (020-7626 1274, bevismarks.org.uk, Aldgate tube, paid entry).

Move on to the Jewish Museum in Camden to explore Jewish culture, heritage and identity. The museum provides a vivid snapshot of Jewish life through its huge variety of well-conceived displays, a blend of traditional items in cases and interactive high-tech exhibits. Be sure to visit the excellent kosher café (£).

Jewish Museum, Raymond Burton House, 129-131 Albert St, NW1 7NB (020-7284 7384, jewishmuseum.org.uk, Camden Town tube).

October

15 October

Movie Magic

Watch a movie or two during the BFI (British Film Institute) London Film Festival, taking place over 12 days in October at venues across London. The highly-regarded LFF champions creativity, originality, vision and imagination by showcasing features, documentaries, shorts, animation and experimental films from around the world. It attracts large public audiences and brings leading international filmmakers, new talent and industry professionals together for its annual celebration of cinema.

London Film Festival (bfi.org.uk/lff, ☏, ①).

Attend a movie marathon at the Prince Charles Cinema (PCC) in Leicester Square. If you can't cope with sitting through, say, four Harry Potter films in one go, the PCC also shows a rotating programme of cult, arthouse and classic films alongside recent Hollywood releases. Plus, it hosts sing-a-long versions of cult musicals such as *The Rocky Horror Show*. Great fun!

Price Charles Cinema, 7 Leicester St, WC2H 7BX (020-7494 3654, princecharlescinema.com, Leicester Sq tube, ☏).

16 October

Grand Designs

Check out über-cool Dover Street Market – not so much a market as a construction site-cum-department store and home to a wealth of cutting edge designers. Set up by Comme des Garçons designer Rei Kawakubo, this six-storey space offers a novel approach to clothes shopping: it's a quirky, design-led store with an edgy street-market feel. But don't let the 'market' tag fool you, either, as prices here aren't cheap.

Dover Street Market, 17-18 Dover St, W1S 4LT (020-7518 0680, doverstreetmarket.com, Green Park tube).

Eat at the marvellous Brasserie Chavot in Mayfair, the latest venture of the illustrious French chef, Eric Chavot, recipient of two Michelin stars. Tacked onto the side of the Westbury Hotel, the charming restaurant occupies a grand room with mosaic floors, soaring Corinthian columns and glittering chandeliers. Chavot is a smart, special-occasion French restaurant – not recommended for dieters. *Magnifique!*

Brasserie Chavot, 41 Conduit St, W1S 2YF (020-7183 6425, brasseriechavot.com, Oxford Circus, ££, ☏).

17 October

Shopping by Appointment

G o (window) shopping in elegant St James's, an area of Westminster bounded to the north by Piccadilly, to the south by the Mall, to the east by Haymarket and to the west by Green Park. It was developed in the 17th century by Henry Jermyn, 1st Earl of St Albans, who created a fashionable residential district for the upper classes, which it remained until the Second World War. It later developed into the upmarket commercial area that we see today, albeit a prestigious one featuring some of London's most luxurious shops (it's as well to leave your credit cards at home on this excursion). It's also home to many of the capital's most exclusive gentlemen's clubs.

Shopping in St James's brings together the best of old and new, with flagship stores providing haute couture alongside family-run businesses, some into their ninth generation. Traditionally known for its shirt-makers, boot and shoe manufacturers, and purveyors of fine perfumes, St James's is synonymous with finely crafted tailoring and good grooming. Its remarkable sartorial heritage has long been an inspiration to fashion, with its dedication to high quality materials and British craftsmanship.

St James's, SW1 (stjameslondon.co.uk/shopping, Green Park or St James's Park tube).

E njoy a luxurious afternoon tea at Fortnum & Mason, London's most exclusive 'grocery store'. Established in 1707 and purveyors to the British royal family, this much-loved department store is renowned for providing its clients with the height of luxury – and the afternoon teas are no exception. Served in the sumptuous St James Restaurant – with resident pianist – it's the ideal setting for one of the great British traditions. You can choose from over 100 different blends of tea from around the globe as well as a fine selection of homemade scones, sandwiches and pastries.

Fortnum & Mason, 181 Piccadilly, W1A 1ER (0845-300 1707, fortnumandmason.com, Piccadilly Circus tube, ££, ☎).

October

18 October

Artful Dodges

Buy a modern masterpiece at the Frieze Art Fair in October, one of the country's leading contemporary art fairs. It shows work from around 1,000 artists, represented by over 150 private art galleries.

Frieze Art Fair, Regent's Park, NW1 (friezelondon.com, Regent's Park tube, ⒤).

Find some treasure at the PAD London Art Fair in Berkeley Square. It's one of London's leading fairs for 20th-century art, design, decorative arts, photography, jewellery and tribal art, from prominent international galleries from around the globe.

PAD London, Berkeley Sq, W1 (pad-fairs.com/london/en, Green Park tube, ⒤).

For those of us for whom the sky isn't the limit, there's the Moniker International Art Fair in Shoreditch. Putting East London on the art fair map, this buying exhibition features works by international artists and challenges traditional conventions with a variety of exhibits and installations.

Moniker International Art Fair, Village Underground, 54 Holywell Ln, EC2A 3PQ (monikerartfair.com, Shoreditch High St tube, free, ⒤).

Moniker International Art Fair

19 October

Medieval Masterpieces

Seek out one of London's 'secret' art collections at the Guildhall Art Gallery, housed in the medieval splendour of the Guildhall built in 1411. The gallery displays around 250 of the collection's 4,000-plus works of art dating back to the 17th century, including paintings by Constable, Millais, Dante Gabriel Rossetti, Solomon, Poynter and Landseer, among others.

Guildhall Art Gallery, Guildhall Yard, off Gresham St, EC2V 5AE (020-7332 3700, cityoflondon.gov.uk > Guildhall, Bank tube, free).

Guildhall

Get stuck into a robust medieval feast at The Jugged Hare, a carnivore's delight where Henry VIII would have felt at home. The 'theatrical' kitchen features a state of the art eight-spit rotisserie and serves spit-roasted meats such as roast suckling pig and spring lamb, plus seasonal British game (e.g. haunch of venison, wood pigeon and wild boar), fish and shellfish.

The Jugged Hare, 49 Chiswell St, EC1Y 4SA (020-7614 0134, thejuggedhare.com, Moorgate tube, ££, ☏).

October

20 October

God's Architect

Celebrate the life of Britain's greatest architect, Sir Christopher Wren, born on this day in 1832. What better way to do this than to glory in the splendour of his masterpiece, St Paul's Cathedral, where Wren was buried on 5th March 1723. Wren's church replaced the previous cathedral, destroyed in the Great Fire of 1666, and was constructed between 1675 and 1710. At 365ft high and set atop the City's highest hill, St Paul's was the tallest structure in London until 1962 and it still dominates the skyline.

Tours of St Paul's take in its magnificent interior, the galleries that wind around its dome, the chapels and the crypt (the largest in Europe). This was the last resting place of some of the nation's greatest heroes, artists and scientists, including (in addition to Wren) Alexander Fleming, JMW Turner, the Duke of Wellington and Lord Nelson, whose black marble sarcophagus occupies centre stage directly beneath the dome. There's a hefty fee to visit the cathedral, but if you attend a service you can 'see' it for free!

St Paul's Cathedral, St Paul's Churchyard, EC4M 8AD (020-7246 8350, stpauls.co.uk, St Paul's tube, paid entry).

October

Take a detour to see another Wren masterpiece, St Stephen Walbrook, also his parish church (Wren lived at 15 Walbrook). It's considered by some to be his finest work, with a dome rivalling St Paul's, and has been open for worship since 1679. This unique church was described by architectural historian Sir John Summerson as 'the pride of English architecture, and one of the few City churches in which the genius of Wren shines in full splendour'. Architectural expert Sir Nikolaus Pevsner rated it one of the ten most important buildings in England.

St Stephens Walbrook, 39 Walbrook, EC4N 8BN (020-7626 9000, ststephenwalbrook.net, Bank tube, free).

21 October

England Expects…

Nelson

Make merry on Trafalgar Day, the anniversary of Britain's greatest naval victory, at the Battle of Trafalgar on 21st October 1805. The British fleet, commanded by Vice Admiral Lord Horatio Nelson (1758-1805), defeated the combined fleets of France and Spain at Cape Trafalgar, off Cadiz in southern Spain. Although England wasn't in imminent danger of invasion, the united fleets of the two old enemies posed a major threat and Nelson vowed to destroy them. Nelson's victory was also his last, as he was killed by a sniper's bullet during the battle.

Nelson joined the Navy at age 12 and rose rapidly through the ranks, serving with leading naval commanders before obtaining his first command in 1778. He was noted for his inspirational leadership, superb grasp of strategy and unconventional tactics, which resulted in a number of decisive victories. He was wounded several times, losing an arm and the sight in one eye. The Battle of Trafalgar was his most celebrated triumph, but Nelson was already famous for winning important battles in Egypt, the Caribbean and Denmark.

Each year the Sea Cadet Corps lead a Trafalgar Day Parade through London to Trafalgar Square. Numerous monuments, including Nelson's Column, have been created in his memory and his legacy remains highly influential to this day.

Take a boat from the Embankment to Greenwich and visit the National Maritime Museum (NMM), where Admiral Nelson's body lay in state in the Painted Hall in January 1806. The Nelson Display at the NMM explores his story through the narrative of the Battle of Trafalgar, his death, funeral and commemoration in the capital. It includes his undress coat worn at the Battle of Trafalgar, with a bullet hole on the left shoulder close to the epaulette. A new gallery, *Nelson, Navy, Nation 1688-1815*, opened on Trafalgar Day 2013.

National Maritime Museum, Park Row, Greenwich, SE10 9NF (020-8858 4422, rmg.co.uk/national-maritime-museum and ornc.org, Cutty Sark DLR, free).

National Maritime Museum (NMM)

22 October

Turning in His Grave?

What would JMW Turner make, one wonders, of the entrants for the Turner Prize on display at Tate Britain? Inaugurated in 1984, the most notorious prize in the world of contemporary art has courted controversy ever since. The shortlist usually features conceptual art – which baffles most of us – but despite the often negative publicity the Turner Prize is always good fun. The winner is assured of instant fame.

Tate Britain, Millbank, SW1P 4RG (020-7887 8888, tate.org.uk, Pimlico tube, free).

Looking for something more naturalistic? Try the Wildlife Photographer of the Year exhibition at the National History Museum, a heart-warming collection of images that magnificently capture the world's wildlife. The annual exhibition consistently shows fresh perspectives on animals, insects, plants and landscapes, brilliantly capturing the most colourful collection of images on display in the capital.

Wildlife Photographer of the Year, Natural History Museum, Cromwell Rd, SW7 5BD (020-7942 5000, nhm.ac.uk/visit-us/whats-on/temporary-exhibitions/wpy, South Kensington tube).

23 October

Delightful Diwali

Join the celebrations for Diwali in Trafalgar Square, the best known and largest annual Hindu festival, lasting five days and celebrated throughout the world. Colourful fireworks are associated with the festival (Diwali translates as 'rows of lighted lamps') and Hindus light oil lamps (*diyas*) and candles around their homes. Diwali also involves the exchange of gifts between friends and relatives.

Hindu Diwali Festival, Trafalgar Sq, WC2N 5DS (diwaliinlondon.com, Charing Cross tube, free, ⒈).

Diwali is a great excuse to visit Tamarind in Mayfair, an award-winning Indian restaurant and the first in the world to be awarded a Michelin star. Dishes are derived from traditional Moghul cuisine, where fish, meat and game are cooked in authentic tandoor ovens, typical of northwest India. One of London's top 'nouvelle' Indian restaurants, Tamarind is a rung (or two) above your local takeaway – and so are the prices.

Tamarind, 20 Queen St, W1J 5PR (020-7629 3561, tamarindrestaurant.com, Green Park tube, £££, ☎).

October

24 October

Breakfast Like a Lord (Mayor)

Get up with the larks and enjoy breakfast at The Fox & Anchor, an attractive heritage pub near Smithfield Market that opens at 7am Mon-Fri (8.30am weekends) and serves a mean 'City Boy Breakfast' (£16.95 – see website). If you aren't an early riser, go for lunch and admire the abundance of dark wood, mosaic tiled floors, etched mirrors and pewter bar.

The Fox & Anchor, 115 Charterhouse St, EC1M 6AA (020-7250 1300, foxandanchor.com, Farringdon tube, ££, ☎).

Drop in on the Lord Mayor of the City of London at his official residence in the Mansion House, a rare surviving grand Georgian town palace built between 1739 and 1752 by George Dance the Elder. The classical Palladian-style building is home to a splendid collection of gold and silver plate, and probably the best collection of Dutch art in Britain. See website for information about guided tours.

Mansion House, Walbrook, EC4N 8BH (020-7626 2500, cityoflondon. gov.uk, Bank tube, ⅰ).

25 October

Falling for Autumn

See stunning autumn colours in the beautiful Kyoto Garden in Holland Park, considered by many to be London's most romantic park. Created in 1991 and immaculately maintained, the garden has a lovely pond with stepping stones and a 15ft waterfall, surrounded by elegant plantings of Japanese shrubs and trees, which put on a ravishing display of colour in autumn.

Holland Park, Ilchester Place, W8 7QU (020-7361 3003, rbkc.gov.uk > leisure and libraries > parks and gardens, Holland Park tube, free).

Learn to shoot clay pigeons at the West London Shooting School in Northolt, one of the UK's best shooting clubs. Founded in 1901, the school provides tailored tuition designed to match your ability and help you develop your own style. The club also has a good (and inexpensive) restaurant.

West London Shooting School, Sharvel Ln, West End Rd, Northolt, UB5 6RA (020-8845 1377, shootingschool.co.uk, South Ruislip tube, ☎).

26 October

Drink with Jeffrey

Prop up the bar at The Coach & Horses, a Victorian pub made famous as Jeffrey Bernard's favourite watering hole (and recreated in the biographical play about Bernard's life, Jeffrey Bernard is Unwell). Now a Soho landmark, the pub fosters its unique identity as a gathering place for writers and thinkers by hosting a fortnightly Private Eye lunch and an excellent piano sing-a-long.

The Coach & Horses, 29 Greek St, W1D 5DH (020-7437 5920, coachandhorsessoho.co.uk, Leicester Sq tube, £).

Spend an entertaining evening at the Soho Theatre in the heart of media land. An exceptional venue for cutting edge new theatre, it has three performance spaces – the 150-seat Soho Theatre, the 90-seat Soho Upstairs and a subterranean cabaret venue, Soho Downstairs. Together they stage at least four shows a night – booking isn't always necessary for the more intimate cabaret shows.

Soho Theatre, 21 Dean St, W1D 3NE (020-7478 0100, sohotheatre. com, Tottenham Court Rd tube, 🎭).

27 October

Curiouser & Curiouser

See the amazing Wellcome Collection, named after Sir Henry Wellcome (1853-1936) and described as a 'free destination for the incurably curious'. One of London's most original and interesting museums, it's an unusual collection of medical artefacts and works of art which 'explore ideas about the connections between medicine, life and art in the past, present and future'.

Wellcome Collection, 183 Euston Rd, NW1 2BE (020-7611 2222, wellcomecollection.org, Euston Sq tube, free).

Step along to The Old Curiosity Shop near Lincoln's Inn. Dating from the 16th century, it's probably the oldest shop in central London, with a precarious overhanging upper storey, uneven floorboards, sloping roof and wooden beams. It's thought to be the inspiration for the shop in Charles Dickens' famous novel, although the name was added after the book was released. It's now a shoemaker's workshop.

The Old Curiosity Shop, 13-14 Portsmouth St, WC2A 2ES (020-7405 9891, curiosityuk.com, Holborn tube, free).

October

28 October

Wonderful Woburn Walk

Get away from it all in Woburn Walk, Bloomsbury, one of London's most original and attractive streets. This lovely Dickensian pedestrian street features beautifully preserved, bow-fronted buildings built by the celebrated architect Thomas Cubitt in 1822. The small street is home to restaurants, bookshops and galleries, and a plaque on one of the buildings marks the house of W B Yeats, who lived here between 1895 and 1919.

Woburn Walk, WC1 (Russell Sq tube).

Be spoilt for choice with lunch at the Brunswick Centre, an iconic '60s shopping mall in Bloomsbury. As well as eclectic offerings of fashion and home stores, it also has the famous Renoir art-house cinema and a wide choice of bars, restaurants and cafés, offering everything from a coffee to a three-course meal. Choose from Apostrophe, Caluccios, Crussh, Fastoche, Giraffe, the Gourmet Burger Kitchen, Nando's, Patisserie Valerie, Starbucks, Strada and YO! Sushi!

Brunswick Centre, WC1N 1AE (brunswick.co.uk, Russell Sq tube).

29 October

Turkish Delight!

Spoil yourself with a Turkish bath at Hamam in Dalston on Turkey's Republic Day. Turkish baths are an ancient method of cleansing and relaxing the body, and were particularly popular in Victorian times when there were many Turkish baths in London. The process is as close as you can get to the baths the ancient Romans enjoyed.

Hamam Turkish Bath, 4A Crossway, Stoke Newington Rd, N16 8HX (020-7249 5554, turkishbathhamam.co.uk, Dalston Kingsland rail, ☏).

Tuck into tasty Turkish food at Antepliler in Upper Street in Haringey, one of several local Turkish restaurants. It's actually three premises: a café, a restaurant and a patisserie where the pistachio and walnut *baklava* is heavenly. The restaurant majors on the cooking of Gaziantep in southeast Turkey, famous for its rich food culture, with dishes cooked in a huge wood-fired oven.

Antepliler, 139 Upper St, N1 1PQ (020-7226 5441, anteplilerrestaurant.com, Highbury & Islington tube, £, ☏).

30 October

One for the Kids

Take your children to the poignant Foundling Museum, Britain's first home for abandoned children, which operated from 1739 to 1954. It was founded by philanthropist Sir Thomas Coram (1668-1751) – who was appalled by the number of abandoned, homeless children living on London's streets – supported by two of the most famous figures in British history: the artist William Hogarth (1697-1764) and composer George Frideric Handel (1685-1759).

Foundling Museum, 40 Brunswick Sq, WC1N 1AZ (020-7841 3600, foundlingmuseum.org.uk, Russell Sq tube).

Move on to Coram's Fields in Bloomsbury, London's first public children's playground and named after Sir Thomas Coram of Foundling Hospital fame. Opened in 1936, it extends to 7 acres and includes a playground, sand pits, duck pond, pets corner, nursery, sports facilities and a café (Mar-Nov). Remember to take the kids with you as adults are only admitted if accompanied by children!

Coram's Fields, 93 Guilford St, WC1N 1DN (020-7837 6138, coramsfields.org, Russell Sq tube, free).

31 October

Trick or Treat?

Enjoy a bewitching few hours at the Magic Circle, founded in 1905, widely acclaimed as the finest magic HQ in the world. The Magic Circle Experience is a tour of the building and museum, while there are regular Meet the Magic Circle evenings performed by some of the Circle's top magicians, plus various other public events throughout the year.

Magic Circle Museum, 12 Stephenson Way, NW1 2HD (020-7367 2222, themagiccircle.co.uk, Euston tube, ☎).

Buy your little angels some old-fashioned treats at Mrs Kibble's Olde Sweet Shoppe, one of London's most nostalgic confectioners, with multi-paned windows, bubblegum-pink stripes and jars of sweet concoctions stacked to the ceilings. The shop is like something out of the '50s, filled wall to wall with old favourites – it even has a fresh fudge counter – and also provides personalised sweet jars and hampers.

Mrs Kibble's, 57a Brewer St, W1F 9UL (020-7734 6633, mrskibbles. co.uk, Piccadilly Circus tube).

October

November

1 November

Skeletons in the Cupboard

skeleton of Charles Byrne, Hunterian Museum

November

Celebrate the Day of the Dead (Mexico's *Dia de los Muertos*) with a ghoulish jaunt around the Hunterian Museum. As might be expected from its location in the Royal College of Surgeons building, this is very much a medical exhibit, one of the world's greatest museum collections of comparative anatomy, pathology, osteology and natural history. It's named after the noted Scottish surgeon John Hunter (1728-1793), whose collection of around 15,000 items was purchased by the government in 1799 and given to the Company (later the Royal College) of Surgeons. (His brother William Hunter's collection forms the basis for Glasgow's Hunterian Museum.)

Be warned, it's rather grisly for some tastes – especially the large selection of preserved human and animal remains. Among the many items on display are a mummified hand, old wax models of dissections, diseased bones and Winston Churchill's dentures!

Hunterian Museum, Royal College of Surgeons, 35-43 Lincoln's Inn Fields, WC2A 3PE (020-7869 6560, rcseng.ac.uk/museums, Holborn tube, free).

November 1st is also All Souls Day – an appropriate date on which to visit Abney Park Cemetery, one of London's 'Magnificent Seven' garden cemeteries created to cope with London's rapid population increase. It was laid out in the early 18th century on the instructions of Lady Mary Abney (and others), becoming a non-denominational garden cemetery in 1840, designed using motifs that weren't associated with contemporary religion.

Today, Abney Park is a romantic wilderness in a grittily urban part of London, every bit as atmospheric and interesting as its more famous 'neighbour', Highgate Cemetery. Its crumbling state adds to its charm, with some magnificent urns, inscriptions, ivy-clad statues and sculptures – leaning, tumbling, falling over and merging with the planting. The park is full of atmospheric walks and picnic spots, and also rich in wildlife.

Abney Park Cemetery, Stoke Newington High St, N16 0LH (020-7275 7557, abney-park.org.uk, Stoke Newington rail, free).

2 November

Invincible Veterans

See some of world's oldest motor vehicles taking part in the world's longest-running motoring event: the Royal Automobile Club's annual London to Brighton Veteran Car Run. It takes place on the first Sunday in November, starting at sunrise from Hyde Park and finishing on the seafront in Brighton. The 55-mile route extends south along the A23 through Lambeth and Brixton, with good vantage points along the way.

Veteran Car Run (veterancarrun.com, ⅈ).

Continue the motoring theme with brunch at Bibendum in magnificent Michelin House in Kensington. This London landmark opened in 1911 as the UK HQ of the Michelin Tyre Company. Its design is Art Nouveau meets Art Deco and since 1987 it has housed the excellent Bibendum restaurant and Oyster Bar – named after the original Michelin man – along with a more informal bistro-café.

Bibendum, Michelin House, 81 Fulham Rd, SW3 6RD (020-7581 5817, bibendum.co.uk, South Kensington tube, £££, ☎).

3 November

Dalston Delight!

Take a stroll around Dalston in East London, taking in some of the area's elegant squares, including early Victorian Albion Square, modern Evergreen Square and De Beauvoir Square with its Regency architecture, the only surviving part of a grand plan in the 1820s to build several upmarket squares. This lovely walk is full of contrast and you can cover the 2 miles in less than an hour. See the website for the route.

Get Walking (getwalking.org/walking-routes/slithery-snakes-dalston-squares).

See a play at the Arcola Theatre in Hackney, one of London's best and most respected fringe theatres. Founded in 2000 and housed in a converted paint factory, Arcola is a favourite of theatre literati – staging work by some of the best living actors, writers and directors – as well as young, upwardly mobile innovators. A theatrical powerhouse.

Arcola Theatre, 24 Ashwin St, E8 3DL (020-7503 1646, arcolatheatre. com, Dalston Kingsland rail, ☎).

November

4 November

Meet Michael Palin

Travel the world for free at Stanfords in Covent Garden, London's leading specialist map and travel book store. The business was started by Edward Stanford in the 1850s as a map publisher; the Long Acre shop opened in 1901 and is the world's largest travel bookshop, selling maps, books, travel accessories and globes. With any luck you might bump into Michael Palin signing his latest tome.

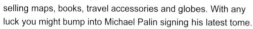

Stanfords, 12-14 Long Acre, WC2E 9LP (020-7836 1321, stanfords. co.uk, Covent Garden tube).

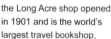

Visit Covent Garden's Jubilee Market in the Jubilee Hall (Grade II listed) built in 1904. It was restored in the '80s and reborn as a 'general market'. On Mondays the market is dedicated to antiques; from Tuesdays to Fridays a general market operates with traders selling clothing and household goods; while at weekends it's the turn of arts & crafts.

Jubilee Market, 1 Tavistock St, WC2E 8BD (020-7379 4242, jubileemarket.co.uk, Covent Garden tube, free).

5 November

Remember, Remember the 5th of November

Pay a visit to Old Palace Yard in Westminster, between the Palace of Westminster and Westminster Abbey, where the perpetrators of the failed Gunpowder Plot – a plan to blow up the House of Lords during the State Opening of Parliament on 5th November 1605 – met their grisly end. Guy Fawkes (aka Guido Fawkes,1579-1606) and his fellow conspirators were tried, found guilty and hanged, drawn and quartered in the yard. It's also where Sir Walter Raleigh was executed in 1618.

Old Palace Yard, Westminster, W1 (Westminster tube).

Celebrate Bonfire Night at one of the capital's numerous fireworks displays held throughout the city, from small local parks to large-scale events. Some, such as the display on Blackheath Common, SE3, are free. They commemorate the capture of Guy Fawkes and the foiling of the Gunpowder Plot, with effigies of Guy Fawkes burned on bonfires while fireworks light up the sky. See the local press for information.

November

6 November

Orient Excess

Admire (and maybe invest in) some exquisite art during the annual ten-day Asian Art in London event, which attracts collectors from around the globe. Items on display range from contemporary art to antiques, and span some 5,000 years of culture in India, China, Japan, the Himalayas and Korea. London's leading Asian art dealers present a series of selling exhibitions, while the major auction houses stage Asian-themed auctions.

Asian Art in London (asianartinlondon.com, ⓘ).

Enjoy a taste of the Orient at the award-winning Cocochan restaurant and bar in the West End, which offers affordable, contemporary, pan-Asian cuisine and classy cocktails. The vast eclectic menu includes light 'snacks' such as dim sum and sushi, along with classic dishes drawn from Japanese, Thai, Chinese, Vietnamese and Indian cuisines. Set menus start from £30 a head, cocktails from £8.50.

Cocochan, 40 James St, W1U 1EW (020-7486 1000, cocochan.co.uk, Bond St tube, ££, ☎).

7 November

Markets & Masters

Check out the goods at Greenwich Market, one of London's best all-round markets which has been trading since 1700. Greenwich comprises three markets: the Antiques and Crafts Market, the Village Market and the Central Market. Tuesdays, Thursdays and Fridays are dedicated to antiques and collectibles, while weekends and Bank Holidays are for arts & crafts. Wednesday is food and homewares day.

Greenwich Market, Greenwich Market, SE10 (020-8269 5096, greenwich-market.co.uk, Cutty Sark DLR).

See the ATP World Tour Finals at the O2 Arena in Greenwich, a tennis tournament contested by the world's eight best men's singles players and doubles pairs. Watching tennis at the O2 is different from watching at a grand slam such as Wimbledon; it's a theatrical affair with the audience plunged into darkness and all eyes on the brightly-lit court below.

ATP World Tour Finals, O2 Arena, Peninsula Sq, SE10 0DX (020-8463 2000, atpworldtour.com/finals, North Greenwich tube, ☎, ⓘ).

November

8 November

The Oldest Show in Town

Have a ball at the Lord Mayor's Show, the oldest, longest, grandest and most popular civic procession in the world. This cavalcade has floated, rolled, trotted, marched and occasionally fought its way through almost 800 years of London history, surviving the Black Death, the Great Fire and the Blitz along the way.

Thanks to the 'caution of King John', each year the newly-elected Lord Mayor of London leaves the City and travels to Westminster to swear loyalty to the crown. With him goes the magnificent procession that has come to be known as the Lord Mayor's Show, involving over 6,000 people including military marching bands, Chinese acrobats, numerous decorated floats and the Lord Mayor himself in his gilded State Coach. Stretching for some 3½ miles, the parade weaves through the City's historic streets from 11am until around 2.30pm, culminating in a spectacular fireworks display.

Lord Mayor's Show (lordmayorsshow.org, ⓘ).

Dick Whittington window

Learn about one of London's most famous Lord Mayors by visiting the church of St Michael Paternoster Royal. First recorded in the 13th century and destroyed in the Great Fire, St Michael was rebuilt under the aegis of Sir Christopher Wren. The church is best known for its association with the fabled Dick Whittington, who was immortalised in a folk tale along with his cat. A fascinating website (purr-n-fur.org.uk/fabled/whittington.html listed) helps sort the man from the myth.

The real Richard Whittington (1354-1423) was a medieval merchant who was elected Lord Mayor of London four times and was also a Member of Parliament. A noted philanthropist, he financed the rebuilding of St Michael's in 1409 and founded the College of St Spirit and St Mary in the church which later became known as Whittington's College. He died in 1423 and was buried in St Michael's.

St Michael Paternoster Royal, 22 College Hill, EC4R 2RP (020-7248 5202, Monument tube, free).

9 November

Funny Goings On

Have a chuckle at the unique Cartoon Museum, which opened in 2006 and is dedicated to preserving the best of British cartoons, caricatures, comics and animation, from the 18th century to the present day. It allows visitors to enjoy the best of original British cartoon and comic art, including a shop packed with humorous books and cards.

Cartoon Museum, 35 Little Russell St, WC1A 2HH (020-7580 8155, cartoonmuseum.org, Tottenham Court Rd tube).

Sup up a pint at The Museum Tavern, an early 18th-century establishment formerly called the Dog and Duck until the British Museum opened its doors across the road. The pub was refurbished in 1855 and retains many Victorian fittings, including attractive etched glass and mirrors, panelled ceilings and the gilt-mirrored, heavy wooden back bar. A good choice for real ale fans, with around seven on tap.

The Museum Tavern, 49 Great Russell St, WC1B 3BA (020-3603 1354, taylor-walker.co.uk/pub/museum-tavern-bloomsbury/c0747, Tottenham Court Rd tube, £).

10 November

Feed Body & Soul

Enjoy an organ concert at St George's Hanover Square, which was composer George Frideric Handel's (1685-1759) parish church – a fine Georgian building designed by John James and completed in 1724. Although largely lacking in ornamentation, the reredos over the altar frames a lovely depiction of *The Last Supper* painted by William Kent, above which is a remarkable Venetian stained-glass window.

St George's Hanover Square, St George St, W1S 1FX (020-7629 0874, stgeorgeshanoversquare.org, Oxford Circus tube, free).

Eat, drink and socialise at the Pollen Street Social bar and restaurant, located in a narrow back street near Oxford Circus. Jason Atherton's lavishly-praised, award-winning restaurant is noted for its wonderfully creative British cuisine and superb wine list (500 bins!). There's also a lovely bar area with tasty cocktails. Set lunch is a steal but booking is essential.

Pollen Street Social, 8-10 Pollen St, W1S 1NQ (020-7290 7600, pollenstreetsocial.com, Oxford Circus tube, £££, 🍽).

November

11 November

Lest We Forget

Armistice Day, better known as Remembrance Day (Poppy Day) in the UK and Veterans Day in the US, commemorates the peace agreement signed between the Allies and Germany which ended World War One. It took effect at the '11th hour of the 11th day of the 11th month' of 1918. It's commemorated by two minutes' silence at 11am and by the laying of wreathes at war memorials throughout London, including the Cenotaph (Whitehall) on the second Sunday in November.

Pay your respects to the fallen heroes of World War One by visiting two of London's finest war memorials, both created by Charles Sargeant Jagger (1885-1934). The Royal Artillery Memorial at Hyde Park Cnr (W1, 1925) shows a dead soldier covered by his greatcoat, while The Great Western Railway War Memorial on platform 1 at Paddington Station (W2, 1922), which depicts a soldier reading a letter from home, is Jagger's most poignant work.

12 November

Walk the Walks

Take a stroll around Gray's Inn Gardens (Mon-Fri, 12-2.30pm), also known as The Walks. They were laid out by Sir Francis Bacon (1561-1626) in 1606 when he was treasurer of the Honourable Society of Gray's Inn, one of the four Inns of Court, and remain among the largest private gardens in London: 5 acres of beautiful parkland guarded by a striking pair of iron gates.

Gray's Inn Gardens, The Walks, Gray's Inn, WC1 (graysinn.info/index.php/the-estate/the-walks, Chancery Ln tube, free).

Dine with Lady Ottoline in a beautifully restored gastropub named after Bloomsbury society hostess Lady Ottoline Morrell who had Aldous Huxley and DH Lawrence in her address book. The upstairs dining room serves imaginative, modern British cuisine, accompanied by a good choice of ales and fine wines. You can also eat in the bar, which has a log fire in winter.

The Lady Ottoline, 11a Northington St, WCIN 2JF (020-7831 0008, theladyottoline.com, Chancery Ln tube, ££, ☏).

Gray's Inn Gardens

13 November

Not Just For Children

Treat your kids to a puppet show at the Little Angel Theatre in Islington, which stages endearing and innovative shows that appeal to adults as well as children. Established in 1961, the internationally-acclaimed Little Angel's 100-seat theatre sits alongside a workshop where new productions and puppets are developed, carved and constructed. Magical!

Little Angel Theatre, 14 Dagmar Passage, Off Cross St, N1 2DN (020-7226 1787, littleangeltheatre.com, Highbury & Islington tube, ⌕).

Take your little ones for a meal at the Rainforest Café, which recreates the Amazon in W1. Once inside you descend into the 'undergrowth', past life-size gorillas, elephants and giant butterflies with flapping wings. The menu keeps up the theme with dishes such as jungle safari soup, rasta pasta, and for the grown-ups, primal steak – all eaten amidst thunder, tropical rain showers and stunning waterfalls. Great fun!

Rainforest Café, 20 Shaftesbury Ave, W1D 7EU (020-7434 3111, therainforestcafe.co.uk, Piccadilly Circus tube, ££, ⌕).

14 November

Boxing Clever

Take a dip or indulge in a spa treatment at York Hall Leisure Centre in Bethnal Green, a unique sporting venue best known for hosting prestigious boxing matches. York Hall is home to Spa London, a highly recommended day spa offering a luxurious experience at an affordable price. In addition to the pool, there's also a fully-equipped air-conditioned gym.

York Hall, 5 Old Ford Rd, E2 9PJ (020-8980 2243, better.org.uk/leisure/york-hall-leisure-centre, Bethnal Green tube).

Go for a healthy lunch just down the road at the vegetarian Gallery Café, which offers an imaginative selection of vegan and vegetarian meals, and has a sunny courtyard for fine days. It's located in St Margaret's House Settlement, a charity based in Bethnal Green since 1889, providing practical initiatives, projects and activities to serve and enable the local community.

Gallery Café, 21 Old Ford Rd, E2 9PL (020-8980 2092, stmargaretshouse.org.uk/gallery-cafe/gallery-café, Bethnal Green tube, £).

November

15 November

Bon Appétit!

Fill up at the BBC Good Food Show at Olympia, London's leading food and wine show. It features all your BBC favourites in the Supertheatre, including a *Great British Bake Off* masterclass with Mary Berry and Paul Hollywood, *MasterChef* cook off hosted by John Torode and Gregg Wallace, *Saturday Kitchen Live* with James Martin, and much more. Plus street food from around the world.

Good Food Show Olympia, Olympia Exhibition Centre, Grand Hall, Olympia Way, W14 8UX (020-7385 1200, bbcgoodfoodshowlondon. com, Kensington Olympia tube, ☷).

Recover from all that rich food at the Evolve Wellness Centre in Kensington, which offers yoga and Pilates classes, holistic natural therapies and lifestyle workshops. Whether your focus is fitness, weight loss, reducing stress or improving your well-being, Evolve can provide you with the tools to build a healthier life.

Evolve Wellness Centre, 10 Kendrick Mews, SW7 3HG (020-7581 4090, evolvewellnesscentre.com, South Kensington, ☏).

16 November

All the Fun of the Fair

Imagine yourself in medieval London by visiting Cloth Fair, a street in West Smithfield with a fascinating past. It's named after the Bartholomew Fair, the country's largest cloth fair which was held annually from 1133 until 1855, when it was banned for encouraging public disorder! Cloth Fair is home to the City's oldest surviving home at number 41, built 1597-1614, while next door (43) is the former home of Sir John Betjeman (1906-1984).

Cloth Fair, Smithfield, EC1 (Barbican tube).

Stroll along Cloth Fair to St Bartholomew the Great (Grade I listed), one of London's oldest churches with a rich history and interesting architecture, particularly its Norman interior. A church was established here in 1123 as part of a monastery of Augustinian canons and the site has been a place of worship since at least 1143.

St Bartholomew the Great, West Smithfield, EC1A 9DS (020-7248 2294, greatstbarts.com, Barbican tube, paid entry).

November

17 November

Hogarth's Hideaway

Take refuge in the former country home of William Hogarth (1697-1764), famous painter, engraver and satirist, who lived in Chiswick from 1749 until his death. A tranquil oasis off the busy A4, the Grade I listed house (built 1713-1717) contains the most extensive collection of Hogarth's prints on permanent public display, while an exhibition documents his life and work.

William Hogarth's House, Hogarth Ln, Great West Rd, W4 2QN (020-8994 6757, hounslow.info/arts/hogarthshouse/index.htm, Turnham Green tube, free).

Spend an evening at The Tabard in Chiswick, a unique Arts & Crafts pub designed by Norman Shaw and built in 1880. On the first floor is the Tabard Theatre, a small fringe theatre operated independently of the pub where top comedians play pre-tour, warm-up gigs. (A tabard, incidentally, is a tunic worn by a herald or royal messenger.)

The Tabard, 2 Bath Rd, W4 1LW (020-8995 6035, tabardtheatre.co.uk, Turnham Green tube, £, ☎).

18 November

Honey for Tea

Treat yourself to a splendid Middle-Eastern feast at Honey & Co, a small café-restaurant run by a husband-and-wife team who were previously head chef and pastry chef at Ottolenghi. Don't let the tiny room or basic décor put you off – the food here is big, bold, colourful and fresh, and a real treat for the taste buds.

Honey & Co, 25A Warren St, W1T 5LZ (020-7388 6175, honeyandco.co.uk, Warren St tube, £).

———————————

Hire a Barclays bicycle (colloquially known as 'Boris bikes') and go on a magical mystery tour of London. It's a great city to explore on two wheels and you don't need to have a planned route or goal – getting hopelessly lost is part of the fun. Boris bikes can be hired from stands throughout the city and returned to any other stand. Free cycling guides can be ordered through the TfL website.

Barclays Cycle Hire (tfl.gov.uk/roadusers/cycling/14808.aspx).

November

19 November

Lighting the Way

Trinity House interior

Take a look around Trinity House, HQ of the General Lighthouse Authority which maintains Britain's lighthouses. Designed by Samuel Wyatt (1737-1807) and built in 1796, its façade includes some of London's best sculptures, but it's the sumptuous interior that's the real star, containing a fine collection of maritime paintings and shipwright models. Tours can be booked via the website.

Trinity House, Tower Hill, EC3N 4DH (020-7481 6931, trinityhouse. co.uk, Tower Hill tube, ☏).

Feast like Henry VIII and his courtiers at a medieval banquet in St Katharine Docks, just east of the Tower of London. You'll be entertained by troubadours, contortionists, magicians, jugglers, minstrels and medieval tumblers at this most royal of banquets, which includes four courses, plus unlimited ale and wine served throughout the meal by dancing wenches. You can even eat in medieval dress.

Medieval Banquet, Ivory House, St Katharine Docks, E1W 1BP (020-7480 5353, medievalbanquet.com, Tower Hill tube, ££, ☏).

20 November

Abracadabra!

Go on the trail of Harry Potter at Leadenhall Market, an ornate, restored Victorian covered market selling fresh food and 'designer' goods. The market was used to portray Diagon Alley, the wizards' 'high street' in *Harry Potter and the Philosopher's Stone*. The entrance to the wizards' pub, the Leaky Cauldron, was filmed at an optician's in Bull's Head Passage in the market.

Leadenhall Market, 1a Leadenhall Market, Gracechurch St, EC3V 1LR (020-7929 0929, leadenhallmarket.co.uk, Bank tube).

Learn how to cast spells at Davenports Magic, London's oldest magic shop, trading since 1899. The staff are professional magicians and can show you a trick or two as you wander around wide-eyed. It's a great place to pick up your magic wand, as well as magic tricks, books, tutorials, magician's kits and a wealth of accessories.

Davenports Magic, 7 Charing Cross Underground Arcade, The Strand, WC2N 4HZ (020-7836 0408, davenportsmagic.co.uk, Charing Cross tube).

21 November

Be Upstanding!

Statue of Lady Justice, Old Bailey

See justice in action at the Central Criminal Court, commonly known as the Old Bailey. The public galleries are open to all on weekdays (10am to 1pm and 2-5pm). Look to the dome above the court to see the famous bronze statue of *Lady Justice*, holding a sword in her right hand and the scales of justice in her left.

Central Criminal Court, Old Bailey, EC4M 7EH (020-7248 3277, oldbaileyonline.org, St Paul's tube, free).

Test your knowledge in a pub quiz at The Punch Tavern, named after the now-defunct satirical magazine (*Punch*), 'created' here in 1841. This magnificent Victorian pub includes a lobby decorated with glazed tiles and an interior that's a riot of etched glass, Art Deco lighting, massive bevelled mirrors, a marble bar, dark wood panelling, and a series of Punch and Judy-themed paintings from 1897.

The Punch Tavern, 99 Fleet St, EC4Y 1DE (020-7353 6658, punchtavern.com, Blackfriars tube, £).

22 November

Fore!

Play a round at Richmond Park Golf Club, set within Richmond Park, the largest of the city's royal parks and a national nature reserve. It's one of London's most beautiful golf clubs, with two 18-hole courses, a driving range and a striking new clubhouse. You don't need to be a member as it's one of the capital's most popular pay-and-play golf destinations.

Richmond Park Golf Club, Norstead Place, SW15 3SA (020-8876 3205, richmondparkgolfclub.org.uk, ☎).

See the 'naked ladies' at York House Gardens in Richmond, set in beautiful grounds on the banks of the River Thames. The gardens were commissioned by Sir Ratan Tata (1871-1918), who installed a group of striking statues of naked female figures representing the Oceanids (or sea nymphs) of Greek mythology.

York House Gardens, Sion Rd, Twickenham, TW1 3DD (08456-122 660, richmond.gov.uk > parks and yorkhousesociety.org.uk, Twickenham rail, free).

23 November

Olde Time Treats

Take time out for lunch at Café des Amis in Covent Garden, a haven of civilisation (with cosy corners and chandeliers) in a sometimes fraught and chaotic corner of central London. It's both a bar and a restaurant, serving solid, tasty brasserie fare, with exceptional value, pre-theatre set menus.

Café des Amis, 11-14 Hanover Place, WC2E 9JP (020-7379 3444, cafedesamis.co.uk, Covent Garden tube, ££, ☎).

Step back in time at a Sunday afternoon tea dance at the Waldorf Hotel. The Waldorf opened in 1908 and its tea dances were all the rage with the smart set; it's easy to imagine yourself back in the roaring '20s as you nibble finger sandwiches in the historic Palm Court to the accompaniment of a five-piece band. Dances take place once a month (see website for dates).

Waldorf Hotel, 21-23 Aldwych, WC2B 4DD (020-7836 2400, waldorfhilton.co.uk/dining-bars/tea-dance.html, Covent Garden tube, £££, ☎).

24 November

Ship Ahoy!

Take the kids on a tour of *HMS Belfast*, a Royal Navy light cruiser that's now a remarkable museum ship moored on the Thames. Named after the city where she was built, *Belfast* was commissioned in August 1939, just before the outbreak of the Second World War. Retired in 1963, she opened as a museum in 1971. Visitors' rations (but alas no rum) are available in the Walrus Café.

HMS Belfast, The Queen's Walk, SE1 2JH (020-7940 6300, iwm.org.uk/visits/hms-belfast, London Bridge tube).

Golden Hinde

Look around the *Golden Hinde*, a replica of the galleon in which Sir Francis Drake (1540-96) circumnavigated the globe. Drake was a notorious privateer, authorised by Elizabeth I to attack and loot ships belonging to England's enemies, i.e. the Spanish, but is most famous for his role in the defeat of the Spanish Armada in 1588.

Golden Hinde, 1 & 2 Pickfords Wharf, Clink St, SE1 9DG (020-7403 0123, goldenhinde.com, London Bridge tube).

November

25 November

To Boldly Go…

Travel through the universe with the help of the Peter Harrison Planetarium at the Royal Observatory (Greenwich), one of the world's most important historic and scientific sites. London's only planetarium takes you on amazing journeys to explore and experience the wonders of the night sky, combining real images from spacecraft and telescopes with advanced computer-generated imagery, projected onto a fully immersive dome.

Royal Observatory, Blackheath Ave, SE10 8XJ (020-8858 4422, rmg. co.uk/royal-observatory, Cutty Sark DLR).

———————

Eat and drink at the centre of Greenwich Mean Time with a visit to the 16 Seconds West Brasserie at the National Maritime Museum. It serves the best of contemporary British cuisine using locally-sourced ingredients, while its eclectic and diverse wine list includes wines from producers originating along the Prime Meridian line.

Sixteen Seconds West Brasserie, National Maritime Museum, Park Row, SE10 9NF (020-3641 7729, 16secondswest.co.uk, Cutty Sark DLR, £).

26 November

Bordeaux & Borscht

Experience a private 'tasting' of fine wines at The Sampler in South Kensington, a wine merchant with a cellar containing over 1,500 classic, unusual and interesting wines. Around 80 are available to try at any one time, with tasting samples costing from 30p. Catering for everyone from novices to oenophiles, the unpretentious Sampler is the ideal place to experiment with wine.

The Sampler, 35 Thurloe Place, SW7 2HP (020-7225 5091, thesampler.co.uk, South Kensington tube, £).

———————

Swap wine for vodka at **Daquise**, a highly-rated Polish restaurant in South Kensington, run by a legendary Polish family. With traditional dishes such as borscht, steak tartar and herring – and courses interspersed with vodka shots – this is the place expatriate Poles go to reminisce and enjoy some of their favourite national dishes.

Daquise, 20 Thurloe St, SW7 2LT (020-7589 6117, daquise.co.uk, South Kensington tube, ££, ☏).

November

27 November

Give Thanks with the Yanks

Give thanks at the American Church in London on Thanksgiving Day, which is celebrated on the fourth Thursday of November. It's one of the most important national holidays in the US, and has its roots in 17th-century religious and cultural traditions, which celebrated the harvest and the preceding year. Today it's all about food and family, and is feted with parades and pumpkin pie.

American Church in London, 79a Tottenham Court Rd, W1T 4TD (020-7580 2791, amchurch.co.uk, Goodge St tube, ⓘ).

Book a special Thanksgiving dinner at Christopher's in Covent Garden. It's one of the capital's best American restaurants, housed in a Grade II listed building with an interesting history – it housed London's first licensed casino in 1870. You can eat casually in the Martini Bar or go à la carte in Christopher's elegant dining room.

Christopher's, 18 Wellington St, WC2E 7DD (020-7240 4222, christophersgrill.com, Covent Garden tube, £££, ☎, ⓘ).

28 November

Soho, So Good

Treat yourself to scrumptious cakes at Maison Bertaux, an eccentric Soho landmark established in 1871, claimed to be London's oldest patisserie. It's certainly one of the best, with a lovely old world atmosphere, unpretentious and relaxed, with a reputation for serving excellent teas. The cakes, croissants and pastries are heavenly. *Parfait!*

Maison Bertaux, 28 Greek St, W1D 5DQ (020-7437 6007, maisonbertaux.com, Leicester Sq tube, £).

Victoria & Albert Museum

Try a night at the (Victoria & Albert) museum on the last Friday of the month and enjoy an eclectic range of free entertainment, including live performances, cutting edge fashion, debates, guest DJs, late-night exhibitions, one-off displays and installations. All that, plus a bar and food. Who needs the pub when you can have a super evening's entertainment at the V&A?

Victoria & Albert Museum, Cromwell Rd, SW7 2RL (020-7942 2000, vam.ac.uk/content/articles/f/friday-late, South Kensington tube, free).

November

29 November

Lighting Up Time

Say 'ahh!' at the Christmas lights which shimmer across the West End from the end of November, with Oxford Street, Regent Street and Bond Street all competing to put on the best display. The lights are switched on by celebrities, who ceremoniously push a button to turn them on around town – see the website or local press for information – and stay lit until Twelfth Night.

Christmas Lights (timeout.com/xmaslights).

Celebrate Christmas a month early with a glass of bubbly and something to eat at one of the many bars or restaurants in Selfridges department store. Your choice includes Harry Gordon's Bar, the celebrated Hix Restaurant Champagne & Caviar Bar, the Corner Restaurant and Champagne Bar, the Oyster and Champagne Bar and the Wonder Bar, plus there's also a wealth of cafés and fast food outlets. *Santé!*

Selfridges, 400 Oxford St, W1A 1AB (020-7318 2476, selfridges.com, Marble Arch tube, £-££).

30 November

His Finest Hour

Explore the Churchill War Rooms on the anniversary of the birth of Sir Winston Churchill (1874-1965), one of England's greatest sons. One of five branches of the Imperial War Museum, this exhibit comprises the Cabinet War rooms, an underground government command centre during the Second World War, and the Churchill Museum, devoted to the life of Sir Winston.

Churchill War Rooms, Clive Steps, King Charles St, SW1 2AQ (020-7930 6961, cwr.iwm.org.uk, Westminster tube).

Toast Winnie at The Churchill Arms, an attractive Fuller's pub dating from 1750 – Churchill's grandparents were regulars here in the 19th century and it was renamed in Churchill's honour after the Second World War. The pub's most famous for its exterior, festooned with hanging baskets (and lights at Christmas) and a regular winner in the London in Bloom competition.

The Churchill Arms, 119 Kensington Church St, W8 7LN (020-7727 4242, churchillarmskensington.co.uk, High St Kensington tube, £).

December

1 December

Humungous Harrods

Get in a bit of early Christmas shopping at Harrods, the world's most famous department store with over one million ft² of selling space spread across 330 departments, making it the largest department store in Europe. Harrods' motto is *Omnia Omnibus Ubique* – All Things for All People, Everywhere – and several of its departments, including the one devoted to Christmas and the glorious Food Hall, are deservedly world famous.

Harrods, 87-135 Brompton Rd, SW1X 7XL (020-7730 1234, harrods. com/food-and-wine, Knightsbridge tube).

Take your pick of Harrods' many fine eateries for lunch. A good choice is Galvin Demoiselle on the ground floor, a spacious, grand-café-style restaurant with tasteful blue banquettes and marble-topped tables. It's yet another venture from the Galvin brothers, offering their trademark gourmet French cuisine and high-quality ingredients, from simple salad niçoise to tempting tarte tatin. Not cheap but a wonderful place for a treat.

Galvin Demoiselle, Harrods (harrods.com/content/the-store/ restaurants/galvin-demoiselle, ££, ☎).

2 December

Tasty Thespians

Try the pre-theatre menu at Hawksmoor, located in the old Watney-Combe brewery near Seven Dials. The restaurant specialises in generous steaks (supplied by award-winning butcher Ginger Pig), cooked on a charcoal grill, with good-value 'express' menus for theatregoers – or you can drop into the bar if you just want a burger and beer.

Hawksmoor, 11 Langley St, WC2H 9JG (020-7420 9390, thehawksmoor.com/locations/seven-dials, Covent Garden tube, ££-£££, ☎).

See a show at the Donmar Warehouse in Covent Garden, a 250-seat, not-for-profit theatre which has become one of the UK's leading producing houses. For over 20 years this award-winning playhouse has presented some of London's most memorable theatrical experiences, showcasing the talent of many of the industry's most creative artists, including Kenneth Branagh and Sir Ian McKellen, and building an unparalleled catalogue of work.

Donmar Warehouse Theatre, 41 Earlham St, WC2H 9LX (0844-871 7624, donmarwarehouse.com, Covent Garden tube, ☎).

3 December

Eat With Tomorrow's Masterchefs

Experience fine dining at student prices when you visit the Phoenix, Lewisham College's training restaurant. You'll enjoy a three-course meal and silver service, presented to the highest standards, overseen by professional chefs – Gordon Ramsey and Angela Hartnett are just two of the big names who've worked with the students here. The Phoenix is also available for private hire.

Phoenix Restaurant, Lewisham College, Lewisham Way, SE4 1UT (020-8694 3294/3071, lesoco.ac.uk/college-life/facilities/cafes-and-restaurants, St Johns rail, £, ☎).

Dance to vintage American music at the Rivoli Ballroom, London's only '50s ballroom to survive intact into the 21st century. It's been restored to its former glory, with plush red velvet, gold-framed walls, crystal chandeliers and oversized Chinese lanterns, and has a welcoming vibe. Whatever your step you can indulge it here, including salsa, ballroom, Latin, country, jive, swing, old time or tango.

Rivoli Ballroom, 350 Brockley Rd, SE4 2BY (020-8692 5130, therivoli. co.uk, Crofton Park rail, ☎).

4 December

East End Culture

Explore the East End art scene on the first Thursday of the month, when over 170 galleries and museums throughout East London stay open until 9pm, with free events, talks, exhibitions and private views in a district-wide celebration of culture and learning. The First Thursday programme changes continually, but whenever you go you can expect to enjoy arts shows, musical performances and perhaps even a few free drinks. Check out the website for information.

First Thursdays (firstthursdays.co.uk).

Head for Whitechapel Gallery, one of Britain's most innovative and influential art galleries. Founded in 1901 and housed in a striking building designed by Charles Harrison Townsend, the gallery majors in contemporary art. It's noted for its groundbreaking temporary exhibitions which have included Picasso's *Guernica* in 1938 and featured British icons such as Lucian Freud, Gilbert and George, and David Hockney.

Whitechapel Gallery, 77-82 Whitechapel High St, E1 7QX (020-7522 7888, whitechapelgallery.org, Aldgate East tube, free).

December

5 December

Foodie Fantasy

Buy some delicious artisan produce at Borough Market, London's most lauded food market. A treasure trove of quality British and international produce, it's where cooks, gourmets and foodies come to discover the tastes, aromas, textures and colours that only fresh, seasonal food can offer. You can buy everything here from cheese and charcuterie to spices and seafood, but plan to arrive early.

Borough Market, Borough High St, SE1 9DE (020-7407 1002, boroughmarket.org.uk, London Bridge tube).

Eat at The Table Café in Borough, one of the Southbank's hidden gems. New chef Cinzia Ghignoni (who's worked with Angela Hartnett) has created a new and exciting menu and wine list that continues the restaurant's commitment to sustainable sourcing and quality British ingredients. (The award-winning weekend brunch is a local favourite, as are the live Saturday evening jazz sessions.)

The Table Café, 83 Southwark St, SE1 0HX (020-7401 2760, thetablecafe.com, Southwark tube, £, ☎).

6 December

Gallic Gastronomy & Ghosts

Take someone special to lunch at Le Cercle. Close to Sloane Square, it's an enticing, elegant French restaurant and lounge bar, serving award-winning, tapas-sized plates, plus fine wines and classic cocktails. The vast menu makes deciding what to order difficult, although you're unlikely to be disappointed. It isn't a cheap venue, but the fixed price menus are good value.

Le Cercle, 1 Wilbraham Place, SW1X 9AE (020-7901 9999, lecercle. co.uk, Sloane Sq tube, ££, ☎).

Go ghost-hunting by bus… on a sightseeing tour that takes in the darker side of London, and entertains passengers with comic-horror theatre. It all takes place aboard a classic '60s Routemaster bus which whisks you between London's historic murder, torture and execution sites, from the Houses of Parliament and Westminster Abbey to St Paul's Cathedral and the Tower of London. En route, you'll learn about the grisly skeletons in the capital's cupboards.

Ghost Bus Tours (theghostbustours.com/london.html, ☎).

7 December

Who Needs Snow?

Have fun with your children in Hyde Park's Winter Wonderland, when the park becomes a magical world with fairground rides, a giant Ferris wheel, a circus and a skating rink. There's also a traditional Christmas market and, of course, Santa's grotto, plus a Victorian bandstand illuminated by over 100,000 lights – the largest of its kind in the UK.

Winter Wonderland, Hyde Park, W2 2UH (hydeparkwinterwonderland.com, Hyde Park Cnr tube, free, ⓘ).

Treat the kids to a meal at Sticky Fingers, Rolling Stone Bill Wyman's ribs 'n' burger restaurant in Kensington – a Mecca for rock fans and children. It's regarded as one of London's most exciting restaurants (rather than just another celebrity hangout), with tasty American-inspired food, including tender steaks, delicious spare ribs and award-winning burgers. Children love it, and it's also good value.

Sticky Fingers, 1a Phillimore Gardens, W8 7QB (020-7937 8690, stickyfingers.co.uk, High St Kensington tube, £, ☎).

8 December

A Towering Sight

Visit iconic Tower Bridge – constructed between 1886 and 1894 – for a unique view of London. The Tower Bridge Exhibition uses film, photos and interactive displays to tell its story, while the high-level walkways serve as viewing galleries, offering stunning views of the Thames and the City. If you're lucky you may see the bridge being raised, which occurs around three times a day.

Tower Bridge Exhibition, Tower Bridge Rd, SE1 2UP (020-7403 3761, towerbridge.org.uk/tbe, Tower Hill tube).

Come back down to earth with a pint at The Anchor Tap, named after one of the many breweries that sprang up in Southwark from the 16th century onwards. The traditional Sam Smith's pub is a down-to-earth antidote to the proliferation of trendy bars in the area, offering a warm welcome, a beer garden and decent pub grub.

The Anchor Tap, Horsleydown Ln, SE1 2LN (020-7403 4637, Tower Hill tube, £).

December

9 December

Drink With the Nobs

Buy a bottle (or three) of fine wine at Berry Bros & Rudd, Britain's oldest wine and spirit merchant (established 1698) which has traded from the same premises for over 300 years. You'll be in esteemed company; Berry Bros holds Royal Warrants for HM the Queen and Prince Charles, while former customers have included Lord Byron and the Aga Khan.

Berry Brothers & Rudd, 3 St James's St, SW1A 1EG (0800-280 2440, bbr.com, Green Park tube).

Enjoy a pint and a pie at The Guinea in Bruton Place. Established in 1675, it's long been a popular spot with the smart set. It has a small bar and a well-regarded (if rather expensive) restaurant, although you can eat splendidly in the bar on weekdays. The Guinea is particularly famous for its award-winning steak and kidney pies.

The Guinea, 30 Bruton Place, W1J 6NL (020-7409 1728, theguinea. co.uk, Bond St tube, ££, ☎).

10 December

Congenial Chiswick

Enjoy a leisurely lunch at The Bollo House, a community-centred gastro pub in Chiswick with a homely atmosphere and friendly service. Offering excellent seasonal food alongside quality wine, beers and spirits, there's no better place to while away a lazy afternoon with loved ones (or a good book), and forget the stresses of the world.

The Bollo House, 13-15 Bollo Ln, W4 5LR (020-8994 6037, thebollohouse.co.uk, Chiswick Park tube, ££, ☎).

Shake a leg with the professionals at the Rambert Dance Company in Chiswick, the national company for contemporary dance. Founded by Marie Rambert in 1926, it's the most creative dance company working in Britain today. If you want to learn or develop dance skills, its Learning & Participation department runs weekly evening classes in contemporary dance at all levels, from beginners to advanced/professional.

Rambert Dance Company, 94 Chiswick High Rd, W4 1SH (020-8630 0600, rambert.org.uk, Turnham Green tube, ☎).

11 December

Passport to Pimlico

Chill out in St George's Square Gardens, Pimlico, an elegant square that provides a welcome respite from London traffic. Dating from 1839 and designed by builder Thomas Cubitt – whose stucco houses define Pimlico – it was once London's only residential square open to the Thames and had (until 1874) its own pier for boats and steamers. It remains a highly desirable place to live.

St George's Square Gardens, SW1 (8am to dusk, Pimlico tube, free).

Quench your thirst at The Morpeth Arms, an elegant Young's pub with a fascinating history. It was built in 1845 on the site of the old Millbank penitentiary – beneath the pub there's a corridor of holding cells. It's rumoured to be haunted by former prisoners, who were incarcerated here prior to being transported to Australia. (The origin of POM is thought to be 'Prisonor of Millbank').

The Morpeth Arms, 58 Millbank, SW1P 4RW (020-7834 6442, morpetharms.com, Pimlico tube, £, ☎).

12 December

Southbank Spectacular

Take the whole family to the Southbank Centre Christmas Market, held on the Queen's Walk along the Thames (from the London Eye to Waterloo Bridge). It's a traditional, German-style Christmas Market, thoroughly festive and beautifully lit, with rows of authentic wooden chalets selling a wide range of unique, hand-crafted gifts and unusual Christmas presents – plus bratwurst and *glühwein* (mulled wine). *Frohe Weihnachten!*

Southbank Centre Christmas Market, Southbank Centre, Belvedere Rd, SE1 8XX (christmasmarkets.com/uk/london-southbank-christmas-market.html, Waterloo tube, ⓘ).

Detour to the Hayward Gallery (named after Sir Isaac Hayward, former leader of the London County Council) at the Southbank Centre, an outstanding example of '60s Brutalist architecture which opened in 1968. The gallery doesn't have a permanent collection but hosts a number of major contemporary exhibitions each year, and has a long history of presenting work by the world's most adventurous and innovative artists.

Hayward Gallery, Southbank Centre, Belvedere Rd, SE1 8XX (020-7960 4200, ticketing.southbankcentre.co.uk/find/hayward-gallery-visual-arts, Waterloo tube).

Tracy Emin, Hayward Gallery

December

13 December

Brick Lane Bonanza

Brick Lane is also the heart of the East End's Bangladeshi-Sylheti community, and you can enjoy a great curry in one the many authentic, inexpensive restaurants.

Brick Lane Markets, Shoreditch, E1 6QL (visitbricklane.org and trumanbrewery.com, Shoreditch High St tube).

––––––––––

Once you're done shopping, get some mates together and head to the All Star Lanes in Brick Lane, a classy ten-pin bowling alley with a difference. In addition to bowling there's pool, an American-style diner and a bar serving fantastic cocktails, plus karaoke booths where you can sing along to over 5,500 tunes. There's even a private room with its own bowling lanes. The atmosphere is relaxed and fun, but nothing like a traditional bowling alley.

All Star Lanes, 95 Brick Ln, E1 6QL (020-7426 9200, allstarlanes. co.uk/venues/brick-lane, Shoreditch High St tube, £, ☏).

Explore Brick Lane Markets at the weekend, a chaotic, colourful bazaar in Tower Hamlets crammed with second-hand furniture, unusual clothes, arts & crafts, bric-a-brac and junk. The joy is that you never know what you'll find as Brick Lane sells everything from period furniture and vintage threads to kitsch collectibles and old LPs – plus a vast range of street food. Street performers enhance the vibrant atmosphere of the lane, which is famous for its graffiti artists such as Banksy, D'Face and Ben Eine.

The name Brick Lane is derived from the brick and tile manufacturers based here in the 15th century, but later became better known for beer. When Benjamin Truman (1699-1780) established the Black Eagle Brewery at 91 Brick Lane in the 1720s, it was the largest in London, covering 11 acres. It closed in 1988 and the Grade II listed building is now a vibrant arts and events centre, housing over 250 businesses, ranging from art galleries to bars, restaurants and shops.

December

14 December

Charity Begins at School

St John's Old School

Raine Street School

G o back to school in Wapping, home to two remarkable 18th-century charity schools:

St John's Old School was founded in 1695 (although the current building dates from around 1765) and was a Bluecoat charity school, named after the blue costumes that pupils wore. These schools were distinguished by their Bluecoat statues and St John's has two of the finest in London. Note also the separate entrances for boys and girls – children were segregated in schools until the middle of the 20th century, and even entered school via different doors.

Raine Street School was established in 1719 and named after its founder Henry Raine (1679-1738), a wealthy Wapping brewer (the street also bears his name). The original school building is now a community centre, although the school still exists at a new location in Bethnal Green. The school motto can be seen over the door: 'Come in and learn your duty to God and man' and in niches on either side are statues (copies of the originals) of a boy and a girl in the school uniform, similar to those at St John's.

St John's Old School, Scandrett St, Wapping, E1 and Raine Street School, Raine St, Wapping Ln, Wapping E1. Wapping rail.

H ave a peek at Tobacco Dock (Grade I listed), a fascinating brick and timber built warehouse constructed in 1811 to store tobacco and wine. It was restored in 1990 in an attempt to turn it into an exclusive shopping complex, but this failed and it's now deserted most of the time. Note the fine tiger statue outside the north entrance, which commemorates an incident in the late 1800s when an escaped tiger seized a nine-year-old boy in its jaws – his life was saved by the heroic intervention of animal trader Charles Jamrach.

Tobacco Dock, 50 Porters Walk, Wapping Ln, E1W 2SF (020-7680 4001, tobaccodocklondon.com, Shadwell DLR, free).

December

15 December

Tea & Talk

Indulge in a delicious afternoon tea in the Rose Lounge at the Sofitel Hotel, a hidden gem in St James's. Decorated in pink and cream with stunning displays of fragrant roses, the setting is enhanced by the gentle sound of a harp, making it the perfect spot for a luxurious afternoon tea, including 'Parisiennes' pastries and a champagne cocktail. Heavenly!

Rose Lounge, Sofitel Hotel, 6 Waterloo Place, SW1Y 4AN (020-7747 2238, thebalconlondon.com/roselounge/roselounge.shtm, Charing Cross tube, ££, ☎).

Attend a free public lecture at Barnard's Inn Hall in Holborn, the home of Gresham College. Founded in 1597 by Sir Thomas Gresham (1519-1579), the college is London's oldest higher education institution, where professors have given free public lectures (more than 100 a year) for over 400 years. The historic hall dates from the late 14th century.

Gresham College, Barnard's Inn Hall, Holborn, EC1N 2HH (020-7831 0575, gresham.ac.uk, Chancery Ln tube, ☎).

16 December

Brollies & Bowlers

Buy a hand-crafted umbrella – an item which ***always*** comes in handy in London – at James Smith & Sons, the home of British umbrellas. Founded in 1830, it remains a family run business and has been making umbrellas, sticks and canes for over 175 years. The historic shop (1867), with its original hand-crafted fittings, is a nostalgic reminder of Victorian times.

James Smith & Sons, 53 New Oxford St, WC1A 1BL (020-7836 4731, james-smith.co.uk, Tottenham Court Rd tube).

Need a bowler to go with your new brolly? Visit James Lock & Co, established in 1676 and the oldest hat shop in the world (it's also the world's oldest family-owned business). Over the years, Lock & Co have supplied headwear to the cream of London society, including Winston Churchill, Charlie Chaplin, the Duke of Wellington and Admiral Lord Nelson.

James Lock & Co, 6 St James's St, SW1A 1EF (020-7930 8874, lockhatters.co.uk, Green Park tube).

17 December

Winter Warmers

W arm up for Christmas at Spitalfields Winter Festival, a celebration of music and song – including festive carols – at various venues, including Hawksmoor's ecclesiastical masterpiece Christ Church, Old Spitalfields Market and Spitalfields City Farm. The annual winter festival takes place each December and encompasses an eclectic mix of styles, periods and presentations, which bring together global and local artists in one of London's most creative corners. Previous year's performances have included everything from baroque to Scottish reels and even opera for the under-twos – and there are always some free events. An intimate and heart-warming end to the year.

Spitalfields Winter Festival, Spitalfields, E1 (spitalfieldsmusic.org. uk/whats-on/winter-festival, Shoreditch High St tube, ☎, ①).

S oak up the atmosphere of Dennis Severs' House on a Monday evening pre-Christmas tour: one of London's most singular attractions, in one of its most magical properties. Part exhibition, part installation, the house is a work of fantasy, designed to create an atmosphere redolent of the 18th century. It was the brainchild of American artist Dennis Severs, who purchased the house in the '70s, when the old Huguenot district of Spitalfields was rundown. While living there, Severs imagined a family of Huguenot silk weavers who once lived there and, room by room, brought them back to life.

You're instructed to remain quiet while exploring this 'still-life drama' – Severs was known to eject visitors who talked too much – and touching objects isn't encouraged; as such it's the antithesis of a modern hands-on museum. The atmosphere of a bygone age is best maintained if you refrain from looking out of the windows, which allows the 21st century to intrude. Even so, the candlelit tours are nostalgic (if expensive), and Christmas is a special time to visit. Enchanting!

Dennis Severs' House, 18 Folgate St, Spitalfields, E1 6BX (020-7247 4013, dennissevershouse.co.uk, Liverpool St tube, ☎).

December

18 December

It's Behind You!

Buy some Christmas reading at Foyles' flagship store on Charing Cross Road, founded in 1903 and one of Europe's largest bookshops. With five floors and over 200,000 titles, Foyles has something for even the most discerning of readers, plus a wide range of gifts and stationery, magazines, printed music, CDs and DVDs, and more. There's also a café, gallery and an events space.

Foyles, 113-119 Charing Cross Rd, WC2H 0EB (020-7437 5660, foyles.co.uk, Tottenham Court Rd tube).

Book to see a traditional Christmas pantomime at one of London's theatres, such as the Leicester Square Theatre or the Shaw Theatre (Camden). Panto is a form of musical comedy, mostly performed during the Christmas season, combining topical humour with a story based on well-known tales such as Cinderella or Aladdin. It employs men dressed as women, girls playing boys and features songs, slapstick and dancing. Kids love it – and so do most grown-ups also.

Big Panto Guide (bigpantoguide.co.uk/london.php, ☎).

19 December

From Poems to Ponies

Eat, drink and read at the Poetry Café in Covent Garden, run by the Poetry Society, whose mission is to advance the study, use and enjoyment of poetry. There are poetry readings most evenings plus a range of events, but you don't need to be a poet or even a poetry lover to enjoy the café's coffee, pastries and delicious vegetarian cuisine.

Poetry Café, 22 Betterton St, WC2H 9BX (020-7420 9888, poetrysociety.org.uk, Covent Garden tube, £).

Trot along to the London International Horse Show at Olympia, the annual equestrian 'Christmas Party' featuring top-class show jumping, dressage and driving, plus 'behind the scenes' access to the warm-up ring, an 'equestrian' shopping mall, and a host of cafés, bars and restaurants. The show concludes on Sunday with a spectacular festive parade featuring hundreds of horses.

Olympia Horse Show, Olympia Exhibition Centre, Grand Hall, Olympia Way, W14 8UX (0871-230 5580, olympiahorseshow.com, Kensington Olympia tube, ☎, ①).

20 December

Ice-Skating with the Impressionists

Step inside the Courtauld Gallery at Somerset House, which conceals a gem of an art collection ranging from the early Renaissance to modernist works of the 20th century. Its highlights include a splendid array of Gothic and medieval paintings, plus Renaissance masterpieces by artists such as Cranach and Brueghel, and one of London's best collections of Impressionist and post-Impressionist art.

Courtauld Gallery, Somerset House, Strand, WC2R 0RN (020-7848 2526, courtauld.ac.uk, Temple tube).

Take to the ice outside Somerset House, where the grand courtyard is transformed into a magical 10,000ft² ice-skating rink from November to January. The majestic backdrop of Somerset House combined with the wonderful musical accompaniment – anything from classical to the latest disco sounds – creates a fabulous festive occasion. Club nights feature some of the UK's hottest DJs for late-night skate sessions. There's also a skate school and a bar.

Somerset House Ice Rink (somersethouse.org.uk/ice-rink).

21 December

Larger Than Life

Immerse yourself in a film at the IMAX Cinema in the Science Museum, South Kensington. The huge IMAX screen – ten times larger than average – is one of the few places in London where you can enjoy the full cinematic experience in 3D. Films focus on nature, the oceans and outer space – where you feel you're right in the middle of the action.

IMAX Cinema, Science Museum, Exhibition Rd, SW7 2DD (020-7942 4000, sciencemuseum.org.uk, South Kensington tube).

Take your kids to eat in the museum's Deep Blue café-restaurant, which offers superb views of the hi-tech Wellcome Wing. The décor is so **very** blue you'll feel like you're underwater, but the family menu is down to earth, offering both full meals and snacks. As well as burgers, pasta and pizza for the kids, there's a selection of wine and beer for grown-ups.

Revolution Café & Deep Blue, Science Museum (0870-870 4868, £).

December

22 December

An American Genius in London

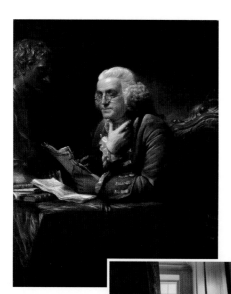

L earn about one of America's founding fathers with a tour of Benjamin Franklin House. This architecturally-important (Grade I listed) house was built around 1730 and is the only surviving home of Benjamin Franklin (1706-1790), statesman, philosopher, writer and inventor. Franklin was born in Boston, Massachusetts, but lived and worked in this house for 16 years until the eve of the American Revolution (it was also the first de facto US embassy). He was a key founder of the United States of America and the only statesman to sign all four documents that created the new nation. As a scientist, he was a major figure in the American Enlightenment and the history of physics for his discoveries and theories regarding electricity.

This inventive museum comprises several sections, including the Student Science Centre which allows the recreation of experiments from Franklin's time in London. Its most compelling attraction is the Historical Experience which takes a 'museum as theatre' approach. You're 'accompanied' by an actress who plays Polly Hewson, Franklin's landlady's daughter, who became like a daughter to him. This live performance, with lighting, sound and visual projections, brings the whole 18th-century experience to life.

Benjamin Franklin House, 36 Craven St, WC2N 5NF (020-7839 2006, benjaminfranklinhouse.org, Charing Cross tube, ☏).

E at your way around the southern Mediterranean, courtesy of Moro in Exmouth Market. Established in 1997, it serves a delectable fusion of Spanish, Middle Eastern and North African (expertly balanced) flavours, much of it cooked in a wood-fired oven or char-grilled, accompanied by a superb Iberian wine list. Moro's buzzy and sensual dining room is one of London's hottest tickets, so be prepared to book well in advance. You can also eat at the bar from the excellent tapas menu. *Fantástico!*

Moro, 34-36 Exmouth Market, EC1R 4QE (020-7833 8336, moro. co.uk, Farringdon tube, ££, ☏).

23 December

Growing Old Gracefully

Grab a few moments' peace at St Etheldreda's, London's oldest Catholic church. Built around 1250, it's one of only two London buildings to survive from the reign of Edward I. It was a spiritual sanctuary during the Middle Ages and the interior still evokes an acute sense of age and mystery. St Etheldreda's also boasts a fine musical tradition, with regular choral recitals.

St Etheldreda's, 14 Ely Place, EC1N 6RY (020-7405 1061, stetheldreda.com, Chancery Ln tube, free).

Have lunch with a side order of history at the Bleeding Heart, one of the City's finest French restaurants. The building contains a warren of rooms, beamed ceilings, cobblestones and a 600-year-old medieval crypt. The yard it stands in is allegedly named after a 17th-century beauty who was murdered there.

Bleeding Heart Restaurant, Bleeding Heart Yard, off Greville St, EC1N 8SJ (020-7242 2056, bleedingheart.co.uk, Farringdon tube, £££, 🍽).

24 December

On Christmas Eve…

Cram in some last-minute shopping at Westfield London, one of the capital's largest shopping malls. As well as some 265 shops, it houses a designer 'village' selling over 40 luxury brands, more than 60 places to eat and drink, a 17-screen Vue cinema and a luxury spa. Westfield is open Mon-Sat, 10am-10pm and Sun noon-6pm.

Westfield London, Ariel Way, Shepherd's Bush, W12 7DS (020-3371 2300, uk.westfield.com/london, Shepherds Bush, White City, Wood Ln or Shepherd's Bush Market tube).

Attend Midnight Mass at majestic St Paul's Cathedral, a moving and uplifting experience. On Christmas Eve, Sir Christopher Wren's masterpiece is lit by candlelight and filled with the soaring voices of the Cathedral choir, to mark the first Eucharist of Christmas. If you cannot make it on this special evening, Christmas celebrations are held in the cathedral throughout December (see website).

St Paul's Cathedral, St Paul's Churchyard, EC4M 8AD (20-7246 8350, stpauls.co.uk, St Paul's tube, free).

December

25 December

Water Wheels

See one of London's more curious Christmas traditions take place in Hyde Park, as members of the Serpentine Swimming Club dive into the chilly lake to compete for the Peter Pan Cup. First contested in 1864, the 100-yard handicap takes its name from the cup presented by *Peter Pan* author JM Barrie in 1904. The race starts at 9am and (fortunately) only members can take part.

Peter Pan Cup, Serpentine, Hyde Park, W2 2UH (serpentineswimmingclub.com, Knightsbridge tube).

Join the Southwark Cyclists on their annual Mithrasmas Mass Ride from Greenwich to central London via Putney. The ride takes place along virtually traffic-free mostly Thameside roads – an unusual but enjoyable way to spend Christmas morning. Starting at Cutty Sark Gardens (SE10, 10am) – you can also join in at London Bridge – it stops for refreshments at the Duke's Head pub in Putney, before ending at a restaurant on the Edgware Road. Merry Mithrasmas!

Southwark Cyclists (southwarkcyclists.org.uk).

26 December

Sharpen Your Elbows!

Get ready to grab a bargain at the Christmas-New Year sales. Most of London's major stores, such as Harrods, Selfridges, Liberty and Harvey Nicks – as well as the Westfield malls – start their end of year sales on Boxing Day. Some stores open early and most have a few heavily-discounted items to draw in the crowds, so you'll need sharp elbows and a reliable alarm clock if you're planning serious retail therapy.

———————

Go football crazy on Boxing Day, when there's a full programme of football, and watching a Barclays Premier League match is a holiday highlight for many sports fans. If you're lucky you may obtain tickets to see one of the capital's finest, be it Arsenal, Chelsea, Crystal Palace, Fulham, Spurs or West Ham – assuming they're still in the Premiership by the time you read this – although you could have just as much fun at Brentford or Barnet…

Premiership (premierleague.com, ☎).

27 December

Horses for Courses

Watch the racing at Kempton Park – the nearest racecourse to central London – during the William Hill Winter Festival on the 26-27th December. The King George VI Chase on Boxing Day is the showpiece event, but there's some excellent jump race action on both days. There's a wonderful view of the racecourse from the excellent Panoramic Restaurant (££, ☎).

William Hill Winter Festival, Kempton Park, Staines Rd East, Sunbury-on-Thames, TW16 5AQ (01932-782292, kempton.co.uk/winter-festival).

––––––––––––

Blow your winnings on a delicious curry at Indian Zest in nearby Sunbury-on-Thames. Balancing traditional Indian cuisine with contemporary techniques, the restaurant offers a series of intimate dining rooms, subtly decked out in colonial style with Indian artefacts and prints. Good cooking and fine wines, friendly service, reasonable pricing and a refined, elegant ambience elevate Zest well above your average high-street curry house.

Indian Zest, 21 Thames St, Sunbury-on-Thames, TW16 5QF (01932-765000, indianzest.co.uk, Sunbury rail, ££, ☎).

28 December

Rock Around the Clock!

Boogie along to the Hard Rock Café on Old Park Lane – the one that started it all in the '70s when Eric Clapton donated a guitar which was hung on the wall. Visit for the atmosphere, the memorabilia, live music in the basement bar and the legendary burgers. Don't forget to visit the Vault, where some of the most valuable rock ephemera is displayed.

Hard Rock Café, 150 Old Park Ln, W1K 1QZ (020-7514 1700, hardrock.com/locations/cafes3/cafe.aspx?LocationID=91&MIBEnumID=3, Hard Park Cr tube, ££, ☎).

––––––––––––

Rock around the clock at Crobar in Soho, London's 'best-loved rock n' roll bar', where the jukebox is loaded with classics and the best contemporary sounds. This fabled heavy metal/goth hangout is famous for its beer, bourbon, live bands and party animals – and its five-hour (4-9pm) Happy Hour. It's open until 3am. Rock on!

Crobar, 17 Manette St, W1D 4AS (020-7439 0831, crobar.co.uk, Tottenham Court rd tube, £).

December

29 December

Barrow Boys & Baristas

Visit historic Leather Lane Market, one of London's lesser-known but most interesting markets. Down to earth and slightly scruffy, but incredibly diverse, Leather Lane sells everything from fruit and vegetables to DVDs and T-shirts, all at bargain prices. Open weekdays from 10am to 3pm, it's a breath of fresh air – and because it caters to the lunchtime trade, there's also some good grub.

Leather Lane Market, Leather Ln, EC1N 7RJ (leatherlanestars. wordpress.com/the-market, Chancery Ln tube).

———————

Fancy yourself as a barista? Learn how to brew the ultimate cup of coffee at the London Barista Resource & Training School (BRAT), run by Prufrock Coffee, established in 2009 and famous for its ground-breaking brews. BRAT was launched in 2011 and offers group classes, Saturday/Sunday school and private training aimed at baristas, business owners – and coffee fiends.

London Barista Resource & Training School, 23-25 Leather Ln, EC1N 7TE (020-7242 0467, prufrockcoffee.com/prufrock-the-london-brat, Chancery Ln tube, ☎).

Leather Lane Market

30 December

Walk with Dickens

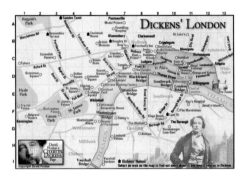

Walk the streets of London in the footsteps of Charles Dickens accompanied by author and broadcaster Richard Jones. A Blue Badge Guide, Jones offers a series of entertaining, informative walks themed around England's greatest novelist, from the crowded streets to secret backwaters, where Dickens' novels and personal life were played out. As befits the writer who created Ebenezer Scrooge, there are also some special Christmas walks.

Charles Dickens London Tours & Walks (dickenslondontours. co.uk, ☎).

———————

Warm up with a meal at the acclaimed Princess of Shoreditch, a handsome gastropub occupying a lovely light-filled 250-year-old building with a spiral staircase linking the downstairs bar and the upstairs dining room. It's a proper pub with a good choice of real ales and an interesting wine list, but the big attraction is the delicious seasonal food.

The Princess of Shoreditch, 76 Paul St, EC2A 4NE (020-7729 9270, theprincessofshoreditch.com, Old St tube, ££, ☎).

31 December

Happy Hogmanay!

Get in an early toast to Hogmanay at Albannach, an outpost of 'Scottishness' deep in the middle of enemy territory, close to Trafalgar Square, generally regarded as the geographical heart of the Sassenach capital. It dubs itself the 'Albannach Restaurant and Whisky Bar', and is split into various drinking and eating areas. It's a slick place – with a smart-casual dress code – which specialises in Scotch whisky, but you can also try Irish and Japanese examples as well as bourbon (over 120 in total). The Albannach also serves cocktails (not all whisky based) in its vaulted cocktail bar.

You can also eat well from a menu catering to homesick Scots, with Scottish specialities such as haggis, venison and salmon. This isn't a budget destination, as you might guess from its prime location, but given the quality of the décor, service, drinks and food, it isn't particularly expensive either.

Albannach, 66 Trafalgar Sq, WC2N 5DS (020-7930 0066, albannach. co.uk, Charing Cross tube, ££, 🖥).

See the new year in with the Mayor's spectacular New Year's Eve Firework Display, which lights up the night sky for miles around with a display of stunning pyrotechnics. Launched from the foot of the London Eye and from rafts on the Thames, the explosive display is visible from most vantage points in central London – if you can see the London Eye you'll be able to see the show. If you want to watch from the embankment, you'll need to get in place by 9 or 10pm, as access to each zone is closed as soon as it's full and many Thameside bars (etc.) are ticketed on the night. Public transport is the best (only?) way to get to and from central London.

New Year's Eve Fireworks (london.gov.uk/get-involved/events/nye).

December

TOWER BRIDGE

INDEX

Index

Index

Index

Index

London's Secrets

LONDON'S HIDDEN SECRETS

ISBN: 978-1-907339-40-0, £10.95

Graeme Chesters

A guide to London's hidden and lesser-known sights not found in standard guidebooks. Step beyond the chaos, cliches and queues of London's tourist-clogged attractions to its quirkier side.

Discover its loveliest ancient buildings, secret gardens, strangest museums, most atmospheric pubs, cutting-edge art and design, and much more: some 140 destinations in all corners of the city.

LONDON'S HIDDEN SECRETS VOL 2

ISBN: 978-1-907339-79-0, £10.95

Graeme Chesters & David Hampshire

Hot on the heels of London's Hidden Secrets comes another volume of the city's largely undiscovered sights, many of which we were unable to include in the original book. In fact, the more research we did the more treasures we found, until eventually a second volume was inevitable.

Written by two experienced London writers, LHS 2 is for both those who already know the metropolis and newcomers wishing to learn more about its hidden and unusual charms.

LONDON'S SECRET WALKS

ISBN: 978-1-907339-51-6, £11.95

Graeme Chesters

London is a great city for walking – whether for pleasure, exercise or simply to get from A to B. Despite the city's extensive public transport system, walking is also often the quickest and most enjoyable way to get around – at least in the centre – and it's also free and healthy!

Many attractions are off the beaten track, away from the major thoroughfares and public transport hubs. This favours walking as the best way to explore them, as does the fact that London is a visually interesting city with a wealth of stimulating sights in every 'nook and cranny'.

LONDON'S SECRET PLACES

ISBN: 978-1-907339-92-9, £10.95

Graeme Chesters & David Hampshire

London is one of the world's leading tourist destinations with a wealth of world-class attractions: amazing museums and galleries, beautiful parks and gardens, stunning palaces and grand houses, and much, much more. These are covered in numerous excellent tourist guides and online, and need no introduction here. Not so well known are London's numerous smaller attractions, most of which are neglected by the throngs who descend upon the tourist-clogged major sights. What London's Secret Places does is seek out the city's lesser-known, but no less worthy, 'hidden' attractions.

320 PAGES, PRINTED IN COLOUR

LONDON'S SECRETS: MUSEUMS & GALLERIES

ISBN: 978-1-907339-96-7, £10.95

Robbi Atilgan & David Hampshire

London is a treasure trove for museum fans and art lovers and one of the world's great art and cultural centres, with more popular museums and galleries than any other world city. The art scene is a lot like the city itself – diverse, vast, vibrant and in a constant state of flux – a cornucopia of traditional and cutting-edge, majestic and mundane, world-class and run-of-the-mill, bizarre and brilliant.

So, whether you're an art lover, culture vulture, history buff or just looking for something to entertain the family during the school holidays, you're bound to find inspiration in London. All you need is a comfortable pair of shoes, an open mind – and this book!

LONDON'S SECRETS: PUBS & BARS

ISBN: 978-1-907339-93-6, £10.95

Graeme Chesters

British pubs and bars are world famous for their bonhomie, great atmosphere, good food and fine ales. Nowhere is this more so than in London, which has a plethora of watering holes of all shapes and sizes: classic historic boozers and trendy style bars; traditional riverside inns and luxurious cocktail bars; enticing wine bars and brew pubs; mouth-watering gastro pubs and brasseries; welcoming gay bars and raucous music venues. This book highlights over 250 of the best.

LONDON'S SECRETS: PARKS & GARDENS

ISBN: 978-1-907339-95-0, £10.95

Robbi Atilgan & David Hampshire

London is one the world's greenest capital cities, with a wealth of places where you can relax and recharge your batteries. Britain is renowned for its parks and gardens, and nowhere has such beautiful and varied green spaces as London: magnificent royal parks, historic garden cemeteries, majestic ancient forests and woodlands, breathtaking formal country parks, expansive commons, charming small gardens, beautiful garden squares and enchanting 'secret' gardens. Not all are secrets, of course, but many of London's most beguiling green spaces are known only to insiders and locals.

320 PAGES, PRINTED IN COLOUR

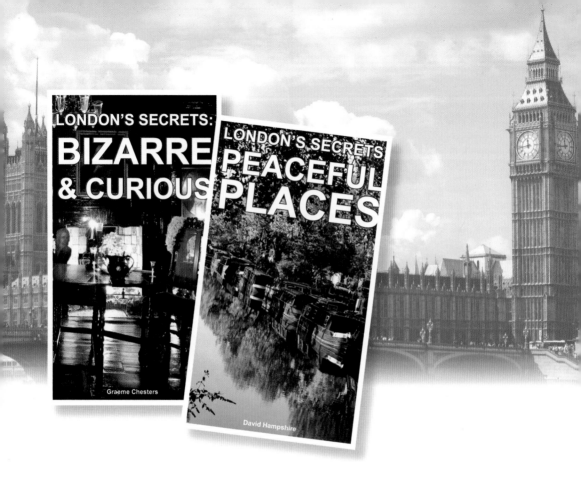

LONDON'S SECRETS: BIZARRE & CURIOUS

Graeme Chesters

ISBN: 978-1-909282-58-2, £11.95, 320 pages

London is a city with 2,000 years of history, over which it has accumulated a wealth of odd and strange buildings, monuments, statues, street trivia and museum exhibits, to name just a few examples. This book seeks out the city's most bizarre and curious sights and tells the often fascinating story behind them, from the Highgate vampire to the arrest of a dead man, a legal brothel and a former Texas embassy to Roman bikini bottoms and poetic manhole covers, from London's hanging gardens to a restaurant where you dine in the dark. *Bizarre & Curious* is guaranteed to keep you amused and fascinated for hours. Printed in colour.

Published Spring 2014

LONDON'S SECRETS: PEACEFUL PLACES

David Hampshire

ISBN: 978-1-907339-45-5, £11.95, 256 pages

London is one of the world's most exciting cities, but it's also one of the most noisy – a bustling, chaotic, frenetic metropolis where it can be difficult to find somewhere for a bit of peace and quiet. Until now. *Peaceful Places* contains over 200 'secret' locations throughout the city, from gardens and churches to libraries and cafes, hotels and spas to shops and galleries – and much more. So whether you're seeking somewhere to recharge your batteries or have a nap, a place to read or study, or a tranquil spot for a break from shopping or to eat your lunch, *Peaceful Places* will steer you in the right direction. Printed in colour.

Published Summer 2014